TRANSFORMING OUR IMAGE,
BUILDING OUR BRAND

TRANSFORMING OUR IMAGE, BUILDING OUR BRAND

The Education Advantage

VALERIE J. GROSS

 LIBRARIES UNLIMITED

AN IMPRINT OF ABC-CLIO, LLC
Santa Barbara, California • Denver, Colorado • Oxford, England

Library of Congress Cataloging-in-Publication Data

Gross, Valerie J.
  Transforming our image, building our brand : the education advantage / Valerie J. Gross.
    p. cm.
  Includes index.
  ISBN 978-1-59884-770-3 (pbk.) — ISBN 978-1-59884-771-0 (ebook)
1. Librarians—Public opinion—United States. 2. Librarians—Professional relationships—United States. 3. Public libraries—Public relations—United States. 4. Public libraries—Aims and objectives—United States.
  Z682.G84 2013
  027.473—dc23   2012027282

ISBN: 978-1-59884-770-3
EISBN: 978-1-59884-771-0

17 16 15 14 13   1 2 3 4 5

This book is also available on the World Wide Web as an eBook.
Visit www.abc-clio.com for details.

Libraries Unlimited
An Imprint of ABC-CLIO, LLC

ABC-CLIO, LLC
130 Cremona Drive, P.O. Box 1911
Santa Barbara, California 93116-1911

This book is printed on acid-free paper ∞

Manufactured in the United States of America

All images, photos, reproductions, correspondence, forms, and so forth, relating to Howard County Library System, used by permission.

*In admiration and with appreciation
to the extraordinary Howard County Library
System team. Your professionalism, innovation,
creativity, and collaboration is reflected in these pages.
You are, quite simply, the very best.*

CONTENTS

ACKNOWLEDGMENTS

Writing this book has been an honor and a privilege, encompassing the contributions of many.

First and foremost, I express my profound gratitude to Howard County Executive Ken Ulman and the Howard County Council for recognizing Howard County Library System (HCLS) as a major component of Howard County's strong education system, along with our A+ partners, Howard County Public School System and Howard Community College. I thank them for their steadfast support—most notably the top priority they place on allocating County funding that affords us the opportunity to deliver excellence in public education for everyone.

I am also appreciative of the Maryland State Legislature's Howard County Delegation for the state funding we receive, and thank all elected officials—local, state, and federal—for participating in our many signature events.

The Third Pillar of HCLS's curriculum would shine far less brightly without the supplemental funding provided by our devoted Friends of Howard County Library, philanthropic partners, and sponsors. Thank you, for enabling the "extras" that add professional polish to all that we do.

For the grant funding that bolsters our budgets, thank you to our grantors, including the Maryland Department of Labor, Licensing & Regulation and Maryland State Department of Education.

For their innovation, creativity, collaboration, and willingness to venture into uncharted territory, I express deep appreciation to the HCLS Board of Trustees and the spectacular HCLS Leadership Team, educators, and support staff who make it all happen with apparent ease—the mark of true professionals. It is with immense pride that I tell anyone who will listen about all of your fine work, and how privileged I am to have the opportunity to work with you.

For being world-class customers and for their tremendously gratifying support, I thank the dynamic people who live and work in Howard County.

For publishing the October 2009 feature article, "Transforming Our Image Through Words that Work," that prompted exuberant feedback, I thank *Public Libraries*, especially editor Kathleen M. Hughes.

I express sincere appreciation to everyone at ABC-CLIO, most notably editor and visionary Barbara Ittner. Sent after reading the aforementioned article, her unexpected e-mail, "I wonder if you might expand this idea into a book," could not have been more inspiring.

I am enormously indebted to the impeccable editing talents, candid opinions, and sacrificed evenings and weekends of the following HCLS staff members: Lisa Bankman, Ann Gilligan, Christie Lassen, and my assistant extraordinaire, Stephanie Shane. I am also incredibly fortunate that my writer/editor dad, Leonard Gross, was willing to impart his ever-appreciated suggestions.

Many thanks to the following organizations, whose invitations to present Transforming Our Image keynotes, workshops, and webinars motivated me to take this message even further: Alaska State Library, California Public Library Directors, Chester County Library and District Center (Pennsylvania), College of DuPage (Illinois), Delta Township District Library (Michigan), Detroit Library Cooperative (Michigan), Infopeople Project (California State Library), The Library Network (Michigan), Maryland Association of Public Library Administrators, Maryland Library Association, Mideastern Michigan Library Cooperative, Montgomery County-Norristown Public Library (Pennsylvania), New Hampshire Library Association, Oxford Public Library (Michigan), Pennsylvania Library Association, Public Library Association, Suburban Library Cooperative (Michigan), Urban Libraries Council, West Virginia Library Association, Wicomico Public Library (Maryland), and Woodlands Library Cooperative (Michigan).

Thanks also to attendees and participants from across the United States and Canada, with an extra thanks to those who took the time to send feedback and ask follow-up questions.

For their unique contributions, I thank Karen Hiser, who, writing on behalf of the West Virginia Library Commission, asked whether I could teach a "program—oops!—I mean workshop"; Victoria Ashford of FearlessLeading, who observed that the prune industry had transformed its image by renaming its product "dried plums;" and Andrea (Andie) Philo of the Norristown Public Library (Pennsylvania), who alerted me to the *Modern Family* episode containing the infamous line, "I thought that was the bathroom for homeless people."

For informing me of their successes with this philosophy, and for allowing me to quote them, I thank Sabrina Smith, Communications Facilitator at Citrus Libraries (Florida); Barbara Roberts, Director of Library Services at Palm Springs Public Library (California); Barbara Dimick, Director, Madison Public Library (Wisconsin); Laura Raphael, Readers' Library Department, Central Library, Tulsa City-County Library; and Doreen Hannon, Director of the Salem-South Lyon District Library (Michigan). Thanks also to Ann Wiegand, Library Manager of the Lewisville (Texas) Public Library, for conveying her library system's successes with signage and title modifications to incorporate self-explanatory strategic vocabulary.

Thank you to my parents, Leonard and Irene Gross, for their words of encouragement, and for teaching me that "avec de la patience, on arrive à tout."

For their unwavering support—and for just being—I express abundant heartfelt gratitude to my husband, Tri Nguyen, and son, David. I thank Tri for his sound advice, and David for his interest and ideas, not to mention his predictable wit ("So when's the movie coming out?").

Lastly, I extend a sincere note of appreciation to you, the reader. Although not an exact analogy, the philosophical question "If a tree falls in a forest . . ." comes to mind. Indeed, it is you who gives meaning to the ideas contained herein. Thank you for your time and consideration.

INTRODUCTION

If you watch the ABC hit comedy *Modern Family,* you may recall the episode where Phil and Claire issue a decree that the entire family will forgo using personal electronic devices for one week.[1] Their kids are none too pleased.

Middle school student Alex complains, "How am I supposed to do my homework? I have a huge science paper due." Fumbling about for viable alternatives, her mother comes up with, "What do you think the public library is for?" Bored, high school student Haley responds, "*I thought that was the bathroom for homeless people.*"

Taking ourselves lightly, we laugh at the exaggeration. Nonetheless, "bathroom for homeless people" underscores that our profession could benefit from an image transformation, and also that we have our work cut out for us.

Now for the good news. We have the power to dispel—permanently—all misperceptions, and be *fully* valued. How? By adopting a new approach: the "Three Pillars Philosophy."

This book describes the philosophy, explains why it works, and, for those desiring to give it a try, offers some guidance for implementation.

Although developed for public libraries, tailored slightly, the concept works for all library types. It's easy, effective, and costs little to implement. Neither does it require that we change anything we do.

What does it involve? Paying attention to *what we say.*

While there is no question that what we do and how we do it is critically important, how we *talk about* what we do can mean the difference between conveying partial or complete value.

Our choice of words can therefore mean the difference between receiving minimum and maximum funding, because what is valued gets funded.

In a nutshell, the Three Pillars Philosophy harnesses the power of language. The power stems from positioning all that we do under three, easy-to-remember "pillars," and replacing typical library terms and phrases with bold, compelling, and descriptive terminology that commands value and *that people understand.*

The philosophy recognizes that the vocabulary we choose has the power to shape in others the perceptions that we want.

What is the reality we want? Picture a world where:

- *Everyone* understands who we are, what we do, and why it matters.
- *Never again* must we justify our very existence, or *explain* why we are "essential."

- Respect and visibility position us center stage to *what the world values most*.
- We receive top funding priority.
- Disproportionate budget cuts are *relegated to history books*.
- Respect and funding *match our true value*.

Would this not be sheer paradise?
Again, some good news. The Three Pillars Philosophy can take us there.

ADDING WIND TO YOUR SAILS

Many library systems have achieved great successes with their current strategies in terms of stature and allocated funding. Others may be struggling.

It is also important to note that some library systems already incorporate pieces of this philosophy into their culture and marketing efforts. If you are in this category, the ideas that follow will seem more familiar and a logical next step.

For others, the approach might seem foreign and quite different from present practices, requiring some adjustments.

Wherever you fall along this spectrum, consider giving pieces of the philosophy a try. As you begin to achieve even greater successes, you will likely be convinced that, whatever your starting point, adopting a few more of the concepts will only add wind to your sails.

The approach has worked remarkably well for Howard County (Maryland) Library System.[2] Others who have tried the approach report similar results.

PRECISION

Librarianship is a proud profession, and rightly so. We know our full value. Yet others do not necessarily see it. There exists a disconnect between how we are currently perceived, and our true image and worth.

The Three Pillars Philosophy accurately communicates our worth so that others assign us our full value. It creates a connection by:

- aligning *everything* we do with what people know and value, education, and
- switching to a strategic, intuitive vocabulary that conveys the precise message we intend.

For external audiences (e.g., customers, funders, media), the Three Pillars Philosophy achieves:

- greater respect,
- heightened perceived value, and
- maximized funding.

Internally, benefits of the Three Pillars Philosophy are equally significant. For library staff, Board members, Friends and Foundation board members, and volunteers, embracing this approach

- establishes a distinctive sense of purpose;
- instills great pride in ourselves, our work, and our profession; and
- makes work more meaningful and fun.

The tremendous power, effectiveness, and simplicity of this approach is that *the very words we use* convey the true value of our jobs, work, and profession—even to the Haleys of this world!

CURRENT IMAGE: MEDIA

As *Modern Family* illustrates, the media typically paint an undervalued—even derogatory—image of libraries.

A similar example occurred on *The Tonight Show with Jay Leno*. In his opening monologue on May 11, 2010, Mr. Leno commented on the impending reduction to the Los Angeles Public Library's operating budget, deadpanning that the cut could affect "as many as nine people."[3] Like "bathroom for homeless people," while an obvious exaggeration, this joke implies that few people find anything of value in or about public libraries.

How best to reverse this trend? Addressing misperceptions through smart use of language will result in the media's *accurate* portrayal of us because (1) they will know our value and it will no longer occur to them to write these types of lines, and (2) until such time, as audiences begin to fully respect and understand us, the intended jokes will no longer generate laughs, effectively teaching the script writers to omit them.

CURRENT IMAGE: ELECTED OFFICIALS— DISPROPORTIONATE CUTS

The media influences the general public, including elected officials, who determine funding based on the value they assign.

Disproportionate budget cuts to libraries—even the elimination of funding—at local, state, and federal levels over the past several years point to the most serious result of being undervalued. These imprudent funding decisions provide the greatest motivation to quell misperceptions once and for all.

Consider the views of two elected officials who proposed steep budget cuts. Their comments reflect an image of us that is far from our true worth.

Bridgeport (Connecticut) Mayor Bill Finch was quoted in *American Libraries* in 2008 as announcing, "We are getting back to basics: police, fire, and education. We will not try to be all things to all people. Libraries are not essential services."[4]

Similarly, *The Washington Post* in 2009 included the following quote from Fairfax (Virginia) County Executive Anthony H. Griffin: "Parks and libraries are essentially discretionary programs."[5]

Likewise, Prescott, Arizona City Council member John Hanna, who supported charging a fee to use the library, is quoted in 2010 as asserting, "I actually consider this library as a luxury, because you do not need it to live. People need to realize . . . if you don't pay, you can't play."[6]

As to Federal funding for libraries, allocations were frozen in 2010 while "education" received a $400 billion increase.[7] A similar fate awaited us in 2011 and 2012.

Why such a grim forecast? In his 2011 State of the Union address President Obama again ranked "education" as his top priority, specifically mentioning schools and colleges (but not libraries).[8] Correspondingly, his proposed Fiscal Year 2012 budget included a *$26.8 billion increase* for "education,"[9] and a *9.5 percent cut* ($20.3 million) to library funding.[10]

It is also important to note that Congress took this one step further, proposing to eliminate *all* funding for the Institute of Museum and Library Services.[11]

Regardless of the eventual outcome of comments and proposals such as these (and, fortunately, not all came to pass), have you ever wondered why such short-sighted measures are contemplated in the first place?

In each of these cases, elected officials clearly do not understand our full value.

OUR PROFESSION'S RESPONSE TO DATE

How have we as a profession responded to date? Typical recommendations found in library literature as a means to refute misperceptions include:

- Tell them why libraries are important.
- Tell them that our programs and services are essential.

- Tell them we are the heart of Main Street.
- Tell them public libraries are one of the greatest tools our nation has.
- Tell them your story.

While this advice is not bad, neither does it immediately convey our full value. Note that each of the above suggestions requires further explanation.

NO EXPLANATION NEEDED

At Howard County Library System (HCLS), we became convinced that there had to be a simpler, more effective solution than continually explaining why we are "essential." In 2001, we began delving into an idea.

It occurred to us that schools, colleges, and universities do not need continually to justify their existence and explain their value. Why not? Because everyone knows who they are, what they do, and why they are important.

They are what the world values most: education. The very word conveys instant value, receiving the highest funding priority. The word is self-explanatory.

We pondered, "Wouldn't it be great if, like the schools, people simply assigned us our true value?" Our idea began to crystallize, and we thought, "Why not us? We, too, are education—education for all ages!"

We observed that while *we* viewed ourselves as education (after all, "lifelong learning" was our mission), we were not perceived by others as such. We were viewed as a "community service," which is often understood to be a "social service."

Additional misperceptions proliferated, such as, "With the Internet, we'll need fewer library branches, not more." (We noted that this inaccurate conclusion was not similarly applied to the County's proposed public school's capital projects.)

We realized that our everyday vocabulary might be the root of these misperceptions, and that if we wanted others to recognize our full value, we would need to modify our language.

Some quick research determined that "education" was not in our vision or mission statements. Neither was it anywhere on our website to describe what we then called our "programs and services."

Thus commenced our quest to reposition ourselves as a vital component of education.

We began by aligning ourselves with the commonly understood definition of education (i.e., "formal" education that leads to a degree). We developed and launched A+ Partners in Education, a comprehensive partnership with the Howard County Public School System (HCPSS) and Howard Community College (HCC).

Once firmly established as partners with HCPSS and HCC, we began expanding our vision to position *all that we do* under the *complete* definition of education, teaching our community that everything about us is their highest priority. (This vision ultimately led to the development of the Three Pillars, a visual with three categories under which all that we do falls, and which comprises the complete definition of education.)

Simultaneously, we started analyzing our language, experimenting with replacing common library language that tended to trivialize our value. We replaced those words with smart, value-enhanced, and intuitive vocabulary that immediately conveyed our value to the listener and reader.

We were taken by surprise.

The approach worked time and again. Respect for HCLS began to grow. Visibility increased. Appropriate levels of funding followed.

SHAPING THE VISION

Results were so successful that I was invited to speak on the topic at more than 20 library associations conferences and meetings throughout the United States, including Alaska, California, Illinois, Maryland, Michigan, Pennsylvania, Virginia, and West Virginia from 2006 to the present.

In addition, it was my privilege to present webinars on the approach for the Urban Libraries Council;[12] the Public Library Association,[13] where colleagues representing 42 of our 50 states attended, as well as the provinces of Alberta, British Columbia, and Ontario; and a New Hampshire Library Association Conference.[14]

Participant feedback from each of these venues, combined with responses to a *Public Libraries* feature article, "Transforming Our Image Through Words That Work: Perception is Everything,"[15] has shaped and strengthened the vision tenfold.

The result? A philosophy that can be adapted by any library system, large or small.

STRAIGHT LINE

The pages that follow aim to impart the "what," "why," and "how" of this simple, effective strategy so that your library system can benefit from implementing the concepts, in whole or in part.

While it has taken HCLS 10 years to develop, implement, and refine the Three Pillars Philosophy, it is likely that you can attain similar results in far less time, as you can learn from our trials and errors.

Furthermore, you will have the advantage of seeing where the vision leads, and can therefore take the fastest route (i.e., a straight line!).

Although many examples included in this book reflect HCLS's experiences with the approach, also included are the remarkable successes of several other library systems that have begun applying the concepts.

INDISPENSABLE

It is not merely fortuitous circumstances that moved HCLS from "Community Services" to the "Education" section of the County's Operating and Capital budgets, or allowed us the opportunity to win the Howard County Chamber of Commerce "Educator of the Year" award.

Neither is it coincidental that HCLS has been allocated generous funding in good economic times and has received relatively minor cuts in more challenging times.

Rather, these, and the following successes that transpired over the past decade, are the direct result of what we do, how we do it, and how we talk about what we do: the application of carefully selected words that enhance our perceived value. For recognizing that we are education, and for the operating and capital funding allocated to us, we express our profound gratitude to our tremendously supportive elected officials.

Here are some recent statistics for HCLS. Between 2002 and 2012:

- Items borrowed *doubled* (3.6 million to 7.1 million)
- Physical visits *tripled* (934,000 to 3 million)
- Classes and events attendance *tripled* (73,190 to 250,000)
- Research assistance interactions *doubled* (759,650 to 1.8 million)
- Operating budget funding from the County nearly *doubled* ($8.8 million to $17 million)
- Friends of HCLS experienced a *500 percent budget increase* ($15,000 to $100,000)
- Capital budget: *142,000 additional square feet* of building space in our Master Plan (up from zero), with the first project—a new $28 million, 63,000 sq. ft. branch—opened in December 2011

This book illustrates that by choosing smart, self-explanatory vocabulary that people understand and value, we have the power to transform our image, positioning ourselves as indispensable.

Without changing anything we do, we can be viewed precisely for what we are: *education*—a timeless, economic imperative that merits immense respect and maximized funding.

NOTES

1. *Modern Family*, "Unplugged," season 2, episode 5 (ABC), October 20, 2010.

2. Located in central Maryland's Baltimore–Washington metropolitan area, Howard County Library System's six branches deliver high-quality public education to a culturally and socioeconomically diverse population of 282,000 residents.

3. *The Tonight Show with Jay Leno* (NBC). May 11, 2010.

4. *American Libraries*, June/July 2008, p. 26.

5. Derek Kravitz, "Fiscal Outlook Grim for 2 Fairfax Agencies," *Washington Post*, November 15, 2009, washingtonpost.com/wp-dyn/content/article/2009/11/14/AR2009111402355.html.

6. *American Libraries*, April 2010, p. 24.

7. Norman Oder, "Federal Library Funding Frozen, as Expected, in President's Budget," *Library Journal*, February 1, 2010, http://www.libraryjournal.com/article/CA6717179.html.

8. Remarks by the President in State of Union Address. January 25, 2011. The White House, Office of the Press Secretary, Washington, DC. http://www.whitehouse.gov/the-press-office/2011/01/25/remarks-president-state-union-address.

9. The President's Budget for Fiscal Year 2012, Office of Management and Budget. http://www.whitehouse.gov/omb/budget.

10. Michael Kelley, "Obama Proposes $20.3 Million Reduction in Library Funding," February 14, 2011, http://www.libraryjournal.com/lj/home/889254-264/obama_proposes_20.3_million_reduction.csp.

11. FY 2011 Continuing Resolution for the FY 2011 budget. Amendment #35, would eliminate all funding for the Institute of Museum and Library Services (IMLS), including Library Services and Technology Act (LSTA) funding.

12. Urban Libraries Council Webinar: "The Power of Strategic Language in Education" (February 24, 2010).

13. Public Library Association Webinar: "Transforming Our Image: No Explanation Needed," November 15, 2010 (Chicago: American Library Association, November 15, 2010), repeated on May 18, 2011 with an added "Implementing the Vision" segment.

14. New Hampshire Library Association Fall Conference Webinar: "Transforming Our Image—Part I: Building Our Brand: The Education Advantage; Part II: Implementing the Vision" (November 4, 2011).

15. Valerie J. Gross, "Transforming Our Image through Words that Work: Perception is Everything," *Public Libraries* 48, no. 5 (September/October 2009), pp. 24–32.

PART I

OVERVIEW—THE WHAT AND WHY

1

THE POWER
OF LANGUAGE

Words carry immense power. Our choice of words can mean the difference between others perceiving us as marginal and ordinary, or as indispensable and extraordinary.

If I were to say to you, "I'm going to give you a *nutritious* snack," how would you respond?

Without knowing what the snack is, would you necessarily be thrilled?

What if I said, instead, "I'm going to give you a *delicious* snack"?[1]

Would your ambivalence now turn to delight?

If you eat only healthy foods, perhaps "nutritious" is the perfect adjective to entice you.

However, if you enjoy an occasional Mrs. Fields cookie, as I do, you will probably be far more eager with anticipation upon hearing "delicious"—yet it's the very same snack.

Such is the power of language. Changing one word can elicit a more favorable response, turning a perceived ordinary into an *anticipated extraordinary.*

THE WORLD OF POLITICS

In the political arena, carefully crafted language can mean the difference between uncertain and strong support.

For example, how likely would you be to vote in favor of "drilling for oil"?

While a number of factors might influence your level of support at any given time, what image does the phrase bring to mind?

Do you remember the television show from 1962 to 1971, *The Beverly Hillbillies*? If so, you may already be singing the show's theme song to yourself. You possibly visualize Jed Clampett and Granny celebrating oil spewing from the ground. This image—underscored by your recollection of the disastrous 2010 Gulf of Mexico oil spill—likely persuades you to lend only minimal support.

But what if, instead, you were asked to vote in favor of "careful exploration of energy"?[2]

Does this altered language increase your level of support? Almost certainly.

In this case, the terminology immediately shifts your mind to images of environmentally friendly exploration practices.

Although you recognize that drilling for oil will be part of the mix, your focus centers on the positive, such as clean solar energy, triggering greater—or even full—support.

This more astute approach garners optimal support.

THE BUSINESS WORLD

Examples of the power of language in the world of business are equally compelling.

For instance, which would you prefer buying? A "used car" or a "certified pre-owned vehicle"?[3]

When asked this question, one workshop participant remarked, "A used car is a used car is a used car," and granted, he is right. I include the example nevertheless, as we can learn from the rationale behind the strategy.

Consider that "used" can denote both "pre-owned" and "not clean," with the latter adding a negative association.

By contrast, "pre-owned" indicates precisely that and nothing more, consequently evoking an image that is likely to be more appealing to the buyer. Sellers prefer this, as the prospect of yet another sale increases.

Adding "certified" conveys professionalism and completeness, which is not only attractive to the buyer, but also holds the seller to a higher standard.

Similar strategies drive the film industry. Success in Hollywood is dependent on consumers spending money to attend, purchase, or download the cinematic works studios produce. The industry's tactics include grabbing your attention at the outset with smart movie titles.

To illustrate the psychological effect of language, based on title alone, would you race to the box office to buy tickets to see a movie called *$3,000*?

What if that same movie were called *Pretty Woman*? Now would you be more inclined to go?

While hard to imagine, *Pretty Woman,* the hit 1990 romantic comedy starring Julia Roberts and Richard Gere, was initially pitched as *$3,000*.[4] What a difference a title can make!

GENERIC VS. EVIAN

One of the most conspicuous examples from the business world comes from the bottled water marketplace. While somewhat less popular these days, the industry can teach us a powerful lesson, as companies created tremendous prestige for an ordinary product.

If you have ever shopped for bottled water, you know that some brands command more than three times the price of their generic counterparts.

Have you ever wondered why people choose to invest in these drinks when less expensive alternatives are readily available?

Thinking that taste might be the reason, I compared Evian and generic bottled water in a blind taste test. To my surprise, I actually preferred generic brands over Evian.

With taste being more or less equal, what is it that elevates Evian? Customer perception.

Customers invest in pricey bottled water because they perceive it as more valuable. Just as important, they take pride in being associated with it.

To create its desired image, Evian and similar brands incorporate clever use of language in their marketing.

Pick up any bottle of Evian water, examine its label and, through language, you'll experience "from the French Alps," "purity," "rejuvenation," and "detox with Evian."

These masterful words evoke positive images with which customers aspire to associate.

In short, strategic language contributes to Evian's perceived worth, and to the reasons why it rises far above the perceived value of generic bottled water brands.

What can libraries learn from Evian? We can learn that:

- Our choice of language can mean the difference between our being viewed as "generic" or "Evian."
- Achieving "Evian" status can attain for us greater respect and bolstered funding.

IMAGE TRANSFORMATIONS

Perhaps smartest of all is what we can learn from three industries that revolutionized their image by harnessing the power of language.

Prunes to Dried Plums

How did the prune industry transform its product's image from wrinkly and medicinal—and mainly for the senior market—to a tasty dried fruit for everyone? By renaming its product.

The lowly prune has evolved into the classier "dried plum."

I personally appreciate this rejuvenated terminology, as I love dried fruit of all kinds. Placing a bag of "dried plums" in my shopping cart is now perceived as healthy and hip as a package of dried pears or apricots.

Liquor to Spirits

Sensing growing negative connotations with the word "liquor," the liquor industry decided to transform its image. Exchanging the term "liquor" for "spirits" accomplished this feat.[5]

The result? Gone are images of bottles in brown paper bags and alcoholics.

The term "spirits" has replaced negativity with cheerful mental pictures of sophistication, style, camaraderie, and friends laughing while clinking glasses after proposing a toast.

Gambling to Gaming

As a final example, the gambling industry orchestrated arguably the most brilliant image transformation of all.

Applying a unified approach, the industry replaced "gambling" with "gaming."[6]

In doing so, the industry rid itself of links to pawn shops, addiction, and broken families.

"Gaming" traded these depressing images with the perception of fun, choices—even family vacations!

POWERFUL LANGUAGE FOR OUR PROFESSION

As an introduction to how the library profession can benefit from harnessing the power of language, take a few moments to think of what you say when asked, "What does your organization do?"

Pare your answer down to just a handful of sentences.

Now, pretend you work at ABC Public Library. At a Chamber of Commerce breakfast, you meet State Senator Jones, who chairs the Budget and Taxation Committee. The Senator and her colleagues will be voting later that morning on a proposed 10 percent cut in state funding to libraries (while "education" is slated to receive flat funding).

Conversationally, she says, "So tell me. What does ABC Public Library do?"

You respond with your prepared talking points.

Like many people, and most politicians, Senator Jones understands little about the value of libraries. She thinks that libraries loan books (i.e., that's *all* they do), that the need for libraries is therefore diminishing due to the Internet and e-books, and that libraries could easily be run by far fewer librarians and more volunteers.

If you were this elected official, would your response:

1. Impress you?
2. Convey a complete, succinct summary of what public libraries do in language you understand and value?
3. Sway you effectively toward a "no" vote on cuts?
4. Equip you to not only justify a "no" vote to your colleagues, but also to persuade them to join the "no" camp?
5. Increase your respect for libraries?

To assess your response's impact on the Senator, score your answers to the above questions on a scale from 1 to 10, with 10 being the strongest.

Now replay this same scenario with the following script:

Senator Jones: So tell me. What does ABC Public Library do?
You: We deliver equal opportunity in education—to literally *everyone* in ABC. Our educational mission and curriculum comprises three pillars.

- Our first pillar, *Self-Directed Education*, includes fiction and nonfiction materials in all formats, such as books, e-books, and specialized online research tools—all that our experts make conveniently accessible to *you*, our customer.
- Pillar two, *Research Assistance & Instruction*, includes personalized research assistance and award-winning classes taught by library instructors for students of all ages.
- And our third pillar, *Instructive & Enlightening Experiences*, includes the cultural and community center concepts, partnerships, and signature initiatives, such as author events that bring people together to discuss ideas.

Placing yourself back in Senator Jones's shoes, ask yourself the same five questions, then compare the effect of this revised response to that of your earlier answer.

Has the overall score increased? I'll bet your answer is, "Yes!"

Senator Jones will now assign greater value and respect to what we do as a direct result of our choice of carefully selected value-enhanced vocabulary. The language speaks for itself, requiring *no further explanation*.

Simply by using dynamic, understandable language, we have inched the Senator's views one step away from "generic" (with its corresponding frugal funding levels) and one step closer to "Evian" (with its optimal funding levels).

This is the power of the Three Pillars Philosophy, which you have just seen in action with Senator Jones.

Apply it in real life and you will have your audience spellbound.

Although we'll scrutinize numerous terms common to the library profession along with recommended replacements, let's begin by analyzing the most commanding word. The term is the essence of the Three Pillars Philosophy and key to our image transformation.

The magic word is *education*.

NOTES

1. Frank Luntz, *Words that Work: It's Not What You Say, It's What People Hear* (New York: Hyperion, 2007), p. 206.

2. Luntz, *Words that Work*, p. 285.

3. Luntz, *Words that Work*, p. 259.

4. Stephanie Palmer, *Good in a Room: How to Sell Yourself (And Your Ideas) and Win Over Any Audience* (New York: Doubleday, 2008), p. 51.

5. Luntz, *Words that Work*, p. 131.

6. Luntz, *Words that Work*, p. 129.

THE THREE PILLARS PHILOSOPHY

Quite simply, the Three Pillars Philosophy positions public libraries as education, with library staff as educators.

Intrigued, you may be wondering, "How can this be?"

EDUCATION—THE COMPLETE DEFINITION

The concept becomes self-evident when one moves beyond the more limited definition of education (i.e., a course of study leading to a formal degree), focusing instead on the word's complete definition, which includes:

- Information about a subject matter
- Knowledge acquired by learning
- Activities of educating, instructing, or teaching
- Activities that impart knowledge
- The process of acquiring knowledge
- An enlightening experience

Are you not pleasantly surprised to discover that *everything we do* falls squarely under education—*what the world holds in highest esteem*?

If you aren't yet energized by this epiphany, I will happily bet my island in Tahiti that you soon will be once you experience the remarkable power of this theory.

WE *ARE* EDUCATION

Firmly establishing ourselves as education benefits us tremendously because in so doing, we convey our full value *with a single word*.

It is important to emphasize the difference in meaning between the strong, assertive phrase, "We *are* education," and what we tend to say in our profession, such as "We play *a role in* education," "We are *an* educational *resource*," or "We *support* education."

These more common phrases diminish our value. They imply that only schools "are" education.

While it's true that we take immense pride in the effective manner in which we "support" and augment the curriculum of schools, colleges, and universities, we also deliver a unique curriculum to our entire customer base—"students" of *all* ages.

The Three Pillars Philosophy establishes public libraries as educational institutions *on an equal footing with the schools.*

We are education in our own right.

THE THREE PILLARS

At Howard County Library System (HCLS), when we recognized that we fell solidly under education, we began conceptualizing an image that would convey—at a glance—our overall curriculum and value.

This idea resulted in the "Three Pillars" (Figure 2.1), with each pillar representing a distinct, equally important curriculum segment.

Most important, the image effectively communicates who we are, what we do, and why it matters.

Pillar I, *Self-Directed Education,* includes what comes to mind for most people when they think of public libraries: books.

Included are:

- Fiction and nonfiction materials in all formats—print, electronic, audio, and visual
- Specialized online research tools, e-readers, and the Internet accessed from the library through public access computers

Essentially, everything our customers find on their own, thanks to the expertise of our staff—who acquire, organize, and enable convenient and friendly access—falls under this first pillar.

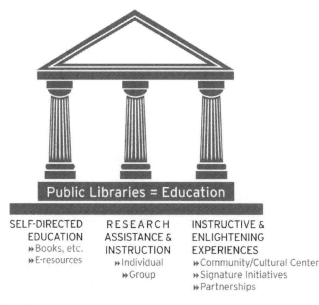

Figure 2.1   The Three Pillars.

Pillar II, *Research Assistance & Instruction,* includes the personalized research assistance we deliver to our customers, as well as the classes, seminars, and workshops we teach or facilitate.

Pillar III, *Instructive & Enlightening Experiences,* includes the cultural and community center concepts; partnerships that leverage funding and expertise (e.g., A+ Partners in Education,[1] Choose Civility,[2] Well & Wise[3]); and signature initiatives, such as Battle of the Books,[4] Summer Reading Kickoff, and notable author events that bring people together to discuss ideas.

THE THREE PILLARS—TAILORED

While the generic version of the Three Pillars image can be used for statewide and national purposes, the visual can be tailored for local use, reflecting a library system's brand.

For example, we incorporated HCLS's logo (see Figure 2.2) and "corporate colors" to individualize the Three Pillars for use when we are representing just our library system (see Figure 2.3).

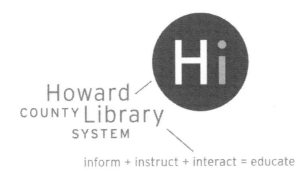

Figure 2.2   HCLS's logo.

Figure 2.3   The Three Pillars—tailored.

Figure 2.4   The Three Pillars—all libraries.

We have also developed a third Three Pillars visual that includes all libraries (see Figure 2.4), to use when public and governmental libraries might be seeking state funding collectively, or developing a combined strategic plan at the statewide level.

This visual can also be adopted by our academic library colleagues.

Each of these images proves to be powerful and persuasive when requesting funding (see the following flyer examples, Figures 2.5–2.7). In addition, the visuals serve as the foundation of impressive presentation outlines.

These images are available to download at hclibrary.org. Various ways of incorporating the pillars into presentations and budget testimony are included in chapters 8 and 9.

PUBLIC LIBRARIES = EDUCATION
Three Pillars

Howard
COUNTY Library
SYSTEM

inform + instruct + interact = educate

A major component of Howard County's strong education system, Howard County Library System (HCLS) delivers *high-quality public education for all ages* through a curriculum that comprises three pillars:

I. *Self-Directed Education* through vast collections of items in print, audio and electronic formats; and thousands of specialized online research tools (e.g., *Wall Street Journal* and *Access Science*).

II. *Research Assistance & Instruction* for individuals and groups. This pillar includes classes, seminars and workshops for all ages, taught by HCLS Instructors.

III. *Instructive & Enlightening Experiences* through cultural and community center concepts, events, and partnerships—such as *A+ Partners in Education*, *Well & Wise*, and *Choose Civility*.

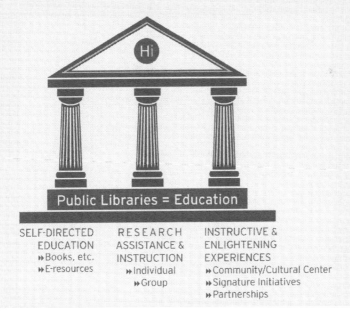

Figure 2.5   Three Pillars flyer tailored for a specific library.

PUBLIC LIBRARIES = EDUCATION
Three Pillars

A major component of [Your State Here]'s strong education system, public libraries deliver *high-quality public education for all ages*. The role of public libraries is best illustrated by the image below, with three pillars that comprise our overall educational mission and curriculum:

I.   *Self-Directed Education* through vast collections of items in print, audio, and electronic formats; and thousands of specialized online research tools (e.g., *Wall Street Journal* and *Access Science*).

II. *Research Assistance & Instruction* for individuals and groups. This pillar includes classes, seminars, and workshops for all ages, taught by library instructors.

III. *Instructive & Enlightening Experiences* through cultural and community center concepts, events, and partnerships.

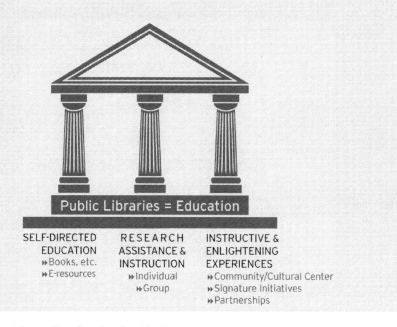

Figure 2.6   Three Pillars flyer for all public libraries.

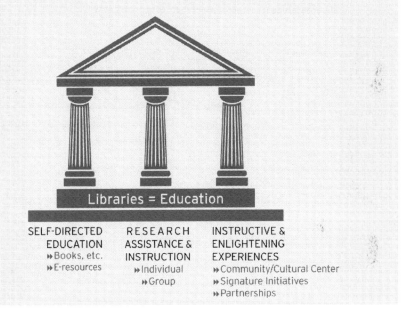

[Your State Here] LIBRARIES = EDUCATION
Three Pillars

A major component of our state's strong education system, [Your State Here]'s public, academic, school, and governmental libraries deliver *high-quality education* through a curriculum that comprises three pillars:

I. *Self-Directed Education* through vast collections of items in print, audio, and electronic formats; specialized online research tools; and preservation of materials in all formats.

II. *Research Assistance & Instruction* for individuals and groups. This pillar includes classes, seminars, and workshops for all ages, taught by library instructors.

III. *Instructive & Enlightening Experiences* through cultural and community center concepts, events, and partnerships.

Libraries = Education

SELF-DIRECTED EDUCATION	RESEARCH ASSISTANCE & INSTRUCTION	INSTRUCTIVE & ENLIGHTENING EXPERIENCES
▸Books, etc.		
▸E-resources	▸Individual	▸Community/Cultural Center
	▸Group	▸Signature Initiatives
		▸Partnerships

Figure 2.7   Three Pillars flyer for all libraries.

TIMELESS AND INDISPENSABLE

A key advantage of the Three Pillars Philosophy is that the theory's timelessness translates to our being viewed as indispensable for centuries to come.

First, education—our mission, plain and simple, under this approach—is timeless. Two hundred years from now, the education we deliver will *still* be critical to economic advancement and quality of life.

In addition, the process of obtaining education is perpetual, which further solidifies our indispensability. To quote Bel Kaufman, "Education is not a product: mark, diploma, job, money—in that order; it is a process, a never-ending one."[5]

Likewise, each of the headings is timeless. For instance, Self-Directed Education is not tied to any particular format. It represents *all* formats—including those yet to be invented—and will evolve over time. Consequently, what happens to the beloved paper book is irrelevant!

Research Assistance & Instruction is also timeless. Although this second pillar will always be a component of our curriculum, as with Pillar I, it will inevitably change, depending on an era's technology, research, and teaching developments.

Pillar III's heading, Instructive & Enlightening Experiences, is just as enduring, as we are social beings, enjoying and needing in-person connection. Technology will never replace face-to-face dialogue and human interaction. Bringing people together enables the exchange of ideas, a critically important component of our educational mission that will always be valued.

Each of the pillars can also be categorized as "self-education," meaning taking the initiative to educate oneself continuously to improve one's intellect and quality of life. As Isaac Asimov famously said, "Self-education is, I firmly believe, the only kind of education there is."[6]

BALANCE

The emphasis we place on our curriculum within each pillar will vary from decade to decade.

Take, for example, the Research Assistance aspect of Pillar II. Twenty years ago, those planning to vacation in Mexico needed our Research Specialists' expertise to assist them in finding the peso's exchange rate against the dollar. Now, vacationers conduct this type of research on their own.

However, our experts are still needed for more complex research, such as when a customer brings in a 17-page article about the Emperor Haile Salassie and wants to find the full text of a citation for the Emperor's speech that ran in the *New York Times* on July 2, 1936. Unlike most of our customers, our Research Specialists know how to navigate the appropriate specialized online research tools to locate the entire speech.

At the same time, the role of instructor under our second pillar has *expanded* in recent years, with the number of classes we teach and events we hold for customers of all ages on the increase in response to demand.

Similarly, the prominence of any one of the pillars will shift over time.

Right now, Pillar I is still our strongest, although Pillars II and III are gaining strength. As we evolve, we can respond to the times, always applying the appropriate balance among all three.

STOP 'EM DEAD IN THEIR TRACKS: SAY ALL THREE

Conveying all three pillars simultaneously is most effective. Why? Because the trio conveys our complete curriculum, that each pillar is part of the whole, and that each is equally important.

Concurrent presentation of the pillars will also effectively stop—once and for all—*all speculation about the future of libraries based on the future of the printed book.* How many times have we heard that e-books mean the end of public libraries?

Were we to collectively convey our curriculum in terms of the Three Pillars, eventually:

- FOX-TV would cease broadcasting television segment headlines, such as "Are Libraries Necessary, or a Waste of Tax Money?" and reporter Anna Davlantes would forever eliminate from her scripts comments such as, "With the Internet and e-books, do we really need millions for libraries?"[7]
- *Newsweek* would stop crafting headlines, such as "Farewell, Libraries?" in an online article about e-books beginning to outsell hardcovers.[8]

This is because currently, FOX and *Newsweek* reporters think that all we do is loan books—which does not even represent the full picture of Pillar I.

Similarly, concurrent presentation of the pillars will put a stop to those who illogically proclaim, "I get everything I need off the Internet. Why do we need public libraries?"

Once people understand that we, like the schools, *are* education, and that our curriculum comprises all three pillars, such absurd comments will cease. (Would people ever assert such remarks about schools—as in, "My child gets everything off the Internet. Why do we need public schools?" Of course not!)

SO LONG, DEFENSIVENESS!

With the Three Pillars approach, we have the power to finally put an end to needing to *constantly be on the defensive.*

Instead, we will be in a strong, offensive position that will be impervious to all new technologies and future developments guaranteed to come our way.

Like the schools, our value will be fully understood. Our future will be solid.

REPOSITIONING OURSELVES AS EDUCATIONAL INSTITUTIONS—SUGGESTED PHRASES

To give you an example of strong phrases that will reposition your library system as an educational institution, try some of these phrases:

- We are a *major component of [your county/city/state]'s strong education system.*
- We deliver *equal opportunity in education.*
- We deliver *public education* for all.
- We deliver *high-quality public education* for all ages.
- We deliver *excellence in education.*
- We provide *equal access to quality education for all,* regardless of age, background, or means.
- We are a *pillar of education.*
- We are a *cornerstone in the education process.*
- We are *partners in education.*
- We are *education.*
- What's our business? *Education.*
- What's our brand? *Education.*

WHAT ABOUT DISCOVERY, CURIOSITY, AND FUN?

Some of you may be worried that this approach will somehow diminish the wonderfully compelling elements of discovery, curiosity, and fun that we strive to weave into the experiences we create for our customers.

Worry no longer! This is certainly not the case.

In fact, as always, it is imperative that discovery, curiosity, and fun be emphasized for everything we deliver under each of the pillars (fun is especially critical for teens) at every opportunity.

AND WHAT ABOUT OUR RECREATIONAL AND ENTERTAINMENT COMPONENT?

At HCLS, although we try to avoid the words *recreation* and *entertainment* (which can be viewed as discretionary or even frivolous), as always, we infuse the recreation and entertainment factors into our entire curriculum as much as possible, since the most effective type of education is enjoyable.

I, for one, took all of the courses Professor Janice Kosel taught in law school because she was highly entertaining, making the driest of subjects fascinating and fun.

HOW DO WORKS OF FICTION FIT INTO EDUCATION?

Although the educational value of *nonfiction* materials is self-evident, categorizing works of fiction as education has generated some discussion among workshop participants.

For those of you who may not immediately recognize the educational merits of fiction titles, consider that while many customers read, listen to, and watch fiction books and movies for recreational and entertainment purposes, those same experiences are also educational.

For instance, I'm currently listening to Alexander McCall Smith's *No. 1 Ladies Detective Agency* audiobook series. What fun! What superlative writing—which narrator Lisette Lecat brings to life impeccably as she performs the characters. *And what an education!* I have learned about life in Botswana and customs unique to that region. I have also benefited tremendously from the nuggets of wisdom the notable author imparts in every chapter.

Another example showing how fiction is educational comes from an interview I heard on NPR, "Alcohol Abuse Rising Among Women; DUIs, Too."[9] Two authors were being interviewed. Both wanted to warn others about the perils of alcoholism, and also provide hope for successful healing. Host Jaki Lynden observed, "What interests me is that . . . one of you [Rachel Brownell] chose to write about what happened to you in a nonfiction way [*Mommy Doesn't Drink Here Anymore*]. And Michelle [Huneven], you have a story to tell about alcoholism, which you have used in a work of fiction [*Blame*]. Why did you do it the way that you did?"

In other words, both genres can be used to "educate."

A final example, Keith Oatley and Ingrid Wickelgren describe yet another educational component of fictional literature in their *Scientific American* article, "10 Novels That Will Sharpen Your Mind." Research has established that a novel evokes in readers real emotions for a book's characters. Extending beyond the printed page and into real life, this "significant sway over the human mind" improves readers' social skills by instilling in them "a better understanding of other human beings and a deeper empathy for others."[10]

With regard to fiction movies, workshop participants have observed that college film study courses include fiction movies, and that fiction movies—like fiction books—are, in and of themselves, education.

Consider the following. When is Asimov's *I, Robot* education? When:

- Someone discovers the book while perusing the stacks at the library, reads it, and is enlightened?
- The book is discussed as part of a book club discussion held at the library?
- The book is part of the ninth grade English curriculum and the student must write a report and be tested on the book?
- The audiobook is borrowed from the library and listened to on a family trip to the Grand Canyon?
- The DVD is borrowed from the library and is viewed as part of a college course?
- The DVD is borrowed from the library and is viewed in a ninth grade English class to compare to the book?
- The DVD is borrowed from the library to view and discuss as part of a book club discussion held at the library?
- The DVD is borrowed from the library by a customer interested in comparing the movie to the book?
- The DVD is shown as part of a monthly "Cinema Series" held at the library?
- The DVD is borrowed from the library to view at home for the purpose of "entertainment"?

This series of questions points to the answer, "All of the above." Each falls squarely under one of our curriculum's three pillars.

IS READERS ADVISORY EDUCATION?

A few thoughts on Readers Advisory and how this curriculum component falls under education.

As a profession, we shortchange ourselves in this area of expertise. When analyzed, Readers Advisory is actually research assistance that our Instructor & Research Specialists deliver to customers.

In response to customers asking what they should read next, depending on the situation, we respond in one of three ways. We might:

1. Make immediate suggestions (i.e., we know what to recommend based on titles they like, no longer needing to conduct the research because we are such experts in the field)
2. Conduct the research on behalf of customers (e.g., searching NoveList)
3. Teach customers how to conduct the research themselves (either individualized instruction or in a class setting)

If you think about it, each of these three possibilities constitutes research, falling squarely under the second pillar of our curriculum, Research Assistance & Instruction.

At HCLS, we are starting to consider alternate words for this invaluable research we conduct every day. It has occurred to us that "Advisory" can mean a warning—as in Weather Advisory. (If you think of a better term, do let us know!)

COMMUNITY/CULTURAL CENTER

Many public libraries highlight the growing importance of the library as a "community center" and "cultural center." While important in and of themselves, when linked with education, the roles increase in value exponentially. This is because education is what is valued above all else.

Under the Three Pillars Philosophy, Community/Cultural Center falls under the third pillar, and is always presented as such, as in, "And the third pillar of our educational mission, Instructive & Enlightening Experiences, includes the Community Center and Cultural Center concepts— bringing people together to discuss ideas—as well as our signature initiatives and community partnerships."

How does one position Community Center under education? By emphasizing that connecting people is central to education, and that both formal and informal discussions with others that follow an author event or film showing are a key part of the educational experience.

Similarly, Cultural Center is inevitably stronger when it is positioned squarely as part of our third educational pillar.

This same strategy can be applied to the components of all three pillars. For example, we all take pride in the collection of books we lend. Instead of merely stating that your books are second to none, say you deliver Self-Directed Education in world-class fashion, and that your stellar book collection is a key component of this first pillar of your educational mission. The full value of the books will be more accurately communicated and perceived.

CRYSTAL CLEAR

Schools, colleges, and universities do not need to constantly explain what they do. Their inherent value is *fully* understood. No one looks at them with a puzzled look, sheepishly asking, "Tell me again what you do?" or "Remind me again why you are essential?"

Everyone knows what schools do. Schools simply are essential. People understand this without needing any explanation.

Repositioning public libraries as education accomplishes for us this same innate understanding.

As education, our actual value will be immediately understood through our *crystal clear* vision: We are education. Our transformed image will speak for itself.

THREE PILLARS PHILOSOPHY IN ACTION

Our first attempt at applying this new approach at the state level occurred prior to the 2008 elections.

As a member of the Maryland Library Association's (MLA) Legislative Panel, I attended a meeting where the MLA president presented some questions she had prepared to pose to each gubernatorial candidate.

One of the questions read:

Where would you rate libraries in importance, relative to other state services?

I noted that, while the question was good, perhaps it could be strengthened to capitalize on an ideal teaching opportunity.

The suggestion involved:

- Beginning with a strong statement that would teach the candidates who we are in an impressive, memorable way.
- Following the statement with a question infused with value-enhanced terminology, which would require the candidates to repeat the terminology in their responses—which we could then quote!

We edited the question to:

Public libraries are *pillars of education*. In your administration, how would you *enhance* public libraries, and how would you incorporate public libraries as you further the *educational goals* for the state?

This approach worked well for Doreen S. Hannon, Director of the Salem-South Lyon District Library in Michigan. Ms. Hannon organized and moderated a "Candidate Meet & Greet"[11] prior to the November 2010 elections, opening the forum with the statement, "Everything we do is education."

She then posed the very question above as edited to the 13 participating candidates. Results show that through her choice of language, Ms. Hannon successfully taught the candidates that public libraries are what they value most: education. As predicted, the candidates repeated the desired language.

Here are three sample responses:

- The incumbent State Representative for the 66th District, Bill Rogers began his response with "Public libraries have always held an important role in the educational process."
- Similarly, running for State Representative for the 66th District, James Delcamp stated, "We need to recognize libraries as teaching and learning institutions and expand their role. I'd like to think of them as mini community colleges."
- Most impressively, incumbent State Representative for the 38th District, Hugh Crawford declared emphatically: "*Everything* is on the table *except* Medicaid and education, and within the umbrella of education are *public libraries*. This cannot involve a cut to library funding. I will work to reverse that."

HIGHEST PRIORITY

The most important reason to reposition ourselves as education stems from the fact that education is universally valued, typically commanding the highest priority, including funding.

Nelson Mandela once said, "Education is the most powerful weapon which you can use to change the world."[12] Similarly, President John F. Kennedy declared, "Our progress as a nation can be no swifter than our progress in education. The human mind is our fundamental resource."[13]

Not surprisingly, education took center stage in President Barack Obama's 2011 State of the Union address, when he proclaimed, "We need to out-innovate, out-educate, and out-build the rest of the world. That's how we'll win the future. . . . Cutting the deficit by gutting our investments in innovation and education is like lightening an overloaded airplane by removing its engine. It may make you feel like you're flying high at first, but it won't take long before you feel the impact."[14]

Similarly, in his 2012 State of the Union address, President Obama set forth a vision for "the America within our reach: A country that leads the world in educating its people."[15]

When unveiling his Fiscal Year 2012 budget, which included a $26.8 billion increase[16] for education, Mr. Obama emphasized:

- "Education is an investment we need to win the future,"[17] and
- "Even as we cut out things that we can afford to do without, we have a responsibility to invest in those areas that will have the biggest impact in our future, and that's especially true when it comes to education."[18]

A final example from the highest elected office, when refuting opposing views questioning the role of federal government in education, President Obama asserted, "Let me make it plain: We cannot cut education."[19]

Why is it that these leaders do not include public libraries when they speak of education? *Because we have not yet effectively conveyed to them the precise message that we are education.*

SAY THE MAGIC WORD

My counterpart from a neighboring library system not too long ago commented that Maryland state legislators don't understand our value.

I remarked, "But we are their highest priority—education."

Sighing, she responded, "Yes, but they don't see us that way."

She's right, and here's why. As with elected officials at the Federal level, we have not yet succeeded in teaching them.

Contributing to the disconnect is that, to date, we have not said the magic word. A perusal of library websites and conference topics points to the fact that not many of us ever use the word *education* to describe ourselves.

When *education* does appear, the word tends to reference elementary, middle, and high schools, as well as institutions of higher education. Rarely is education used in connection with libraries to describe our very essence.

Incidentally, as in a number of states, Maryland public libraries are governed by the Annotated Code of Maryland. The Education section of the code specifies that "Public library resources and services are essential components of the educational system."[20]

Also important to note, New York's Supreme Court of Suffolk County recently ruled that public libraries are educational institutions, and librarians, educators.[21]

While such legislation and case law has the potential of influencing elected officials—indeed the general public—to value us on par with schools, in reality, this is not the case. Instead, people are mystified as to why we fall under education, because "they don't see us that way."

So what is the solution? We can easily teach them by:

- Saying and writing the word *education* early and often, reinforcing the word's complete definition through our use and application of the term.
- Positioning all that we do under this complete definition, embracing and conveying the Three Pillars vision that succinctly articulates our full value.

RESULTS

Compare the previously mentioned quote of Bridgeport Mayor Bill Finch in *American Libraries*, "We are getting back to basics: police, fire, and education. We will not try to be all things to all people. Libraries are not essential services,"[22] to Howard County Executive Ken Ulman's views.

As a preface, Mr. Ulman has appreciated that HCLS *is* education for the past 10 years—first as a County Council member, and now as County Executive.[23] While we have assisted with the alignment by saying and writing the word *education*, Mr. Ulman places us under education because it makes sense.

One of our strongest supporters, Mr. Ulman regularly acknowledges us as a major component of education—the driving force of the county's award-winning quality of life.

Six months into his new County Executive position, Mr. Ulman wrote to his constituents: "We are continuing our dedication to quality education. Education is the engine which drives our quality of life. We are fortunate to have a public school system, library system and community college which are all nationally recognized, but these institutions cannot continue to thrive without strong support from the County . . . I am proud that my budget reflects the high priority I place on education."[24]

Last year, when *Money* magazine ranked Howard County the second best place to live in the United States,[25] Mr. Ulman stated, "Our lowest unemployment rate of 5.2 percent in the state, our #1 nationally ranked library system, and #1 public school system in the state are just a few reasons why Howard County is such a special community."[26]

Equally impressive, in a *Corridor, Inc.* article featuring Mr. Ulman and three other newly elected central Maryland County Executives,[27] the reporter asked the officials, "What's the number one attribute of your county?" While Ulman's counterparts answered "its beauty," "the whole community spirit," and "the schools," what was the first thing Mr. Ulman mentioned? The library system!

Lastly, ever since 2007 when the County Executive moved HCLS from the Community Services section of the County's Operating and Capital budgets to the Education section, joining the school system and community college in this category, County Executive Ulman has included the following language in the proposed countywide budgets he submits to the County Council:

April 2009

The education system comprised of our local schools, community college and library is one of our County's greatest strengths. Maintaining the excellence of these educational institutions is of highest priority.[28]

April 2010

Our top-ranked educational system—comprised of our local schools, community college and libraries—remains a top priority . . . Maintaining the excellence of these institutions is our highest priority.[29]

April 2011

Our top-ranked educational system—comprised of our local schools, community college and libraries—is one of Howard County's greatest strengths. Maintaining the excellence of these institutions is our highest priority.

Howard County's schools are the best in Maryland, in large part because of wise investments in our educational system. Howard Community College is also an essential part of our community's educational partnership. Our Library System, also among the best in the country, is another important educational partner and an essential ingredient in the success of our community.[30]

April 2012

This budget provides record funding for Howard County's Educational partnership, which includes Howard County Public School System, Howard Community College, and Howard County Library System. Education is at the heart of our community's success today and into the future. [31]

A final example of the effect of the Three Pillars Philosophy on local elected officials, the *Columbia Flier* summarized County Council Chair Calvin Ball's priorities as education and public safety, with the following description of education. "Ball said his commitment to funding education is shown not only in his support for the public schools, but for the county library and Howard Community College."[32]

We have also been successful in applying the Three Pillars approach to fully convey our value to the State and Federal elected officials representing Howard County.

It's exciting to think about how we might all join forces to attain—across the board—the assigned value we deserve!

CONVINCED?

Hopefully the successes we've seen in Howard County will persuade you to give the Three Pillars Philosophy a try.

Following the June 8, 2010, Michigan Director's Summit,[33] which included a "Transforming Our Image" workshop, Cecelia Ann Marlow, Director of the Cromaine Library in Hartland, Michigan decided to apply the concepts. Summarizing the results, she wrote:

When I met with Mike Malott, news editor of the *Livingston County Daily Press-Argus*, about our building and millage renewal ballot proposals, I used the concepts of self-directed education, research specialists, and classes led by esteemed and qualified instructors. Mike commented that he had not heard public libraries described in that manner before and responded very positively.

It truly worked and has continued to work with each person with whom I've shared these principles.

Just using the terms that others recognize *rather than the library lingo we toss about so casually and with so little effectiveness* is making a difference not just in how others perceive us, but how we perceive and value ourselves . . .

One of my trustees has now incorporated [education] into his talks with the community about our library and, especially, our renovation and expansion project—a tough sell in Michigan's economy. His terms, [such as] "citadel of self-directed education," he has found are quite effective.[34]

Note that Ms. Marlow is referencing the entire Three Pillars Philosophy, which also includes applying Supporting Strategic Vocabulary.

NOTES

1. Valerie J. Gross, "A⁺ Partners in Education: Linking Libraries to Education for a Flourishing Future," *Public Libraries* 44, no. 4 (July/August 2005), pp. 217–22.

2. Valerie J. Gross, "Choose Civility: Public Libraries Take Center Stage," *Public Libraries* 50, no. 4 (July/August 2011), p. 30–37.

3. Well & Wise website: http://hocowellandwise.org/.

4. HCLS Battle of the Books 2011, http://www.flickr.com/photos/hocolibrary/sets/72157626462634340/.

5. Self-Education Quotes, "What Great Thinkers Have to Say About Independent Learning," http://selfmadescholar.com/b/2007/03/09/self-education-quotes-what-great-thinkers-have-to-say-about-independent-learning/.

6. Self-Education Quotes.

7. "How the World Sees Us," *American Libraries* 41, no. 8 (August 2010), p. 22.

8. Malcolm Jones, "Farewell, Libraries?," *Newsweek*, August 5, 2010, http://www.newsweek.com/2010/08/05/farewell-libraries.html.

9. "Alcohol Abuse Rising Among Women; DUIs, Too," *National Public Radio, Weekend Edition Sunday*, October 4, 2009, http://www.npr.org/templates/story/story.php?storyId=113479801.

10. Keith Oatley and Ingrid Wickelgren, "10 Novels That Will Sharpen Your Mind," *Scientific American,* December 9, 2011, http://www.scientificamerican.com/article.cfm?id=fiction-stories-that-sharpen-your-mind.

11. "Candidate Meet & Greet, Salem-South Lyon District Library, Michigan," September 23, 2010, http://vimeo.com/15289219.

12. "Nelson Mandela." Thinkexist.com. http://thinkexist.com/quotation/the_greatest_glory_in_living_lies_not_in_never/148833.html.

13. "John F. Kennedy." Great-Quotes.com. Gledhill Enterprises, December 13, 2011, http://www.great-quotes.com/quote/1299200.

14. "Obama State of the Union Speech 2011: Full Text & Video," http://www.huffingtonpost.com/2011/01/25/obama-state-of-the-union-_1_n_813478.html.

15. "Full Transcript: Obama's 2012 State of the Union Address," *USA Today,* January 25, 2012, http://www.usatoday.com/news/washington/story/2012-01-24/state-of-the-union-transcript/52780694/1.

16. The President's Budget for Fiscal Year 2012, Office of Management and Budget, http://www.whitehouse.gov/omb/budget.

17. Obama delivers remarks on education and key budget priorities, Speech Transcripts, February 14, 2011, http://projects.washingtonpost.com/obama-speeches/speech/561/.

18. Jackie Calmes, "Obama's Budget Focuses on Path to Rein in Deficit," *New York Times,* February 14, 2011, http://www.nytimes.com/2011/02/15/us/politics/15obama.html.

19. Gail Russell Chaddock, "No Child Left Behind: Why Congress Will Struggle to Hit Obama's Deadline," *The Christian Science Monitor,* March 14, 2011, http://www.csmonitor.com/USA/Politics/2011/0314/No-Child-Left-Behind-Why-Congress-will-struggle-to-hit-Obama-s-deadline.

20. Annotated Code of Maryland Education, Volume §23–101.

21. Michael Kelly, "New York Court Declares That Libraries Are Educational Institutions," *Library Journal,* June 2, 2011, http://www.libraryjournal.com/lj/home/890854-264/new_york_court_declares_that.html.csp.

22. *American Libraries,* June/July 2008, p. 26.

23. For much of Maryland, local government typically operates at the county level. Twenty-three counties and Baltimore City make up Maryland's 24 main local jurisdictions. Governance is either by a multimember Board of County Commissioners or, as is the case for Howard County, divided between a county executive and legislative council.

24. "Ken Ulman's First Six Months in Office," County Executive Ken Ulman, e-mail message to his constituents, June 26, 2007.

25. Pieter van Noordennen et al., "100 Best Places to Live in America," *Money* 39, no. 7 (2010), p. 64.

26. "Howard County—'Top Five Places to Live in America!,'" County Executive Ken Ulman, e-mail message to his constituents, July 12, 2010.

27. Amrit Dhillon, "The Exec Files," *Corridor Inc* 2, no. 2 (February 2007), p. 16.

28. "FY 2010 Operating Budget," Howard County Executive Ken Ulman, April 20, 2009, p. v.

29. "FY 2011 Operating Budget," Howard County Executive Ken Ulman, April 21, 2010, p. v.

30. "FY 2012 Howard County Proposed Budget," Howard County Executive Ken Ulman, April 20, 2011, p. 42.

31. "FY 2013 Howard County Proposed Budget," Howard County Executive Ken Ulman, April 20, 2012, p. x.

32. Lindsey McPherson, "GOP Challenger Faces Uphill Battle in District 2," *Columbia Flier,* October 14, 2010, p. 12.

33. Michigan Directors' Summit, "Building Partnerships and Forging New Alliances During Turbulent Fiscal Times," June 8, 9:30 A.M. to 4 P.M., sponsored by the Detroit Library Cooperative, Mideastern Michigan Library Cooperative, Suburban Library Cooperative, and The Library Network.

34. Cecilia Ann Marlow, Library Director, Cromaine Library, Hartland, Michigan. Report as forwarded in her July 8, 2010, e-mail to me, "Promised Follow-up on Directors' Summit." Used with permission.

3

SUPPORTING STRATEGIC VOCABULARY— KEY TERMS

In addition to positioning all that we do under education, the Three Pillars Philosophy involves exchanging some of our long-standing words and phrases—language we use without thinking— for a value-enhanced vocabulary.

You may wish to view the recommended lexicon outlined in the next three chapters as brilliant supporting actors, whose performances merit accolades on their own while elevating the star.

Many of these terms further associate us with education. Others correlate with business principles. Still others are simply stronger, more notable terms than the ones we currently say.

All of these smart words share two common elements. Like *education*, they convey our importance with precision, requiring no explanation to do so. Speaking for themselves, these words catapult our perceived value to that ideal Evian level.

Let's begin by analyzing the effect of a term most of us use daily without thinking.

WHAT DOES "STORYTIME" MEAN?

Have you ever asked yourself what the word *storytime* means to someone who has no idea what libraries do? Most likely, you haven't, simply because it hasn't occurred to you to ask the question.

What does *storytime* mean to the uninitiated? Workshop participants have noted that the word conveys the obvious "a time at which a story is told," as well as "play," "recreation," and "babysitting."

One workshop participant from Oxford, Michigan, summed it up in a single word. Raising her hand with a look of astonishment, she said, "Nothing."

By "nothing," she meant that *storytime* trivializes the value of what storytime really is—not only content, but also the staff expertise that is involved.

It was, for her, an epiphany.

At Howard County Library System (HCLS), we reacted similarly to a 2006 *Baltimore Examiner* article, which prompted us to begin contemplating the meaning of *storytime*.

Highlighting HCLS and what we then called our "Character Counts storytime," the piece featured a captivating photo of an impressively large group of kindergarteners. The children were listening attentively as then County Executive James Robey (now a State Senator) read *Curious George at the Fire Station,* where Curious George sets off a false alarm. The inquisitive monkey ultimately redeems himself by rescuing a puppy—a benevolent feat that teaches an important lesson in building a compassionate character.

You're thinking that this sounds like great publicity!

Yes and no. Although pleased with the article's visibility and accompanying photo, we looked at the headline, "Story time with County Executive Jim Robey,"[1] and shook our heads.

Storytime fell short of conveying the full educational value of what had taken place. We thought, *"Surely we can do better than this!"*

Reasoning that the reporter used *storytime* because we did, we realized that any changes we might desire from others, including reporters, would first need to occur internally.

Five months later, a different headline caught our attention. Entitled "A Little Song: Kindermusik Classes Pair Parents and Their Tykes for Musical Playtime,"[2] the newspaper article described a class developed for Howard Community College (HCC).

Intrigued, we observed that this "milk and cookies"–themed class looked quite like HCLS's Play Partners storytime for infants and toddlers. The class involved stories, music, rattles, songs, movement, and social interaction.

If these components were indistinguishable from our Play Partners, what were the differences? We identified three.

- Kindermusik was called a *class* (as opposed to a *storytime*).
- The class was *taught* by an *instructor* (compared to *presented* or *done* by a *programmer*).
- The class cost $225 for a 14-week session (whereas our admission is free).

Storytime → Children's Classes

We resolved then and there to start calling storytime a class.

Upon learning about this plan, a skeptic advised, "If you're going to call them classes, you'll need teaching objectives."

Our response? "You're right! Teaching objectives. Great idea!"

From the same "Kindermusik Classes" article, we gleaned phrases, such as "the class teaches cognitive, physical, social, musical, and language skills," and "teaches them to be expressive and creative in the thought process."

Starting with this, we compiled a list of what we teach in our children's classes:

- Creative expression
- Social skills
- Thought process development
- How to follow instructions
- Civility (e.g., empathy, tolerance, kindness)
- Color recognition
- Subject areas—including *math* and *science*
- The foundations of reading
  - Listening comprehension
  - Sounds in words
  - Vocabulary building
  - Print awareness
  - Alliteration
  - Rhythm
  - Rhyme
  - Letter and number recognition

Not only did we begin infusing these objectives into our vocabulary, we also added the following descriptions to *source*, our quarterly classes and events guide:

- *Infants through 23 months:* Classes for infants and toddlers teach social skills, listening comprehension, and the foundations of reading through letters, numbers, and vocabulary (see Figure 3.1).

infant - 23 months

Classes for infants and toddlers teach social skills, listening comprehension, and the foundations of reading through letters, numbers, and vocabulary. An adult must accompany children under age 3.

Figure 3.1   Children's classes description (infant–23 months).

- *Preschool:* Preschool classes teach creative expression, social skills, listening comprehension, and the foundations of reading through letter and number recognition, and vocabulary building.
- *Kindergarten through fifth grade:* Kindergarten through fifth grade classes teach subjects— including math and science—through children's literature and creative expression, as well as cognitive, social, and communication skills.

As predicted, reporters picked up on our revised vocabulary, resulting in far more accurate and impressive descriptions of our children's classes. We were pleasantly surprised to see that *class* soon replaced *storytime* in the press, as in "Library has classes for ages 3–5,"[3] a newspaper article that included, "Classes for preschoolers . . . are designed to teach creative expression and social skills, increase comprehension and lay the foundation for reading through number recognition, and build vocabulary," and "'What's in My Art Box?' a class for ages 3–5," as well as, "'Storybook Friends' for ages 2–5 . . . offers a story and a craft to enjoy with your child."

From our perspective? A major milestone (and near perfection!).

Will I Like Saying "Children's Classes"?

Transitioning from saying *storytime* to *children's class* does take some getting used to. At first, *children's class* will seem a bit peculiar.

However, sooner than you might think, the phrase will roll off the tip of your tongue, making *storytime* the odd-sounding term.

Eventually, you will like saying *children's class*, because you'll enjoy and take pride in the:

- Added value the community will assign to both the classes you teach, and *you*, the experts who develop, teach, support, and promote them.
- Heightened level of respect allocated by the community to you and your entire library system.
- Increased funding that is inevitable. (How can I be so sure about this? Because, as illustrated by the Evian example, people fund that which they perceive as valuable *at a level they think it is worth.*)

"If I Were Mayor . . ."

If you remain hesitant as to the merits of parting with *storytime*, remember that, while there's nothing wrong with *storytime*, our overriding goal is to capitalize on the power of smart terminology to communicate accurately the complete value of what we do in order to maximize funding.

Each staff member must care deeply about optimal funding, as it affords us the opportunity to flourish and deliver excellence under each of our Three Pillars.

Optimal funding ensures us our jobs and our future.

So if you are on the fence, ask yourself, "If I were mayor, county executive, city/county council, state/federal legislator, governor, or President of the United States, which would I fund more?"

- *storytime*, or
- *children's classes* that teach creative expression, social skills, the foundations of reading, and any subject matter—including math and science—through children's literature?

Hopefully, you'll conclude that *children's classes* is the more convincing choice. This example of strategic vocabulary needs no explanation.

A boost in perceived value is crucial, as increased funding inevitably follows.

We'll be analyzing a number of terms in the next two chapters. While it is likely that you'll immediately see the benefits of substituting stronger vocabulary for each, if at any time uncertainty sets in, ask yourself, "If I were mayor . . ."

WHAT DOES "PROGRAM" MEAN?

We'll next examine another word we use without much thought in our profession.

What does *program* mean to the nonlibrary connoisseur?

When asked this question, workshop participants answered:

- A radio or television show
- A thin book or a piece of paper that gives an audience information about a performance or event
- A computer-related series of coded instructions or operations controlling the functions of an electronic device

Our Oxford, Michigan, colleague who had instantly grasped the merits of replacing *storytime* with *class*, raised her hand again.

This time, her resigned, "Nothing," was delivered with a slight smile and shake of the head.

She understood that our profession's most frequent application of *program* (e.g., "I'm doing a genealogy program tonight.") substantially diminishes the importance of both content and staff expertise.

Beer Appreciation, Juggling, and Happy Hair

At HCLS, we began questioning our use of the word *program* in response to a 2007 newspaper article entitled, "HCC brews an eclectic mixture of classes."[4]

The article highlighted a number of classes at HCC, including one called Beer Appreciation.

Perusing HCC's Fall 2007 Noncredit Classes catalog,[5] we located the class and its synopsis, which included: "Learn a brief history of the Nectar of the Gods. Join Nick 'The Baltimore Beer-trekker' Nichols as you taste a variety of beers from microbrews to imports. Participants must be 21 or older (IDs will be checked). Please bring a glass (not plastic), a bottle of water, crackers, and paper towels. $29. Wed. 6:30 PM–9:30 PM, Oct. 03."

This class brought to mind our comparable "The Science of Homebrew" *program* (minus the "please bring" items).

Similarly, HCC's "Genealogy: Discovering Your Roots," "English Afternoon Tea" (tea party attire optional), and "Creative Giftwrapping" classes costing $46–$99 resembled our line-up of *programs*.

Still other classes could easily have been our programs, including "Juggling," and, my personal favorite, "Happy Hair." ("Frustrated with lifeless hair? Eager to try a new style or color? Come join professional hair stylist Lilly Mariza for an afternoon of sharing tips and techniques for great hair.")

We asked ourselves, "What are the differences between HCC's classes and what we do?"

We found three:

- HCC called them *classes* (and we said "programs").
- The classes were *taught* by *instructors, teachers, faculty members,* or *professors* who *develop* and *teach class content* (while we said "presented" or "done" by a "programmer" who "does" "programming").
- The classes cost from $29 to $99 (whereas our admission is free).

Program → Class, Seminar, Workshop, Event

You have undoubtedly guessed our subsequent actions! We began a concerted effort to cease saying *program,* replacing the "generic" term with *class, seminar, workshop,* and *event*—powerful terms that make an impression (see Figure 3.2). (We also started incorporating *instructor* and *teach* into our everyday lexicon.)

Traditional	Strategic
Program	Class Seminar Workshop Event Initiative Project

Figure 3.2 Traditional to strategic—program to class.

Note, however, that *program* can be used effectively at times when referring to curriculum.

For instance, at HCLS, we could very well say that HCLS Project Literacy is our adult basic education *program* for those who have not graduated from high school, the umbrella under which our *Instructors teach* individualized tutoring sessions, and *classes* for larger groups of students.

For now, however, we call HCLS Project Literacy an *initiative*—simply because we are trying to get out of the habit of overusing the underwhelming word *program* when we really mean *class* or *event.*

The term *project* can also come in handy for variation as we try to wean ourselves from using the nondescript, weaker *program.*

Programming → Curriculum Development

Like the word *program, programming* associates chiefly with radio and television broadcasts, and IT.

To achieve that Evian level of funding, let's trade in our favorite programming phrases—the ones that have nothing to do with IT, as in, "We do children's programming"—for stronger, more accurate ones.

For example, consider replacing "We do programming" with "We teach classes," "We develop class content," or "We develop and teach the curriculum used in our classes and events" (see Figure 3.3).

To illustrate, we previously taught a continuing education class for our own staff called, "Children's Programming." We have changed that to "Children's Classes: Preparing & Teaching Our Curriculum."

Traditional	Strategic
We do programming.	We develop class content. We develop the curriculum for classes. We teach children's classes. We teach classes, seminars, and workshops for all ages.
Our programming is second to none.	Our classes and events are second to none.
"Children's Programming" (a staff continuing education class)	"Children's Classes: Preparing & Teaching Our Curriculum"

Figure 3.3 Traditional to strategic—programming to teach.

If We Say "Classes," Won't People Stop Coming?

Some of you may be asking a question similar to one posed by a workshop participant from West Virginia. She wondered, "But if we call them classes, won't people stop coming? Don't they want to get away from school?"

It has been our experience—and also the experiences of others who have tried this approach—that your audiences will *increase*! Why? Two reasons.

Business as Usual

First, because the people who already attend your *storytimes* and *programs* will keep coming. They will hardly notice the transition to your saying *classes, seminars,* and *workshops* because the transition will be gradual.

What they *will* notice is that your classes are, as always, engaging, enlightening, and worthwhile.

When you give opening remarks at a "storytime," you can, for instance, introduce your new strategic vocabulary by saying, "Welcome to Three, Two, Fun! This morning's class will focus on the colors green and yellow, and number 4."

Although participants will probably not even notice that you said *class,* they will begin assigning a higher estimation to the value of your classes because of your new, value-enhancing terminology.

As they hear you say *class* week after week, they, too, will begin calling storytime a class.

It is true that those who deal with language sometimes notice modified vocabulary. For example, early on in our transition, I was speaking to a reporter about our popular children's classes when she said, "Oh, you call them classes now?" As though we had all along, I responded in my best where-have-you-been voice, "Why, yes!" And that was that! She used *children's classes* throughout her feature article, and from then on.

If it's *program* from which you are transitioning, you can say to your audience, "Welcome to this afternoon's genealogy workshop!" No one will think, "Hey, I thought I had signed up for a *program,* not a *workshop!*" (Also, recall that they know what a workshop is—which is what your program really is!)

Our smart terminology will fly under most people's radar. Although participants will not know why, our new language's effect will enhance perceived value. They will be even more impressed by the instructor and all that they learn in the class—precisely the result we desire.

Standing Room Only

Second, because those who had previously chosen *not* to attend your *programs* now *will* attend your *classes.* This is because of heightened perceived value.

For instance, parents who are increasingly focused on extracurricular activities that build physical and intellectual prowess would not have invested time bringing their children to *storytime* (because they did not understand that it is a class). But they *will* bring them to your children's *classes.* Joining those who already attend, they, too, will keep coming. (This may require that you schedule additional sessions—a great problem to have!)

Best of all, both groups will tell the world how much they value your library and you. They'll rave about the quality education—*and heaps of fun*—you deliver for their children. They'll express their gratitude for the quality education you deliver for all age groups under Pillars II and III through complimentary letters, e-mails, and blog posts.

As your base of fiercely loyal customers grows, this expanded fan club will tell your funding decision makers directly and indirectly how indispensable you are to education and quality of life in your community. Your funding will increase, enabling additional classes, and even more happy customers.

At HCLS, we capitalize on combining the terms *class, education,* and *fun* (especially for children and teens), and also our strong connection with the schools. Figure 3.4 is an example of what we posted on Twitter when schools were closed on November 2 and 5, 2010.

It is important to reiterate that, although we now say *classes,* class content stayed exactly the same. The only variable, our choice of words, serves as a teaching opportunity for others.

HoCo_Library

Did you know that Howard County Library System plans ahead when schools are closed? When school is closed bring your family to HCLS for a fun and educational class.

Schools Closed? Visit Howard County Library System!

Date	Description
11/02/10 11 am and 3 pm Glenwood Branch	*Book Bingo* Play Bingo featuring favorite book characters and maybe win a book! Ages 5 & up; 45 min.
11/02/10 2 pm Central Branch	*Crafts* Drop in and be creative!
11/02/10 2 pm Miller Branch	*Game Day!* No school? Hang out and play board games! Ages 7–10. 2–4 pm
11/02/10 2 pm Savage Branch	*Happily Ever After* Features stories, songs, games, crafts, and a fairy tale ending. Ages 5–10; 60 min.
11/05/10 11 am @ East Columbia Branch 2 pm @ Miller Branch	*Chemistry in the Library—Behind the Scenes with Chemistry* Join chemists from the Army Research Laboratory and the American Chemical Society for hands-on experiments and a celebration of National Chemistry Week. Ages 7 & up; 60 min.
11/05/10 2 pm Savage Branch	*Fairy Fun* Explore the magical world of fairies through stories, music, and activities. Ages 5 & up; 60 min.
11/05/10 2 pm Elkridge Branch	*I Spy with Walter Wick* Celebrate *I Spy* artist and illustrator Walter Wick, then create an I Spy scene. Ages 5 & up; 60 min.

Figure 3.4   Twitter schools closed—classes.

We now hear people saying, "This is such a nice library . . . they teach classes here and everything."

Journalists have a higher regard for us as well. To illustrate, the *Howard County Times* published a front page feature article headlined "Events around county celebrate 40th Earth Day."[6] Accompanied by a close-up color photo of students studying a microscope slide, the newspaper article began,

> Howard County Library is holding several free classes with Earth Day themes throughout April . . . In one class, called "Plants: The Green Machines," Army Research Laboratory chemist . . . will conduct a hands-on photosynthesis experiment with children ages seven and up. Another class, "Happy Earth Day," will feature songs and games about conservation.

Previously, Ms. McPherson would have used *program* and *storytime* for her story. She now uses *class*. Why? Because we do. We say it. We write it.

At HCLS, attendance at our classes has *tripled* since we began branding ourselves as education for all.

Even Oprah

While you are likely convinced that *class* commands far greater respect and value than *program*, if you need a final nudge toward the more strategic term, know that even Oprah Winfrey has recognized the word's added prestige.

Oprah has decided to categorize her 5,000 episodes of "Oprah" *programs* into subject areas, and she will rebroadcast them as *classes*, desiring to create the "World's Biggest Classroom." Her new "The Oprah Class" will "teach people how to live their best lives."[7]

WHAT DOES "REFERENCE" MEAN?

Another long-standing word deserves a dose of scrutiny. What does *reference* mean to most people? Most likely, the dictionary definition:

- A statement about a person's qualifications, character, and dependability
- A person who is in a position to recommend another or to vouch for his or her fitness, as for a job
- An act of referring
- A mention of an occurrence or situation
- A note in a publication referring a reader to another passage or source

Dictionaries do not even mention what *we* mean when we use the word. This is because there's another word that means precisely what we think we're communicating when we say *reference*! That word is *research*.

Research means

- Inquire into
- Attempt to find out in a systematically and scientific manner (as in, "The student researched the history of that word.")
- A systematic investigation to establish facts
- A search for knowledge

Are you surprised to discover that *research*—a term we tend to shy away from because we somehow think it's too "academic"—is actually broadly defined?

The term connotes both complex and general research, which requires either our expert guidance or our conducting the research on behalf of a customer.

Each of these is research, as in, "I need to research . . .":

- The best Metro route to get to the Washington Monument.
- Locations of all public tennis courts in Phoenix.
- The name and address of that new Ethiopian restaurant in Washington DC.
- Authors who write books similar to Alexander McCall Smith, because I loved his books and want to read something equally compelling.
- Primary sources for the Restoration Period in British literature.

Reference → Research

At HCLS, this was a revelation! Once we realized that, unlike *reference*, people understood, respected, and valued *research*, we adopted the more commanding word, phasing out *reference*.

Although this seemed like a bold move initially, *research* has merged with our daily vocabulary. We say *research* easily and with immense pride.

Indeed, *research* aptly describes the major component of our educational mission reflected in Pillar II, Research Assistance & Instruction.

We would all benefit from eliminating *reference* from our lexicon—unless, of course, we are referencing an article in a writing piece, or providing a reference for a candidate who is applying for a job.

Research is far more advantageous, as the self-explanatory, value-laden term demystifies what we do.

Consider replacing the common words/phrases in Figure 3.5 with the recommended strategic vocabulary.

A concluding suggestion: One webinar participant came up with the phrase, "top level web navigation." You may wish to experiment with mixing in this phrase when writing or speaking about the manner in which we deliver first-rate research assistance.

Traditional	Strategic
Reference Department	Research Department Instruction & Research Department
Reference Desk	Research Desk Research Assistance Desk Research IT Desk Customer Service & Research Desk (if combined)
Reference questions	Research questions
Reference Librarian	Instructor & Research Specialist
Reference interview	Research needs assessment
Reference behaviors	Research needs assessment skills
Reference Collection	Research Collection
Reference databases	Specialized online research tools
I do reference.	I assist customers with their research

Figure 3.5   Traditional to strategic—reference to research.

WHAT ABOUT "INFORMATION?"

Since most of us say we are "information professionals" working in the field of "information," assessing the message we send every time we say *information* is especially important.

What does *information* mean?

For most people—I'll assert, for *all* who make our funding decisions—information is ubiquitous. In this 21st century, information is easily obtainable, requiring little expertise.

To illustrate, your State Senator's 10-year-old granddaughter can easily search Google to find when Free Comic Book Day will be next year, which colors combine to make green, or when Albert Einstein was born, not really caring about "authoritative sites."

Also, note that *information* includes the answer to "Where is the bathroom?"

Realizing that this "generic" term falls dangerously short of conveying who we are, what we do, and why it matters, our Oxford, Michigan colleague would likely concede that the term now means practically "nothing."

One can reasonably conclude that our very use of the word *information* is contributing to our diminishing perceived value.

Information → Education/Research

Information should therefore be used in only limited circumstances, such as, "Our research has produced the following information."

In all other situations, *education* and *research* are the preferred strategic terms.

Although these terms may seem bold to you right now, try them! It's high time we receive full credit for what we do. Try switching to the strong, Evian term that is most appropriate, depending on the meaning you intend.

Wherever *information* is used to convey our essence, substitute *education* (as defined by our Three Pillars). Figure 3.6 provides some examples.

Similarly, *research* is valued universally. When you find yourself saying *information* and actually intend to communicate *research*, substitute the latter, as in Figure 3.7.

Traditional	Strategic
We provide access to information.	We deliver equal opportunity in education through our Three Pillars.
We are information professionals.	We are education professionals. We are educators.
Health Information Center	Health Education Center
We are in the business of information.	We are in the business of education.
We provide information.	We deliver high-quality education.

Figure 3.6   Traditional to strategic—information to education.

Traditional	Strategic
Information Department	Research Department Instruction & Research Department
Information Desk/Info. Desk	Research Desk
I work in Info.	I work in Research

Figure 3.7   Traditional to strategic—information to research.

Case Study: Information → Research

Like many of you, at HCLS, we exchanged *Reference Desk* for *Information Desk* somewhere in the 1990s.

Then in 2008, we changed the title of everyone classified as either Librarian or Library Associate to *Information Specialist & Instructor*. Our goal was to indicate that we teach (individually and class settings), and also align our language with our Information Desk signage.

In 2010, we realized we were still shortchanging ourselves.

Our staff determined that *research* was preferable to *information*, concluding that information was passive.

By contrast, they determined that *research* was strong and active. They further noted that both a noun and a verb, the word empowered staff, accentuated staff expertise, and provided clarity for the public, minimizing confusion with Information Technology (IT).

Our initial idea was to move from *Information Specialist & Instructor* to *Research Specialist & Instructor*. While this received enthusiastic support, staff asked whether Instructor could come first (i.e., *Instructor & Research Specialist*) to emphasize their role as educators.

Another outstanding idea, this recommendation was implemented simultaneously with their companion suggestion that *Information Desk* be renamed *Research Desk* (our desks that are combined were relabeled *Customer Service & Research Desk*).

At HCLS, our administrative offices currently are located in a wing off the East Columbia Branch, which means I hear our wonderful branch announcements throughout the day. Recently, I heard the following announcement:

> Chelsea seems to have lost her parents. Would Chelsea's lost parents please come to the Adult Research Desk?

Heightened perceived value for everyone who heard? Most certainly.

WHAT DOES "CIRCULATION" MEAN?

Hearing the word *circulation* triggers in most people thoughts of newspaper distribution or health-related matters, such as blood circulation.

We, of course, say *circulation* to mean items loaned to customers. So why not say *loan* instead! *Borrow* and *customer service* are also good candidates with which to replace circulation.

Circulation → Loan/Borrow/Customer Service

Figure 3.8 provides a list for your consideration.

In addition, consider eliminating the use of the favorite jargon term, "circ." The abbreviation can be heard used as a noun (e.g., "Our circ. is up" or "I work in Circ.") and as a verb (e.g., "We circ. 5,000 at our Central Branch daily.").

Traditional	Strategic
Circulation	Borrowing (e.g., "Borrowing is up this year over last.") Loans (e.g., "Loans are up this year over last.")
Circulation (statistics)	Items borrowed
Circulate	Loan (e.g., "We loan seven million items each year.") Borrow (e.g., "Customers borrow seven million items each year.")
Circulation Department	Customer Service Department
Circulation Clerk	Customer Service Specialist
Circulation Desk	Customer Service Desk

Figure 3.8   Traditional to strategic—circulation to borrowing.

For all of these reasons, and to use self-explanatory terminology, switch to saying *borrowing*, *loans*, and *customer service*—depending on your intended meaning.

Case Study: Circulation → Customer Service → Accounts

Following the November 15, 2010, PLA "Transforming Our Image" webinar, Lewisville (TX) Public Library Manager Ann Wiegand sent me an e-mail outlining her successes with strategic vocabulary relating to the term *circulation*.[8]

Wiegand noted, "Citizens seem to understand newspaper circulation and blood circulation. However, we were constantly explaining library circulation."

Wiegand and her staff first changed the "Circulation" signage to "Customer Service," subsequently electing for "Accounts—Cards & Payments," which they found to be even more self-explanatory.

The former "Circulation Supervisor" position title has been modified to "Accounts Supervisor," in part to incorporate strategic vocabulary, and also to begin aligning the department's jobs with the city's "Cashier" positions, which are assigned a higher pay grade than comparable positions in the library.

Services/Programs and Services → Curriculum

Not too long ago, never thinking twice about it, I said and wrote *programs and services* countless times each week (e.g., "Our programs and services are second to none."). Similarly, I used *services* quite frequently (e.g., "We deliver exceptional library *services*.").

This is actually quite surprising (and a bit embarrassing!) given that, at HCLS, we had already substituted strategic vocabulary for *program* (classes, seminars, workshops, and events) and *programming* (class content, curriculum).

Thank goodness for our forward thinking colleagues at the Chester County (PA) Library System and District Center—especially John Venditta, then Executive Director (now Administrator of the Eastern Shore Regional Library, Inc.), and Peggy Wadsworth, Staff Development Coordinator. Toward the end of a "Transforming Our Image" workshop,[9] they and their fine team shed light on how to catapult these ambiguous, generic phrases into the Evian stratospheres!

Having already analyzed how little meaning the word *program* conveys, the Chester County workshop participants noted that another common library-world term, *service*, fell into the same "conveys-next-to-nothing" category. They were right!

Consider that *services* means: "performance of duties helpful to others."

So what are we actually communicating to our customers—especially those who make our funding decisions—when we say *services*? "Nothing."

Saying *services* essentially places us in the same category as:

- social services,
- citizen services, and
- community services.

While none of these categories is bad, at best, any and all will achieve for us "generic" funding increases, and, at worst, steep budget cuts.

I propose that none will ever be funded on par with education.

So what should we substitute for *services* and *programs and services* to further our connection with education? With *curriculum*. Chester County Library and District Center contributed this gem to the Three Pillars Philosophy!

We've already discussed *curriculum* as a strong replacement for *programming*. By contrast, *curriculum* is recommended here to mean "*all that we do,*" which we have already categorized into our Three Pillars. This is a powerful, sweeping application.

You've seen *curriculum* used in this broad fashion in earlier pages (e.g., "We deliver high-caliber education through a *curriculum* that comprises Three Pillars."). Even if you didn't notice, you were likely impressed. It is a commanding word.

You may be asking the same question Chester County asked, "Does the definition of *curriculum* enable us to use it broadly to mean 'all that we do'?"

Chester County looked it up then and there, determining that we fall squarely under the word's definition, which includes:

- All the courses of study offered by an educational institution. (We've already established that we are an educational institution. We can certainly make a case that "courses of study" includes everything under our Three Pillars.)
- The subjects taught at an educational institution, or the topics taught within a subject. (We have already established that under Pillar II, we teach classes.)

Howard County Council's Budget Hearing
May 1, 2010

Testimony in support of Howard County Library
Valerie J. Gross
Chief Executive Officer, Howard County Library

Howard
COUNTY Library
SYSTEM

inform + instruct + interact = educate

Good morning, Chairperson Watson, members of the
County Council. I am Valerie Gross, CEO of Howard
County Library. Thank you for the opportunity to testify in support of our Library system.

Howard County is *the* place to live—to move to, stay, raise a family, and retire—for many reasons, and the most compelling factor is **high-quality public education**. At Howard County
Library, we are *relentless* about advancing this hallmark, so vital <u>for all ages</u> in today's knowledge-
based economy.

Customers visited our six branches nearly **three million** times last year, attending classes and
events, and borrowing **6.6 million** items—*up 17 percent over the previous year.* (Such impressive
numbers underscore the Library's ability to deliver <u>a remarkable return on taxpayer investment
in education.</u>)

Why such notable statistics? Because our **talented staff** delivers excellence in all areas of our
<u>unparalleled curriculum</u>, which comprises
three pillars:

  I. Self-Directed Education,
  II. Research Assistance & Instruction, and
  III. Instructive & Enlightening Experiences.

The County Executive's proposed FY 11 Operating Budget maintains County funding at
the FY 10 level. While challenging—as many
operating costs continue to rise—recognizing
the economy, we are grateful.

Public Libraries = Education

Combined with efficiencies and short-term
savings, the proposed funding will afford us the
opportunity to <u>maintain our current hours of
operation</u>, and continue to place a *high priority*
on our staff. We look forward to providing you with more details at our work session on May 6.

SELF-DIRECTED
EDUCATION
» Books, etc.
» E-resources

RESEARCH
ASSISTANCE &
INSTRUCTION
» Individual
» Group

INSTRUCTIVE &
ENLIGHTENING
EXPERIENCES
» Community/Cultural Center
» Signature Initiatives
» Partnerships

In any economy, our customer base encompasses people of all ages, means, and backgrounds
who demand that we set our standards high. I urge you to fully fund the County Executive's proposed FY 11 Operating Budget for the Library, and also his proposed Capital Budget, which our
Board Chair will outline.

Thank you for the many ways you demonstrate your support, and for realizing that an investment in Howard County Library is a <u>wise investment for a **smart community**</u>.

Respectfully submitted,

Valerie J. Gross
Chief Executive Officer

Figure 3.9 Budget testimony—"unparalleled curriculum."

- A group of subjects studied. (While Pillar I springs to mind, this could also be Pillar II or III.)
- Any plan of activities.
- Directed and undirected transformative experiences that take place in and outside of school.

With this revelation, at HCLS, we began using *educational mission* and *curriculum* interchangeably, and to define both with the Three Pillars.

Elated to have discovered this new winning word, we coined: "unparalleled curriculum." I tested the effectiveness of this new phrase in testimony I delivered before the Howard County Council at its May 1, 2010, public hearing in support of our fiscal year 2011 budgets. Figure 3.9 shows what I presented.

If you had been a Howard County Council member, would this testimony have persuaded you to fully fund the County Executive's proposed budgets for HCLS?

If you had been a taxpayer in the audience or watching on television, how would "unparalleled curriculum" and the other terms used throughout this testimony have affected your views of HCLS (and the library profession in general)?

While adjusting to *curriculum* takes some time because the phrase *programs and services* is so ingrained, it's well worth the effort. Trying it is the biggest step. Then, it's easy. Stick with it and you'll soon speak the word with ease, as though you'd said it all along.

As shown in Figure 3.10, *curriculum* packs power—almost as much as *education*. (Our budget lobbying efforts, by the way, proved successful!)

Traditional	Strategic
Our *programs and services* are second to none.	Our unparalleled *curriculum* comprises three pillars: Self-Directed Education, Research Assistance & Instruction, and Instructive & Enlightening Experiences.
We provide exceptional *services*.	We deliver an exceptional three-pronged *curriculum*: Self-Directed Education, Research Assistance & Instruction, and Instructive & Enlightening Experiences.
Fully funding our budget will guarantee continuation of our *programs and services*.	Fully funding our budget will guarantee the continuous delivery of *public education for all*.
Our library system comprises six *full-service* branches.	Our library system comprises six branches, each of which features our *full curriculum*.

Figure 3.10 Traditional to strategic—programs and services to curriculum.

CUSTOMER BASE—WHICH WORDS ARE BEST?

We'll conclude our discussion of key terms with an assessment of *customer, patron, user,* and *student*.

Before analyzing the merits of each, it is helpful to note that the Three Pillars Philosophy blends the best of the academic and business worlds.

In addition to adopting strategic vocabulary that assigns high academic standards to our curriculum (i.e., our collection, research, instruction, classes, and events), our lexicon must also include words that emphasize the sound business principles we incorporate into our operations.

Why is this important? Because people invest even more when they are convinced their funds will be well managed.

We therefore benefit from weaving powerful, persuasive business words and phrases into our arsenal of smart terminology.

Examples include "efficiency," "accountability," "fiscal responsibility," "leveraging funding through partnerships," and, that pinnacle to which we all aspire, "extraordinary customer service."

Patron/User → Student/Customer

The terms we assign to our customer base merit careful consideration, as their accompanying underlying messages differ vastly.

Let's first revisit the message we intend to send with any word. To optimize perceived value, we aim to communicate that we run an *efficient and effective educational institution*.

With this goal in mind, which of the terms debated in the profession best reinforce this message? Patron? Customer? User? Student?

Student

You are likely not surprised that an analysis of these terms places *student* at the top of the list. Student should be used at every opportunity, as it *advances our goal of being viewed as education*.

We can easily switch to calling infants through prekindergarten age children our *students* (as in, "Sally is one of our regular 'Three Two Fun!' students at the HCLS Glenwood Branch.").

Referring to those who attend kindergarten through college as our *students* is also easy, because they are already called students in the school setting.

As to our adult customer base, seize opportunities to assign the term *student* when possible (recall that "students" take "Beer Appreciation" and "Juggling" at the community college). For example, at HCLS, we now say:

Students of all ages participate in our four Summer Reading Clubs:

- My World (infants and toddlers)
- One World, Many Stories (ages 3–10)
- You are Here! (6th grade+)
- Novel Destinations (high school and adults)

Customer

When student does not fit, customer is the next best choice. This is because customer is business oriented, which furthers our quest to be perceived as a solid financial investment.

Note that we aim to deliver extraordinary "*customer* service," a business phrase.

In addition, *customer* can mean a person who pays for a good or service. This applies to us, as most customers contribute to the public funding that makes us possible through taxes they pay.

Lastly, like successful businesses, we very much appreciate our customers. Without them, we would be out of business. We therefore develop our curriculum with our entire customer base in mind.

User

User comes in third, for the simple reason the word advances neither of our two highest goals.

Patron

Why does *patron* come in last? Because the term sends a wrong—even dangerous—message.

Connected first and foremost with philanthropy, *patron* associates the library with museums and other arts organizations (e.g., "patron of the arts"), which are funded in great part through private donations made by *patrons, precisely the trend we are aiming to halt in these challenging economic times*—and at all times.

We must therefore actively seek ways to move away from any connection that implies that our operating and capital budgets should be funded with donations. Rather, we should capitalize at every opportunity to establish for public libraries *the same assumptions held for public schools*—that our operating and capital budgets must be *publicly* funded.

If your library system desires to achieve equal footing with public schools, replacing *patron* with *student* and *customer* is a smart first step in this direction.

NOTES

1. Jessie Webb, "Story Time with County Executive Jim Robey," *The Baltimore Examiner,* October 19, 2006, p. 7.

2. Stefanie Ickowski, "A Little Song: Kindermusik Classes Pair Parents and Their Tykes for Musical Play-time," *Howard County Times,* March 1, 2007, p. 24.

3. "Library has Classes for Ages 3–5," *The Baltimore Sun,* June 29, 2008, p. 10U.

4. Jessica Dexheimer, "HCC Brews an Eclectic Mixture of Classes: College Adds Dozens of Non-Credit Courses to Its Catalog for Fall," *The Baltimore Sun,* August 10, 2007, p. G1.

5. Fall 2007 Noncredit Classes, Howard Community College, Howard County, MD, p. 50.

6. Lindsey McPherson, "Events Around County Celebrate 40th Earth Day," *Howard County Times,* April 15, 2010, p. 1.

7. Lisa de Moraes, "Oprah Swoops in to Boost OWN's ratings," *The Washington Post,* July 30, 2011, p. C1.

8. E-mail from Ann Wiegand, Library Manager, Lewisville Public Library, 1197 W. Main St. Lewisville, TX 75067, to the author, dated November 19, 2010. Used by permission.

9. Chester County (PA) Library and District Center Conference Workshop: "Transforming Our Image through Words that Work," April 29, 2010, Exton, PA.

4

SUPPORTING STRATEGIC VOCABULARY—A FEW MORE WORDS

Having analyzed some fundamental expressions we've used habitually for decades, we'll next study a handful of routinely repeated ancillary terms, along with recommended replacements.

We'll also examine the advantages of retaining two long-standing words in our revised lexicon.

ENTERTAINMENT/RECREATION → FUN/ENGAGING/FICTION

While discussed briefly in Chapter 2, *entertainment* and its companion, *recreation*, deserve more scrutiny, as these particular words are exceedingly risky.

Associating any form of *entertainment* and *recreation* with libraries invites diminished funding. Why?

Both fall squarely in the "discretionary" category. (It would be the rare politician who would say, "In these challenging economic times, I'll support budget cuts in all areas—except entertainment and recreation.")

Entertain

Although it will always be advantageous to emphasize that we are education, at times we desire to communicate that our curriculum is "entertaining." This can be accomplished through the application of astute language that conveys both.

The secret to success with this tactic is always to include the word *education*—or another strategic word that everyone connects directly with education (regardless of whether they understand our Three Pillars), such as *class*, *seminar*, or *workshop*—near the word you choose that means *entertain*, preferably in the same sentence.

Generally, it's best to steer clear from *entertain* in all of its forms. So what might we say instead?

For children and teens, fun rules. The enticing word *fun* for these age groups is therefore highly effective. For instance, to a group of 4-year-olds, we might say, "Join us for Go Figure!, a class where you'll learn all about numbers and have loads of *fun!*"

Note, however, that our pitch to parents for this same class would benefit from underscoring the education side of the coin. For example, we could say, "Join us for Go Figure!, a *fun* and educational class for preschool students that teaches basic math concepts through children's literature."

How many strategic words do you count in the version for parents? At least six: *educational, class, students, teaches, math,* and *literature.*

For adults, the word *engaging* works well as a substitute for *entertaining*, as in "Our instructors teach *engaging* classes on a wide variety of subjects." Here, *engaging* joins three powerful words: *instructors*, *teach*, and *classes*.

Fun, engaging, enticing, and *captivating* are excellent alternatives for *entertaining* in many instances. Being selective in this fashion, we can emphasize the characteristics of *entertaining* without sacrificing the Evian funding cachet.

In limited circumstances, *entertain* will be the best choice and can be used without compromising perceived value. For example, if Milkshake, the popular children's musical group, performs at your Summer Reading Kickoff, you might say, "Milkshake *entertained* packed audiences of children and adults alike at the Summer Reading Kickoff, which attracted an audience of 4,000."

While educational as well, Milkshake will have contributed to the day's *entertainment*—along with balloons and dragon dances. This type of entertainment is peripheral, comparable to school assemblies where all students gather in the auditorium or gym for a program that frequently includes entertainment.

Recreation

Likewise, *recreation* and *recreational* are two words we would be better off without. Their perceived value quotient will achieve generic funding at best, and major cuts at worst.

Terms to use instead of *recreation* include *fun* and *enrichment*.

To replace *recreational*, try *engaging, fun, captivating, enthralling, enriching,* and at times, *entertaining*.

Again, it is always advisable to combine these suggested substitutes in the same sentence with *education, class, seminar,* or *workshop*.

Mission/Vision Statements

If your library's mission or vision statements include any form of the words *entertainment* or *recreation*, consider their removal.

Some libraries include a combination of *information, recreation,* and *entertainment* in their mission statements, with a few also including *education*. The former terms weaken the power of a mission or vision statement.

In addition to deleting *entertainment* and *recreation*, try also deleting the generic term *information*. You'll see that removing these words strengthens your statement, placing all of the focus on *education*.

Education says it all.

Traditional	Strategic
Entertain	Engage, captivate, enthrall, enrich (at times, entertain)
Entertaining/Recreational	Engaging, fun, enthralling, captivating, enriching (at times, entertaining)
Recreation	Fun, enrichment (at times, entertainment)
Entertainment DVDs	Fiction DVDs

Figure 4.1   Traditional to strategic—entertain to engage.

ENTERTAINMENT DVDS → FICTION DVDS

Let's take a look yet at what many of us call *entertainment* DVDs.

Although most libraries categorize print materials into *nonfiction* and *fiction*, they label DVDs differently, usually along the lines of *educational/instructional* and *entertainment*.

Why the dichotomy? Perhaps Hollywood has influenced our category choices for DVDs.

At Howard County Library System (HCLS), we pondered this question, electing to apply the print categories to visual materials. Our *educational/instructional* DVDs became *nonfiction* DVDs. Similarly, our *entertainment* DVDs are now *fiction* DVDs.

Nonfiction DVDs

Nonfiction DVDs made sense from both a logical standpoint, and because we assign Dewey numbers to all titles in this category.

Furthermore, this revised language eliminated the unintended message we were sending to our customers with *educational/instructional*—that only this category was educational.

Fiction DVDs

Our move to *fiction DVDs* resulted in consistency. The revised label mirrors the category we assign to our print collection.

In addition, *fiction DVDs* enhanced the perceived educational value of our overall collection. How? Through the resulting "drilling for oil" versus "careful exploration of energy" effect.

We used to say:

Our collection comprises fiction and nonfiction titles in all formats, and *entertainment* DVDs.

We now say:

Our collection comprises fiction and nonfiction titles in all formats.

Our current phrase is shorter, which is typically better. Most importantly, the carefully selected language does not bring attention to this potentially misperceived segment of our collection.

If challenged about the merits of including fiction DVDs in our collection, we are well prepared to articulate our solid argument as to how fiction DVDs are also education, but why not make life easier for ourselves? We can minimize the chances of this happening with clever use of language.

This strategy could potentially have avoided the recent misguided comments offered by a former elected official in Cincinnati.

In the July 27, 2011, Cincinnati.com article "Hamilton Co. Libraries Face Cuts, Closings amid Budget Shortfall," former Ohio State Representative Tom Brinkman was reported as having asserted that "before any branches are closed the library needs to look at its music and video purchases . . . 'They've gotten too far away from their core mission which is providing reading material and materials to help people do research and improve their lives.'"[1]

Two thoughts surface in response to Mr. Brinkman's remarks.

First, blending fiction DVDs into our overall fiction collection can minimize this sort of flawed assertion that audio and visual materials are dispensable. A broad, inclusive collection description does not accentuate any particular collection segment. And second, were Mr. Brinkman to comprehend that our mission *is* education as defined by the Three Pillars Philosophy, he would cease misstating the library's mission.

Although he currently grasps pieces of Pillars I and II, Self-Directed Education and Research Assistance & Instruction, his understanding is incomplete. (Mr. Brinkman does get partial credit for saying *research*.)

Furthermore, because he does not mention anything related to Pillar III, Instructive & Enlightening Experiences, one can reasonably conclude that he does not connect this pillar with our curriculum. While Mr. Brinkman's comments represent the inaccurate views of many, he—and everyone else whose views of libraries are erroneous or incomplete—is teachable!

We can make it easy for the Tom Brinkmans of this world to fully understand our mission, and thus our value, by showing them the Three Pillars visual. At a glance, they will understand our mission.

JUVENILE → CHILDREN'S

On to the analysis of one of the most intriguing terms we use.

Why do we say *juvenile*? Do you, like me, immediately think of the corresponding *delinquent* whenever you hear this word?

People fill in this imaginary blank because the most common definition of *juvenile* is "a young person who has committed a crime or is accused of committing a crime."

Used as an adjective, the word's primary definition reads, "Relating to young people who have committed a crime or who are accused of committing a crime." The secondary definition, "immature" (as in "juvenile behavior"), registers negativity as well.

When introducing children to others, would you ever say, "These are my juveniles, Benjamin and Sarah," or "These are the juveniles who live in our neighborhood"? Unless they were acting immature at the moment, most likely not!

You would say, "These are my *children*."

Likewise, one does not hear the phrase, "Our *juveniles* are our future," but rather, "Our *children* are our future."

How about eliminating *juvenile* and its accompanying negative associations from our vocabulary, substituting the positive word *children*.

Traditional	Strategic
Juvenile Fiction	Children's Fiction
Juvenile books	Children's books
Juvenile materials	Children's materials
Juvenile DVDs	Children's Fiction DVDs Children's Nonfiction DVDs
Juvenile programs	Children's classes Kids' classes

Figure 4.2 Traditional to strategic—juvenile to children's.

Although editing websites, brochures, electronic records, and most signage will be straightforward, if you happen to have "J" (for "Juvenile") on book labels as we do at HCLS, the modification becomes more complicated. The thought of changing all labels to "Ch" (for Children's) is rather a daunting project.

At HCLS, while we are replacing *Juvenile* with *Children's*, we've also decided that book labels will stay the same for the time being—with "J" now able to stand for "Junior!"

DATABASE → SPECIALIZED ONLINE RESEARCH TOOLS

Many workshop participants have asked whether we've found an improvement for *database*, a word many customers find puzzling.

At HCLS, we struggled a bit with this one before coming up with a solution. Although *online research* works at times, this phrase also includes free online sites.

We have found that, while slightly lengthy, the self-explanatory phrase "specialized online research tools" works satisfactorily. See Figure 4.3 for how this replacement can work on a brochure.

Homework or research assistance?

Specialized
Online
Research
Tools

Expanded Academic ASAP
AccessScience
American Periodicals Series
Ancestry.com
Biography Resource Center
Small Business Resource Center
CQ Researcher Gale Virtual Reference
Library HeritageQuest Online Historical
New York Times History Reference
Center: US / History Resource Center:
World Learning Express Library
(LearnATest) Literature Resource
Center LitFinder Live Homework Help
General OneFile Student Resource
Center: Bronze Customer Newspapers
NoveList SIRS Researcher Standard &
Poor's NetAdvantage Teen Health and

Figure 4.3 Traditional to strategic—database to "specialized online research tools" (sample brochure).

CATALOG

The term *catalog*—which brings to mind those voluminous reams of glossy pages marketing Sears Roebuck and JC Penney merchandise—should retire. Nonetheless, it lives on, even at HCLS. We haven't yet come up with a good substitute.

At HCLS, when we need to, we still say *catalog*, albeit mostly *online catalog*. What we do for now is try to avoid saying the word, as in, "Let me check to see if we have that title."

Although some workshop participants have suggested *inventory* and *educational resources index* as possible improvements, these good ideas just don't quite seem to capture the essence of what we mean by *catalog*.

What does Amazon.com call its "catalog?" Amazon.

The hunt continues. If you invent something brilliant, please share it!

LIFELONG LEARNING → LIFELONG EDUCATION

We'll next analyze a phrase we use often, *lifelong learning.*

Although not a bad phrase—and it does possess nice alliteration—note that we do not hear our elected officials say, "My highest priority is learning."

Here's what they do say: "My highest priority is education." And our goal is to insinuate ourselves into their definition of the word.

It is therefore to our benefit to teach people that we are education at every opportunity, which means saying the word *education.*

So think about replacing *lifelong learning* with stronger phrases that include *education*, such as *lifelong education, continuing education, education for all ages, public education for all.* These replacements will elevate your perceived value.

Traditional	Strategic
Lifelong learning	Lifelong education Continuing education Education for all ages Public education for all

Figure 4.4 Traditional to strategic—lifelong learning to lifelong education.

EMERGENT LITERACY → CHILDHOOD EDUCATION

A few years back, I was talking with someone at a summer picnic when I tossed *emergent literacy* into our conversation. Quizzically, she ventured, "What's that?"

After hearing my quick explanation that it's just childhood education, she immediately understood.

At HCLS, we decided to trade the obscure phrase for the more descriptive *childhood education* and *early childhood education.*

If you haven't already, consider implementing this no-explanation-needed exchange.

Traditional	Strategic
Emergent Literacy	Childhood education Early childhood education

Figure 4.5 Traditional to strategic—emergent literacy to childhood education.

READY TO LEARN/READY AT FIVE → WE TEACH . . .

Have you ever stopped to think that the ubiquitous phrases we use related to children entering kindergarten, "ready to learn" and "ready at five," imply that *real* learning takes place in school? The inadvertent message, which slights our importance, stems from the emphasis the phrases place on the future.

We know that the intended meaning of these phrases is laudable—that children benefit academically from mastering age-appropriate childhood education proficiencies in their early years, a component of our curriculum.

But why "ready to learn"? Children are born ready to learn!

What if we were to exchange "ready to learn" for any version of: "We teach . . . the foundations of reading (listening comprehension, sounds in words, vocabulary building, print awareness, alliteration, rhythm, rhyme, letter recognition, and number recognition), creative expression, social skills, thought process development, civility, and a wide variety of subject matters—including math and science—through children's literature."

The result would be to focus on our contributions to the academic success of our children in this age group. We would retain the well-deserved credit, which is what we're after (full recognition for what we do).

And why "ready at five"? Why not, "ready at one" or "ready at three"? Wouldn't it be more advantageous for our image to celebrate the milestones students achieve at all age-appropriate levels thanks to our curriculum?

Traditional	Strategic
Ready to learn; Ready at Five	We teach age-appropriate childhood education proficiencies. We teach the foundations of reading—listening comprehension, sounds in words, vocabulary building, print awareness, alliteration, rhythm, rhyme, letter recognition, and number recognition—creative expression, social skills, thought process development, civility, and broad subject matters—including math and science—through children's literature. Ready at One, Ready at Two, Ready at Three, Ready at Four

Figure 4.6   Traditional to strategic—ready to learn to "we teach the foundations."

FREE → PUBLIC, EQUAL OPPORTUNITY, FREE OF CHARGE

We'll now look at a term that should be used judiciously.

On its face, *free* is a fine word to use. At the same time, we know that delivering our high-quality curriculum costs money.

Mindful that public libraries—like public schools—are not free, at HCLS, we have minimized our use of the word, replacing "free" where possible with the words that mean free, such as the following bolded words:

- **equal opportunity** in education
- **equal access** to high-quality education
- high-caliber **public** education for all

In addition, when people ask how much we charge for our classes (actually a compliment triggered by customers assigning far greater value to your classes when you call them what they really are), we respond, "Your taxes, well invested!"

We do say "free of charge," as with HCLS Project Literacy, our adult basic education initiative, where personalized tutoring and class sessions are delivered at no enrollment cost to the participating students (the initiative is paid with grant and taxpayer funding).

We also combine phrases, such as:

- "We do not charge admission to author events, as we deliver equal opportunity in education for everyone," or
- "We deliver high-caliber public education for all. Admission is free for all children's classes."

Note: We used to add "regardless of means" at the end of some of these phrases (e.g., "high-caliber public education for all, regardless of means") to emphasize *free*, but we now think it's stronger and more positive without that addition.

Traditional	Strategic
Free	Equal opportunity in education Equal access to education Public education for all "We do not charge admission to our author events" "Admission is free for all of our classes"

Figure 4.7   Traditional to strategic—free to equal opportunity.

HELP/SERVE/REACH → ENHANCE/ADVANCE/IMPROVE/DELIVER/TEACH

Although appropriate choices on occasion, *help*, *serve*, and *reach* should always be scrutinized before use. Bland and nebulous, these terms usually downplay what we do.

Enhance, advance, improve, increase, conduct, deliver, assist, instruct, tutor, and *teach* are all vibrant replacements that will strengthen your message.

Thoughts on *Teach*

Although many library staff participating in the workshop had not previously thought to use the strategic word *teach*, they readily acknowledged that we do, in fact, *teach*.

Teach means to:

- impart the knowledge of
- cause to know something
- instruct by precept, example, or experience
- cause to know how
- accustom to some action or attitude
- guide the studies of
- conduct instruction regularly

Workshop participants took immediate pride in the realization that we teach.

Sample Edits

To illustrate the effect of incorporating these stronger terms, here are some examples.

The lackluster phrase we hear in our profession, "We *help* people," can be transformed into far more impressive phrases, such as, "A major component of education, we advance the economy, enhancing quality of life."

Similarly, the nondescript phrase, "The ABC Public Library *serves* 100,000 residents," can be transformed into "At ABC Public Library, we *deliver* equal opportunity in education to our 100,000 residents."

A final example, at HCLS, we made the following edit to the June 2011 *Team Update*, our staff newsletter:

- Before: "Summer Reading is in full swing, and our book promotions are too! We've *reached* more students this year, presenting the game to higher grades in our partner schools."
- After: "Summer Reading is in full swing, and our book promotions are too! We've *taught* more students this year, presenting the game to higher grades in our partner schools."

Traditional	Strategic
Help, serve, reach	Enhance, advance, improve, increase, conduct, deliver, assist, instruct, tutor, teach
"We *serve* 100,000 residents"	"We *deliver* equal opportunity in education to 100,000 residents"
"We *help* people"	"A major component of education, we *advance* the economy, *enhancing* quality of life" "Our instructors *assist* customers with their research"

Figure 4.8   Traditional to strategic—help to advance.

TOUCH → ENHANCE/ADVANCE/IMPROVE

Touch fits into the same undistinguished category as *help* and *serve*. While poignant in certain settings (e.g., sympathy cards), *touch* should be left out of communications representing your library system.

Instead, substitute dynamic language, such as *enhance*, *advance*, or *improve*.

Notice that *change* is not part of the suggested list. Although *change* implies "for the better," the word means "different."

Traditional	Strategic
Touch	Enhance, advance, improve
"We *touch* people's lives"	"We improve people's lives" "We enhance quality of life"

Figure 4.9   Traditional to strategic—touch to enhance.

DO/HOLD/OFFER → INSTRUCT/TEACH/LEAD/FACILITATE

A seemingly innocuous word that actually subtracts value, *do* would not be missed were it to disappear from our lexicon. For instance, the funding power of the typical phrase, "We do good work" upgrades tenfold when exchanged for "We deliver high-quality public education for all."

Although *hold* and *offer* sometimes work well, these terms should be replaced when possible with the more engaging ones, such as *teach, instruct, lead, facilitate, deliver, guide,* and *tutor*.

Traditional	Strategic
Do, hold, offer	Teach, instruct, lead, facilitate, deliver, guide, tutor
"We do programming"	"We teach classes"
"We do good work"	"We deliver high-quality public education for all"
"We hold book clubs"	"We facilitate book discussion groups"
"We offer storytimes"	"We teach children's classes" "Our children's curriculum includes classes for infants through pre-K students"

Figure 4.10   Traditional to strategic—do to teach.

OUTREACH → MARKETING/COMMUNITY EDUCATION

Outreach is one of those words that can cause people to think we are a social service. This is because the term is defined as:

- The act of reaching out
- The practice of providing help
- An organization's involvement with or influence in the community, especially in the context of religion or social welfare
- To provide charitable services to people
- A program, as by a local church or business, for extending assistance and services to the community, especially as an act of charity or goodwill.

Although there's nothing wrong with this connection, saying *outreach* will gain for your library generic funding at best, and steep cuts in the worst of times.

To achieve the higher level of respect and funding we are seeking, libraries would do well to eliminate this indistinct word from their vocabulary.

Give it a try. You'll see that your message will be immediately strengthened if you replace *outreach* with *community education* and *community engagement*, depending on the intended meaning.

Traditional	Strategic
Outreach	Community education, community engagement
Outreach Coordinator	Community Education & Partnerships Coordinator

Figure 4.11   Traditional to strategic—outreach to community education.

REGISTER → ENROLL

For word variation, and also to establish a slightly stronger academic connection when possible, *register* (a terrific word) can sometimes be replaced with *enroll*.

At HCLS, we use *enroll* instead of *register* for our Summer Reading Clubs, as in, "*Enrollment* for Summer Reading Clubs begins June 1."

While *register* is preferable for one-time classes, you might wish to say *enroll* for classes that are grouped in a series.

MEET THE WANTS/MEET THE NEEDS → DELIVER HIGH-QUALITY EDUCATION

Whenever you find yourself saying or writing the phrase *meet the wants* or *meet the needs*, as in "We meet the wants of our customers" or "We meet the needs of our customers," experiment with substituting the more influential statement "We deliver high-quality public education for all."

Although we certainly do meet the wants and needs of our customers, these unremarkable phrases could include social services. *Wants*, the more dangerous of the two, falls squarely into a discretionary category. *Wants* will be the first to get slashed in a bad economy.

Both *meet the needs* and *meet the wants* rank far lower on the funding-persuasion scale than "We design our curriculum to benefit a diverse customer base," or "We deliver high-quality public education for all." (If you really want to crank up perceived value, add " . . . through a curriculum that comprises three pillars: Self-Directed Education, Research Assistance & Instruction, and Instructive & Enlightening Experiences.")

Traditional	Strategic
"We meet the needs/wants of our customers."	"We deliver high-quality public education for all." "We deliver equal opportunity in education." "Our curriculum, which comprises three pillars, is second to none." "We design our curriculum to benefit a diverse customer base."

Figure 4.12   Traditional to strategic—"meet the needs" to "design a curriculum."

BOOKMOBILE → MOBILE BRANCH

At HCLS, we don't have a bookmobile, but if we did, we'd call it a *mobile branch* thanks to the ingenuity of our Pennsylvania colleagues at the Montgomery County–Norristown Public Library.

During a "Transforming Our Image" workshop for library staff, participants informed me that they had coined *mobile branch*, reasoning that the more strategic phrase captured all Three Pillars.

By contrast, *bookmobile* falls under Pillar I—and only a portion of it.

If you have a bookmobile, you may wish to switch to the more comprehensive, enhanced term, *mobile branch*, which conveys that our entire curriculum is delivered on wheels.

Another option would be to always connect *bookmobile* with *mobile branch*, as in, "The bookmobile, our mobile branch, delivers our curriculum to the rural areas.

LIBRARY

What are your thoughts about the perceived value of *library*? Do you think the general public assigns appropriate value to this word?

Although workshop participants have, on occasion, suggested *education center* and *continuing education center* as possible alternatives, they reached a consensus that *library* depicts a positive, venerated image. They concluded that library, which represents knowledge, tradition, and our roots, commands suitable associated value.

For all of these reasons, at HCLS, we have elected to keep *library.*

At the same time, we have taken note of the outstanding *education center* idea, and have woven the phrase into our language as an enhancement. For example, we edited the description of our Central Branch as follows (emphasis added):

Howard County Library System Central Branch

A major destination not only for Downtown Columbia but also for all of Howard County, the Central Branch of Howard County Library System (HCLS) is an *education center* featuring research, instruction, and myriad community and cultural events. Housing over 200,000 items in its various collections, the Central Branch welcomes over half a million visitors each year, with 20,000 children alone attending classes on an annual basis. Conveniently located on major thoroughfares with access to local transit, the Central Branch of HCLS takes pride in offering high-quality public education for all on a daily basis.

Education center in this example provides word variation and description.

BRANCH → EDUCATION CENTER

Another possibility suggested by an HCLS staff member would be to replace *branch* with *education center*.

We considered this, observing that *education center* positions us squarely with what we are—education—and captures our essence in an ideal fashion.

Trying the more academic phrase on for size, we crafted:

- "HCLS delivers a three-pronged curriculum at its six *education centers* located in Columbia, East Columbia, Ellicott City, Savage, Elkridge, and Glenwood," and
- "I'm a Children's Instructor at the HCLS Glenwood Education Center."

We reasoned that the potential substitute for *branch* is effective not only due to the term *education*, but also because of *center*, which emphasizes that we bring people together to discuss ideas through Pillars II and III, Research Assistance & Instruction and Instructive & Enlightening Experiences.

Nevertheless, we chose to retain the word *branch* for the time being, a business term that indicates one of our six locations that comprises our system.

Note, however, that we have eliminated that odd (and common!) "branch library" redundancy. To illustrate, here's a bank analogy.

When referring to Citibank's branch at Geary Boulevard in San Francisco, would you ever say, "I'm going to Citibank's Geary Branch Bank?" Of course not! What you would say is, "I'm going to Citibank's Geary Branch."

As with much of our vocabulary, adding the superfluous *library* many of us repeat after *branch* is most likely out of habit. To illustrate, at HCLS, we used to call our Elkridge Branch the *Elkridge Branch Library*. It's now the HCLS *Elkridge Branch*.

CAMPUS

Another Chester County (PA) Library System and District Center suggestion, *campus* can be added to our strategic vocabulary for an added academic link.

For example, at HCLS, two of our buildings will reside at the same location. Our recently constructed new Miller Branch is adjacent to its previous site. The "old" Miller Branch building will be renovated into the HCLS Administrative Branch. We call this the forthcoming Miller Branch *campus*.

MISCELLANEOUS

Since some workshop participants wondered whether stronger vocabulary could replace the following common words and phrases, we'll address these briefly:

- *Acronyms*—Acronyms should be avoided or defined.
- *E-journals*—This confusing term can be avoided with sentences such as, "That magazine is online as well."
- *Interlibrary loan*—Although appropriate for internal use, when communicating with customers, it's best to sidestep this phrase and, instead, say something like, "This book is not in our collection. We can borrow it from another library system if you like."
- *Periodical or serial*—Consider moving to *magazine* (or *journal*, if scholarly).
- *Resource*—A general term, *resource* should be replaced when possible with more specific words. In addition, be careful with phrases like, "We are an educational *resource*," which falls a few steps below that optimal Evian realm (would the schools ever say they are an educational *resource*?). Rather, assert the strongest phrase of all, "We *are* education."
- *Subject categories such as Humanities or Social Sciences*—Adopting more customer-friendly descriptions like "Cooking," "Pets," and "Travel" is more intuitive for customers. For more scholarly topics, specific categories, such as "Philosophy," "Psychology," "Economics," and "Art" work well.
- *Underserved*—This broad term falls in the same category as *help, serve*, and *outreach*, which reinforces the mistaken view that the library is a social service. Use *economically disadvantaged* if that is your meaning. Although longer, it will elevate the strength of your message.

SPECIAL COLLECTIONS → CENTER

We'll conclude with terms some workshop participants have asked about relating to internal departments called *Collection Services* and also *Special Collections* in many libraries, noting that most people associate these phrases with the collection of fees (e.g., a collection agency).

To project a more positive image, and to incorporate clarifying strategic vocabulary, at HCLS, we've renamed our *Collection Services* department *Data & Materials Processing*.

With regard to *special collections*, a recommended alternative is the word *center*. For instance, at HCLS, our *special collection* in health is now our *Health Education Center*.

Similarly, our *special collection* in history at our new Miller Branch is called our *Historical Center*. We have even added this key *special collection* curriculum component to the branch name: HCLS Charles E. Miller Branch & Historical Center.

Following the November 15, 2010, PLA "Transforming Our Image" webinar, Heather Kearns, Associate Curator of the Alice C. Sabatini Art Gallery Special Collections of the Topeka & Shawnee County Public Library, wrote the following on this topic:[2]

I thoroughly enjoyed *Transforming Your Image*. It struck home with me for many reasons, but primarily because my department, Special Collections, has been struggling with how the public perceives us for a long time.

We are within a public library and include local history, genealogy, non-circulating Kansas Collection (authors from, and books about Kansas), historic artifacts, rare books, book art collection, and the oldest fine art collection in the city (130 years) with over 5,000 works of art and museum collection.

Professionally, the library community understands what we do. The public, however, consistently associates us with fines and fees.

What to call ourselves is a frequent topic. We want to remain true to who we are, keep it short, but also communicate what we actually do, concisely and accurately.

Any suggestions? We consist of three Special Collections Librarians, two art historians, two studio artists, a genealogist and a reference specialist.

Thanks again for such an engaging discussion.

My response to Ms. Kearn's question included the recommendation that they edit *Special Collections* to *Historical Center*, with this as possible wording for their website and brochures:

> The Historical Center at the Topeka & Shawnee County Public Library delivers high-quality specialized education for all, providing passage into the fascinating world of local and regional history—your heritage! We feature:
>
> - Extensive local history and genealogical sources
> - The Kansas Collection (from, by, and about our great state)
> - Rare books and historic artifacts
> - The premier Sabatini Collection of fine art
>
> Our team stands ready to assist you with your research—in person, by phone, and online. We also hope to see you at our classes and events.

I then suggested the following revised titles that incorporate strategic vocabulary to both clarify and elevate perceived value:

- *Associate Curator*
  - Strategic Replacement: *Associate Director & Curator of the Historical Center*
  - Rationale: The strategic suggestion reflects the role's importance.
- *Special Collections Librarians* and also *Reference Specialist*
  - Strategic Replacement: *History Specialist & Instructor* (to replace both)
  - Rationale: The suggested replacement conveys (1) expertise, (2) the delivery of one-on-one research assistance and guidance in the area of history, and (3) the teaching of classes. *Instructor & History Specialist* would be another possibility.
- *Art Historian*
  - Strategic Replacement: *Art History Specialist & Instructor*
  - Rationale: Art Historian conveys working with the art, as opposed to working with the public. The recommended title denotes expertise and instruction of all kinds. *Instructor & Art History Specialist* would potentially be even more compelling.
- *Studio Artist*
  - Strategic: *Studio Artist & Instructor*
  - Rationale: The revised title would improve the perception of the role if the position includes teaching.
- *Genealogist*
  - Strategic: *Genealogy Specialist & Instructor*
  - Rationale: Genealogist, a term that tends to describe people who conduct research for themselves, conveys less expertise than the suggested substitute. In addition, the recommended title conveys that the person teaches others. Reversing the title to *Instructor & Genealogy Specialist* would also be a great choice.

Our titles speak volumes, which is why we'll next delve into why it is to our benefit to strategize in this vital area of our vocabulary as well.

NOTES

1. Sharon Coolidge, "Hamilton Co. Libraries Face Cuts, Closings Amid Budget Shortfall," Cincinatti.com, July 27, 2011, http://www.ongo.com/v/1474482/-1/4BBD41E0351A7F9A/hamilton-co-libraries-face-cuts-closings-amid-budget-shortfall.

2. E-mail from Heather Kearns, Associate Curator, Alice C. Sabatini Art Gallery, Special Collections, Topeka & Shawnee County Public Library, 1515 SW 10th Ave., Topeka, KS 66604, to the author, dated November 16, 2010. Used by permission.

5

STRATEGIC TITLES

A critical component of the Three Pillars Philosophy, job titles present a golden opportunity to harness the power of language to achieve the optimal respect and assigned worth we seek.

Let's begin our assessment of this strategic language segment with a snapshot of what the word *librarian* communicates.

How often do you hear, "I'd love to work in a library so I could read books all day" (or the one I find so amusing, "I'd love your job. It must be quiet and relaxing.")?

This is what many people—including elected officials—think librarians do. They also think we organize, loan, and shelve the books we read all day. That's pretty much it.

Furthermore, they do not differentiate among staff roles. They think that everyone who works at a library is a "librarian." Why do people think this? To a degree, it's because of the broad and ambiguous definition of the word *librarian*.

Consider that *librarian* means all of the following:

- one who cares for the publications and files in a library, whether staff or volunteer
- a person assisting in a library
- a person who processes and organizes information
- someone who works in a library
- a person trained to work in a library, or who maintains a particular collection of books
- a person who is in charge of a collection
- a professional person trained in library science and engaged in library services
- someone who is in charge of a library

In light of this sweeping definition, one can certainly understand why the general public doesn't know what we do, and thinks everyone who works in a library is a librarian—even volunteers!

CURRENT LANDSCAPE

With this as the prevailing picture, is the following viewpoint published in *Library Hotline* really so surprising?

Why are libraries so expensive? It's such a simple idea, get a cheap place where people can donate used books, some volunteers organize them according to the Dewey Decimal system, then some volunteers loan them out to other people. It could be done in an old building with folding tables and used book shelves.[1]

Neither should we be shocked by newspaper headlines like the one *The Wall Street Journal* crafted for an article on self-serve lockers available to customers at the Washington County (MN) Library for picking up requested materials. The unfortunate headline read, "New Library Technologies Dispense with Librarians."[2]

Regrettably, both of the above examples fuel the prevalent misperception that librarianship and the tasks librarians perform are inconsequential, requiring minimal expertise. In fact, both examples imply that "librarians" are expendable, contributing to the disproportionate budget cuts many library systems are facing.

Although we haven't thought much about it, these unfavorable views persist. The indistinct meaning of librarian leads people to draw incomplete and incorrect conclusions when they hear the word *librarian*.

Other common job titles in our profession compound this challenge. Many diminish the significance of the positions they aim to describe (e.g., circulation clerk). Some titles also exacerbate the stereotypes that endure, in spite of our concerted advocacy efforts.

Center stage, our job titles present an ideal strategic vocabulary opportunity to set the record straight. We can capitalize on this power by choosing titles that accurately describe our roles, imparting their full value.

Effective revisions to our titles can shatter detrimental inferences and typecasts once and for all, increasing respect and—that end all and be all—funding.

NEW, SMARTER APPROACH

You may be wondering why, instead of changing our language, we couldn't simply better explain what a librarian does.

While seemingly logical, consider that our profession has tried the "explain why we are important" advocacy approach for decades. What have we accomplished? We have essentially spun our wheels, achieving minimal progress. The "no one understands what we do" refrain keeps coming back.

To continue in the same vein after all this time seems futile. Achieving different results would constitute a steep, uphill climb.

For starters, explaining is incredibly time-consuming. Plus, it's virtually impossible to bend everyone's ear long enough to explain. Even if this were possible, those detrimental, hard-to-shake preconceived notions of *librarian* would inevitably impede progress.

Instead, why not make life easier on ourselves and coast downhill to the finish line with an effective, far easier methodology?

If we expect a different outcome, then we must try a new approach. For job titles, this involves choosing terms that are education and business oriented—strong, authoritative titles our customers will understand, which in turn will garner greater respect, enhanced value, and the funding we deserve.

Here's an example of the tactic's striking impact.

Pretend Ms. Non-Library Connoisseur approaches you and asks, "What do you do?" If you say, "I'm an *instructor*," what will she think? She'll think you teach.

The answer is crystal clear. The picture in her mind will be accurate. No further explanation is required. The word speaks for itself.

By contrast, if you tell her, "I'm a *librarian*," what will she think? She won't really know what you do.

Based on the definition of *librarian*, you could be anything from a volunteer to the person in charge. Most likely, she'll think you read, organize, loan, and shelve books. Further explanation—and lots of it—must take place to correct these misperceptions.

Based on title alone, to which of these positions would she assign a higher salary?

TRANSFORMING OUR TITLES

At Howard County Library System (HCLS), when we recognized that our titles were hindering the image we desired to project, we began deliberating possible alternatives. We also wished to maximize our chances of receiving funding approval for the salary increases we desired to achieve.

We decided to implement title modifications that would command more respect, and therefore greater associated value. Our desire was to convey more effectively the importance of the HCLS team: academic, business-oriented experts delivering high-quality public education for all.

Here are the titles we scrutinized, the alternatives we chose, and some accompanying commentary.

Librarian/Library Associate → Instructor & Research Specialist

At HCLS, our first move several years back took us from *Librarian* and *Library Associate,* to *Information Specialist & Instructor.*

Staff members experienced elevated pride with this first modification. They gained an even greater sense of importance when we further refined the title to *Instructor & Research Specialist.* Our revelation that *research* more accurately conveyed staff expertise prompted this follow-up edit.

You may have noticed that, in addition to replacing *information* with *research*, we reversed the title's word order, placing *instructor* first to emphasize this aspect of the role. This was in response to staff preference.

Our staff members enjoy this new title because it is self-descriptive and value-charged. The title conveys that the person holding the position is an educator who teaches, possessing proficiency and knowledge.

Titles implemented in this category include *Children's Instructor & Research Specialist, Teens' Instructor & Research Specialist,* and for adults, simply *Instructor & Research Specialist.*

Supervisory titles include *Children's Instruction & Research Supervisor* (instead of *Children's Services Supervisor*), and *Instruction & Research Supervisor* (to replace *Adult Services Supervisor*).

People now understand what these positions do. No one asks us anymore whether we sit around reading books all day!

Consider replacing *Librarian* and *Library Associate* with *Instructor & Research Specialist,* an intuitive title that captures and communicates the essence and importance of the role. We've already established that we teach customers one-on-one, as well as in groups—in classroom, seminar, and workshop settings. We also assist with and conduct customer research.

Let's take advantage of a great title that will attain for staff well deserved credit for what they do.

They'll Love It

Your staff will love the new title.

They'll enjoy the heightened respect they will receive from customers, take greater pride in their work, and be energized to perform at an elevated level of excellence.

At HCLS, before we had officially announced we would be rolling out the revised title *Instructor,* two of our then Library Associates approached me right before teaching Kindness Counts, a children's class that was being filmed for inclusion in the documentary, *Rude: Where Are Our Manners?*[3] Beaming, they asked, "Can we use our new titles for the introduction?" to which I responded, "Yes. What a great idea!"

With visible pride, they introduced themselves as *instructors* to the audience of 100 that comprised second grade students, elementary school teachers, parent chaperones, a principal, and a Board of Education member.

They then commenced to teach the class.

Figure 5.1   HCLS instructors teach Kindness Counts, a Choose Civility children's class.

Traditional	Strategic
Librarian, Library Associate	Instructor & Research Specialist, teacher, adjunct faculty, educator, facilitor
Children's Services Supervisor	Children's Instruction & Research Supervisor
Adult Services Supervisor	Instruction & Research Supervisor

Figure 5.2   Traditional to strategic—Librarian to Instructor.

Teacher

Having already established that we are *instructors* who *teach*, let's now examine the word *teacher*, which means:

- one who teaches
- one whose occupation is to instruct

In addition, here's how Vocabulary.com defines *teacher*:

If the guy down the street shows you how to play the guitar and helps you develop a masterful plucking style, then he's your guitar *teacher*.

A teacher is anyone who teaches things. Schools hire people to be teachers, but you don't have to work in a school to be a teacher. You can be a teacher to your children. If you're really good at making pizza, you can be a teacher to an aspiring pizza chef. If you're really passionate about methods of education, then you can become a teacher who teaches teachers how to teach better. Whoa.[4]

Although acknowledging that we fall squarely under the word's definition, some workshop participants wondered whether library staff members could call themselves *teachers* when they are not certified.

Others countered that we are *teachers*, not only in the general sense, but also in our own right as *teachers* at an educational institution. They noted that *teachers* in private schools and professors at colleges and universities are not necessarily certified. Like us, they are simply experts in their fields.

At a Maryland Public Library Administrators conference,[5] one attendee commented that adjunct faculty members who teach noncredit community college classes hold no particular standardized credentials, with knowledge of the subject matter being the hiring requirement.

At HCLS, our titles include the word *instructor*, as opposed to *teacher*. However, we do say that we *teach* classes. We teach them at HCLS branches and in the schools through A+ Partners in Education, our comprehensive partnership with the schools. School teachers invite HCLS instructors to teach A+ Curriculum Classes, which are categorized by age group and subject.

In addition, we say that our profession is *public education*, and that *teaching* is part of our overall curriculum under each of our Three Pillars.

Although we do refer to ourselves as *teachers* occasionally, it's mainly others who bestow the title of *teacher* on us. For example, preschoolers say phrases like, "My favorite library teacher is Miss Ronnie," and parents can be overheard saying, "Sally's favorite part of the day is library school."

We also receive e-mails from customers who call us *teachers*, such as the following one with the subject heading "Kids Classes":

I love the library! My kids love the classes, especially the Baby Signs class at Central and the Book Parade at Glenwood. The library teachers are wonderful![6]

Positive Feedback from School Teachers

Several workshop participants have asked if we have received any feedback from licensed school teachers about the library's use of the word *teacher* when referring to library staff.

At HCLS, we receive only positive responses from certified public school teachers (Maryland uses the term "certified" as opposed to "licensed").

The input we receive is not related to the word *teacher*—or any other word or phrase in our strategic vocabulary—but rather their immense appreciation for the quality of the curriculum our instructors deliver to their students. Many school teachers view us as *adjunct faculty*, with some schools even offering school faculty badges to our instructors.

Why is it that we don't receive pushback about our use of the word *teacher*, or any other smart term to which we have gravitated? It's because the implementation of our revised lexicon is gradual. School teachers—and everyone else—probably do not even notice. They just think more highly of us.

At first, we introduced the title *Instructor*, along with the concept that we *teach*, into our language, with *Librarian* and *Library Associate* still the dominant title terminology. As our application of the smarter title gained wider usage, others began using the new title, which, in turn, continued the strategic vocabulary's forward momentum. Now, *Instructor* is commonplace at HCLS.

In other words, the image transformation occurs in stages, with time for adjustment.

Educator

An exceptional word, *educator* can enhance our image appreciably. Some of us already call ourselves educators. For instance, after confessing in his *Information Today* column that he gave away his secret on how to land the coveted first-in-line spot on Southwest flights, Steven M. Cohen added, "Of course, I told them how. After all, I'm an educator."[7]

While many in our profession might not think to describe themselves as *educators*, when asked whether we are, most would agree. This is an important step in the right direction toward transforming our image that will achieve the level of respect and funding we're after.

At HCLS, we find that when we call ourselves *educators*, the general public assigns greater value to all that we do.

Educator of the Year

That higher value was visible already back in 2003 when we won the Howard County Chamber of Commerce's coveted Educator of the Year Award. Hope Chase, our Head of Youth Services (a position we now call Head of Children's and Teens' Curriculum) was recognized for her leadership in DEAR (Dogs Educating and Assisting Readers). A component of A+ Partners in Education, DEAR links third grade students who need to improve their reading skills with therapy dogs. The students enjoy reading to the loving, patient canines, who never ridicule or criticize (sometimes called Puppy Tails, Reading with Rover, or Paws to Read—many of you have similar initiatives).

A major coup, this first place win proved particularly significant because that was the first time HCLS educators were eligible to receive the award. Previously, only faculty and administrators from schools and institutes of higher education had been nominated. The award therefore indirectly celebrated the collective educational contributions of the entire HCLS team, and the system's overall image as an educational pillar, which had already taken root (our efforts at becoming viewed as a major component of education, along with the schools, had begun only two years earlier).

How did our inclusion in the nomination pool come about? Although I hope you'll find the story interesting, it's included here for one reason: to demonstrate that we have tremendous power to shape our image through the smart application of strategic vocabulary.

A year or so before HCLS received this award, the Chamber of Commerce was looking for a representative for its Education Subcommittee. Thinking my participation would perhaps further HCLS's efforts to be viewed as an educational institution, I volunteered. At a meeting to discuss the 2003 Education of the Year awards, the Chamber of Commerce President asked me whether HCLS staff members could serve as judges.

Seizing what I thought might be an opportunity, I responded, "I'll be delighted to ask . . . However . . . I was hoping that this might present a conflict of interest. You see, I was hoping you might consider allowing *HCLS* educators to be nominated for Educator of the Year."

I followed this remark with several examples of impressive HCLS *educators* and their notable contributions to excellence in *education*, and, of course, a succinct description of how HCLS is a major component of the county's strong education system.

To my pleasant surprise, the committee members—who knew about A+ Partners in Education and so at least had connected HCLS as an educational partner with the school system by that time—were open to the idea.

However, since the brochure for that year's award had already been disseminated, they suggested extending eligibility to HCLS employees the following year, editing the brochure's language accordingly. Pleased, I would soon be ecstatic.

The chair suggested checking the eligibility language in the brochure that had already been mailed to see whether the existing definition might be broad enough to include us yet for 2003. The wording read:

> Anyone who serves in a teaching or administrative capacity as a full-time professional in a Howard County educational facility is eligible.

The committee determined that the parameters included HCLS, and that we could nominate our *educators* already that year.

Discussion on judges resumed, except this time, my wish had come true. HCLS staff members had to be excluded as potential judges due to a conflict of interest.

In two short years, we had made sufficient progress in our efforts to be viewed as education that eligibility for Educator of the Year had become a reality. At the awards ceremony, the audience of 1,000—which included a host of elected officials and community leaders—was introduced in convincing fashion to the notion that, along with teachers and college faculty, we, too, are educators.

Our "stock rating" kicked up a few notches that evening.

Facilitator

A term you may already be using, *facilitator* works well to describe our roles as they pertain to book club discussions, as in "I'm Amy Jones, Instructor & Research Specialist at ABC Public Library's West Branch. Welcome to the Chapter Chats Book Club! I'll be your *facilitator* this evening."

"I'm your *instructor* this evening" works when we are teaching others how to expertly lead a book discussion.

Programmer → Instructor

As with the word *program*, our current use of the term *programmer* conveys little value to the listener in most instances.

The recommendation is therefore to keep *programmer* only for those circumstances where we mean what is commonly understood. Anything IT related would fall into this category. For instance, *Web Programmer* is a title to keep.

For any other title that includes *programmer* (e.g., *Children's Programmer*) and really means a position that develops class content and teaches classes, experiment with migrating to *instructor*, which everyone understands.

Programming can also sometimes be found in our titles. Here again, if the title is IT related, then keeping the term is fine. However, if *programming* means *curriculum* or *instruction*, try replacing it with the more intuitive, value-enhanced term. To illustrate, *Manager of Children's Programming* would become *Manager of Children's Curriculum* or *Manager of Children's Instruction*.

At HCLS, our previously titled *Head of Adult Programming* was best rescripted as *Events & Seminars Manager*.

Traditional	Strategic
Programmer	Instructor, facilitator, educator, teacher, adjunct faculty Web Programmer
Head of Children's Programming	Head of Children's & Teens' Curriculum (or Director or Manager)
Head of Adult Programming	Events & Seminars Manager, Head of Adult Curriculum (or Director or Manager)

Figure 5.3   Traditional to strategic—Programmer to Instructor.

Circulation Clerk → Customer Service Specialist

Our staff who work as *Circulation Clerks* deserve a better title.

Customer Service Specialist works especially well as a replacement, instilling great pride in staff members who hold this position. The revised title's effect on staff is best encapsulated by this recent conversation.

Occasionally, I stop by the Customer Service workroom (formerly Circulation workroom) at the HCLS East Columbia Branch to say hello, and sometimes also to search for interesting just-returned DVDs (my office is adjacent to the branch).

During a recent visit, as I was perusing movie titles, I heard a polite, "Excuse me." I turned towards the voice and found Grace standing next to me. Pointing to her staff name badge, she continued, "Was this your idea?"

Wondering whether she meant her magnetic-backed name badge, the logo on it, or her title, I asked for clarification. She said, simply, "Customer Service Specialist."

Not certain where she was headed, I conceded that, yes, I had suggested the revised title a number of years back, expressing my thanks to the entire HCLS team for having embraced the idea.

"Thank you," were her next words. "It makes me feel so important. That's exactly what I am. A Customer Service Specialist. The customers understand what I do now."

I smiled, adding, "And they respect you more now, too. Do you sense that?"

Grace nodded, "Yes, they do! And that makes me feel proud. And motivated. I love working here."

She hesitated, then asked, "How come other libraries don't say Customer Service Specialist?"

Other Customer Service Titles

Similarly *Circulation Supervisor* can easily transfer to *Customer Service Supervisor*.

In addition, if you don't yet have a systemwide position implementing your Customer Service Philosophy (if you have yet to develop a Customer Service Philosophy, you are welcome to use HCLS's as a start—it's posted at hclibrary.org), you may wish to establish a Head of Customer Service, or a variation on this title, depending on the size of your library system.

Traditional	Strategic
Circulation Clerk	Customer Service Specialist
Circulation Supervisor	Customer Service Supervisor Systemwide position: Head of Customer Service, Customer Service Manager, Director of Customer Service, Chief Customer Service Officer

Figure 5.4 Traditional to strategic—Circulation Clerk to Customer Service Specialist

Cataloger/Cataloging → Data Specialist/ Data Services Department

Let's now take a look at how we might capitalize on strategic vocabulary to enhance the perceived value of the pivotal role of cataloging that, in conjunction with IT, enables that crucial first pillar, Self-Directed Education.

We'll begin by contemplating what the words *cataloger* and *cataloging* convey to a nonlibrary person.

To a nonlibrary person, *cataloger* means "someone who catalogs," or "a person who makes catalogs." And *cataloging*? "That which is cataloged." Neither term says much.

Because the words are not understood, the assumption will be that a *cataloger* involves little training at best, and volunteer work at worst (recall the viewpoint in *Library Hotline*, "get a cheap place where people can donate used books, some volunteers organize them according to the Dewey Decimal system"[8]).

While *cataloger* and *cataloging* may have communicated value when they were first coined, neither term even hints at the sophisticated data integrity and IT skills involved since the card catalog moved online. It would therefore behoove us in these high-tech times to consider alternatives for these long-standing words in order to describe the role and its function more accurately and elevate perceived value.

At HCLS, we replaced *Cataloger* with the more updated *Data Specialist*, a business-related title with an IT component that commands a greater assigned value than *Cataloger*.

We also exchanged *Cataloging Department* for the more 21st-centuryesque *Data Department*. Consider experimenting with some of these updated titles. You'll find that the IT and business connection results in higher perceived worth.

Traditional	Strategic
Cataloger	Data Specialist
Cataloging Department	Data Department

Figure 5.5   Traditional to strategic—Cataloger to Data Specialist.

KEY ADMINISTRATIVE POSITIONS

We come to the final group of titles to analyze, our administrative positions. Arguably the most important category, these visible titles set the tone for how the entire organization is perceived.

In short, when we hand people our business cards, we want them to be duly impressed *from our titles alone*. Ideally, our titles convey that the operation we run is a highly regarded educational institution that incorporates best business practices.

How can we best achieve this? By choosing titles that describe our roles precisely, in bold, authoritative language that is recognizable—titles that are commonly found in the world of academics and business.

With these goals in mind, let's take it from the top.

Director → President & CEO

Not too long ago, my title was *Director*. When I introduced myself as such, the conversation would continue, "Oh! Which department?"

While my response ("Oh, I dabble a bit in all of them.") served to explain, I am eternally grateful to the HCLS Board of Trustees for appreciating the power of titles. The Board recognized that modifying my title would not only clarify my role, but would also enable value-enhanced titles for other administrative positions, and contribute vastly to the desired image transformation for our entire library system.

As *Director*, why did people assume I was in charge of a particular department? Because in the corporate world, and also at colleges and universities, which use many corporate titles, *director* denotes a lower executive-level position that supervises a limited area.

My being called *Director* also hampered our strategic vocabulary efforts relating to certain key administrative position titles. For example, our plan included calling some of our then *"Head of"* positions (e.g., *Head of Human Resources*) what their counterparts were called in the academic and business spheres, such as Director of Human Resources and Director of Public Relations. To assign value-enhanced titles to this group of staff, my position would first need to be revised.

The HCLS Board observed that my counterparts in the college, university, public school, and business setting are called:

- President, and sometimes Chancellor at colleges and universities
- Superintendent, and occasionally Chancellor at public schools
- CEO, President and CEO, and Chairman and CEO in businesses

Unlike *Director*, each of these titles communicates clearly that the role is *the* top position with the highest decision-making authority and greatest responsibility.

Note that *Executive Director*, a title in place for the top position at some nonprofit organizations, is not on this list, likely because the title can also denote lower level management positions (e.g., *Executive Director of Building Maintenance* at a college).

The HCLS Board determined that modifying my title to *President & CEO* would be self-explanatory, describing precisely what I do. The respected title also blends the strongest title from the academic world, president, with the best of the business world, CEO.

Subsequently modifying our *Head of* titles into *Director of* positions would achieve the same objective.

At the time of this discussion, the highest HCLS Board of Trustees officer was called *President*, which meant that a three-step plan would be necessary to accomplish this vision. Here are the steps the Board implemented:

1. Board *President* became Board *Chair.*
2. *Director* was replaced with *Chief Executive Officer* which enabled:
   - Exchanging *Associate Director* for *Chief Operating Officer* and
   - Replacing certain *Head of* positions with *Director of* (e.g., *Director of IT*).
3. Once *Board Chair* had been in place for a year, *CEO* became *President & CEO.*

The HCLS Board took pride in following the lead of New York Public Library and Boston Public Library, where the top position is President and CEO. In addition, Brooklyn Public Library recently conferred the title of President and CEO to its top role.[9]

Now, when we introduce ourselves, people understand what we do. Most importantly, they also now think more highly of HCLS (without realizing why).

Other Common Top-Post Titles → President and CEO

Our entire profession would benefit if everyone were to take a cue from the likes of New York and Boston, working toward establishing *President & CEO* as the most common title for the top role in our respective library systems.

For those of you who already have *CEO* as your top role's title, consider preceding that with *President and* to edge perceived value a little bit higher, and to further strengthen that link to education. *President* by itself works well too.

If *Administrator* is your library system's top job, note that this term falls in the same category as *Director*, in that the term is typically assigned to lower management positions, as is sometimes the case with *Executive Director*. Experiment with moving to *President* or *President & CEO.*

As to *Chief Librarian, City Librarian,* and *County Librarian,* I wonder whether these have been passed along over time without much thought. We've likely never paid attention to the message these titles send. Neither have we put much thought into how we might benefit from beginning to

Traditional	Strategic
Director, Administrator, Chief Librarian, City Librarian, County Librarian, Executive Director	President & Chief Executive Officer President
Assistant Director, Associate Director, Deputy Director	Chief Operating Officer
Head of Accounting	Chief Financial Officer
Head of Human Resources	Director of Human Resources, Chief Human Resources Officer
Head of Public Relations	Director of Public Relations, Chief Public Relations Officer, Chief Marketing Officer
Head of IT	Director of IT, Chief Information Officer, Chief Technology Officer

Figure 5.6   Traditional to strategic—Director to President & CEO.

work toward value-enhanced titles that convey greater stature. Consider that a superintendent of a public school system would not likely be called Chief Teacher, City Teacher, or County Teacher. Neither would a college or university president be called Chief Professor, City Professor, or County Professor.

For library systems that are currently part of government, *President & CEO* or *President* may not be possible in the short-term. If that is the case, then *CEO* (by itself) would be the next strongest title, followed by *Executive Director*. However, you may need to start with the highest title that reports to your mayor or county executive.

INCREASED SALARIES

Some workshop participants asked how our unions responded to job title changes.

While HCLS functions successfully and effectively in a nonunion environment, it stands to reason that unions would welcome the Three Pillars Philosophy, as its application results in the ability to pay people salaries that more accurately reflect the true value of their work.

An increased operating budget means that all budget categories can be bolstered, including the important area of employee salaries, always a top priority, regardless of work structure.

At HCLS, we take pride in the upwardly adjusted salary ranges we can now post for positions. Many of our positions' starting salaries were increased by 15 percent as a direct result of our ability to convey our full value.

EXPANDED APPLICANT POOL

Workshop participants also inquired whether HCLS's Human Resources department welcomed the job title modifications.

Our Human Resources department has been instrumental in both developing and implementing our job title revisions. HR fully embraces the vision because the new titles have instilled greater staff pride, enabled higher salaries, and expanded our pool of qualified applicants.

Since our titles are now self-explanatory, we now receive applications from candidates who previously chose not to apply, including contenders from schools, colleges, universities, and businesses. Unlike before, applicants now see themselves in our positions and apply.

For example, our current *Chief Operating Officer* who hails from the fields of business and government contracts would not have applied had we advertised the position under the role's previous title, *Associate Director*. She would not have understood the position. However, with the revised title of *Chief Operating Officer*—which is precisely what the position is—she understood the role, and applied.

The title made the difference.

CASE STUDY

In January 2011, we advertised an opening for a *Children's Instructor & Research Specialist*, a position commonly called *Library Associate or Librarian* at other library systems.

Learning about the revised title, an HR colleague from a neighboring library system remarked to our Director of Human Resources that she didn't think many people would apply because they would be confused and would not know what the job was.

What actually transpired? The direct opposite! We experienced a 100 percent increase in applicants (a record 66 people applied within two weeks).

Why? People understood the role. The self-explanatory title prompted them to click on the position description, where they also found language they understood.

Figure 5.7 shows the position description we posted.

POSITION DESCRIPTION
Children's Instructor &
Research Specialist

RESPONSIBILITY

- Positions Howard County Library (HCLS) as a major component of public education for all ages
- Effectively lives the Seven Pillars of HCLS's strategic plan: Authentic Values, Strategic Vocabulary, Everyone a Leader, Winning Teamwork, Community Partnerships, The Power of Us, and Fiercely Loyal Customers, motivating others to do so as well
- Fully embraces HCLS' educational mission, effectively communicating our curriculum, which comprises Three Pillars (Self-Directed Education. Research Assistance & Instruction, Instructive & Enlightening Experiences)

ESSENTIAL FUNCTIONS

- Regularly prepares and teaches children's classes for infants through grade 5, including classes related to the Enchanted Garden (science, health, nutrition, and environmental education)
- Visits schools to teach A+ Partners in Education classes, including book promotions, and provide instruction resources for preschool, elementary and middle school students and staff
- Delivers research assistance to the public
- Teaches/facilitates classes, seminars and events for adults related to children's education
- Works at any HCLS Customer Service or Research Desk
- Hosts HCLS branch tours
- Acts as A+ Partnership liaison as assigned
- Participates in special events in the community as assigned

Figure 5.7   HCLS Position Description—Children's Instructor & Research Specialist.

Outside candidates totaled 58, falling into the following categories:

- 33 came from education fields
  - 22 teachers and professors from schools/colleges/universities
    - 9 public school teachers
    - 11 private school teachers
    - 2 college professors
  - 11 public library instructors and research specialists
- 19 were professionals from the following fields: finance, law, marketing, communications, social work, IT, pharmacology, statistics, marine biology, museums, and medicine
- Six were administrative professionals from the private sector (e.g., retail)

In addition, eight internal candidates applied: Customer Service Specialists and part-time Instructor & Research Specialists desiring full-time positions.

Of the 66 candidates, 21 were currently unemployed, and 3 were retirees.

Two variables point to the reason for this record pool of candidates: the job's revised title and a carefully crafted position description. Especially noteworthy, our modified language enabled teachers at schools and colleges to see themselves as potential Instructor & Research Specialists at our organization.

While the state of the economy clearly played a role in the number of applications we received, we disregarded this factor since we had posted an equivalent position twice in the preceding two-year period in an equally depressed economy. The prior postings produced only half as many applications—none from schools, colleges, or universities.[10]

What might one conclude from this analysis? That our smart, self-explanatory language expanded our pool of qualified candidates, a key advantage when desiring to build extraordinary teams.

LIBRARIAN OF THE YEAR → EDUCATOR OF THE YEAR

We'll conclude this section with some thoughts about a truly grand award, which relates to titles in that a title is in the award's name: *Library Journal*'s "Librarian of the Year."

How might our profession benefit if *Library Journal* were to rename this acclaimed honor "Educator of the Year"?

Such a modification would contribute to the successful building of our brand in a major way, unleashing the education advantage. Here's how effective this one edit could be.

Imagine being recognized for "Educator of the Year" before your state legislators. Picture the Senate Majority Leader offering remarks as follows:

> We recognize and celebrate President & CEO Jane Doe of ABC Public Library System, who was named Educator of the Year by *Library Journal*. We thank Ms. Doe for her exemplary leadership in delivering high-quality public education for literally everyone who lives and works in ABC.

What a tribute this would be for Ms. Doe, her library system, and the entire profession.

Just as important, what an optimal teaching opportunity this would present for every single legislator in the room, all of whom determine funding allocations for their state's libraries.

Such a powerful message would advance us one step closer to being recognized as the highest funding priority.

Traditional	Strategic
Librarian of the year	Educator of the year

Figure 5.8   Traditional to strategic—Librarian of the year to Educator of the year.

NOTES

1. *Library Hotline* 39, no. 20, May 24, 2010, p. 6.

2. Conor Dougherty, "New Library Technologies Dispense With Librarians," *The Wall Street Journal*, October 25, 2010, p. A3.

3. *Rude: Where Are Our Manners?* [DVD], by 90th Parallel Film & Television Productions, Toronto, Ontario, CBC Learning, 2008.

4. "Teacher," The Dictionary, vocabulary.com, http://www.vocabulary.com/definition/teacher.

5. Maryland Association of Public Library Administrators Presentation: "Words That Work: Perception Is Everything" (October 3, 2008, Ocean City, MD).

6. "Kids classes," e-mail received in HCLS's general mailbox, askhcl.org, October 5, 2010.

7. Steven M. Cohen, "How Firefox Add-Ons Can Get You on the Plane First?," *Information Today*, November 2008, p. 20.

8. *Library Hotline,* p. 6.

9. Michael Kelley, "Brooklyn Public Library Picks Linda Johnson for Top Spot," *Library Journal,* August 16, 2011, http://www.libraryjournal.com/lj/home/891647–264/brooklyn_public_library_picks_linda.html.csp.

10. This case study reflects the work of HCLS Director of Human Resources Stacey C. Fields.

6

TRICKS OF THE TRADE

We can extend the mileage of our strategic vocabulary efforts by incorporating persuasive linguistic techniques into our communications.

Frank Luntz sets forth expert advice in this area in his "Ten Rules of Successful Communication."[1] By weaving even some of these recommendations into your speeches, conversations, and writing pieces, you will engage the listener and reader more intently and thus more effectively. Here are the rules, along with a few examples of how these snippets of wisdom apply to us.

1. *Simplicity.* While sophisticated word choices are appropriate for certain audiences, simple words tend to be best in most situations. This is because when people do not understand a word, they rarely go to the trouble of consulting a dictionary.

2. *Brevity.* Use short sentences. Drawn out ones can lose a reader's attention.

3. *Credibility.* Fulfilling that which you assert is imperative. For instance, if you say, "We deliver excellence in education," then your customers should experience excellence.

   To a certain extent, this is a self-fulfilling prophecy. Declaring that you deliver excellence sets a standard and expectation your staff will be inspired to attain. As Luntz summarizes it, "The words you use become you—and you become the words you use."[2]

4. *Consistency matters.* The more consistent we can be with our strategic vocabulary, the more quickly we will establish our brand and the sooner we will reap the rewards.

   A time-tested practice, language repetition causes people to remember. To illustrate, what does "good to the last drop" bring to mind? The odds are you knew immediately that the phrase describes Maxwell House coffee. Why is it that you—and many generations before you—make the association so quickly? Because the company has been repeating exactly the same phrase since 1907.[3]

   If everyone in our profession were to begin saying, "We deliver *public education for all*," and "Our curriculum comprises Three Pillars: Self-Directed Education, Research Assistance & Instruction, and Instructive & Enlightening Experiences," these statements would stick in people's memories—including those of elected officials.

   Assume, for a moment, that we were to achieve such collective language alignment. Picture how this would influence funding decisions at state Budget and Taxation Committee meetings across the country. As members debate whether to cut, maintain, or increase funding for libraries, gone would be the misperceptions. This time, they would understand that we are educators who deliver equal opportunity in education for everyone—and would know precisely why education matters. Imagine the positive results!

5. *Novelty: Offer something new.* This is the "Well, I'm impressed!" or "I had never thought about it that way before—of course!" reaction in response to our words.

   The Three Pillars language achieves this type of arresting impression because it encapsulates our essence in fresh, fascinating terms. Try it and you'll see that your revised language will pique people's interest and capture their attention.

   The next time Mr. Event Attendee asks you what you do, experiment with "something new." Tell him you're an educator. He'll probe, "School? College? University?"

   You'll smile and respond, "ABC Public Library—high-quality education for everyone. I'm an Instructor. I teach classes for elementary school students, like 'What's in My Art Box' and 'Spring Into Science.' Plus I assist with research, and also A+ Partners in Education signature events, like Battle of the Books—700 fifth grade students participated last year!"

   How many "something new" words and phrases will he have heard packed in 30 seconds?

   - Educator
   - Education for everyone
   - Instructor
   - Research
   - Teach
   - Classes
   - Science
   - A+ Partners in Education
   - Signature events
   - Battle of the Books
   - 700 students

   Guaranteed, you will have his full attention. His face will be broadcasting, "Wow!"

6. *Sound and texture.* Use alliteration, rhythm, and rhyme to add variety and interest to phrases and sentences. For example, a class where students build model bridges out of spaghetti can be called "Everyday Engineering."

8. *Visualize.* One reason the Three Pillars communicates our curriculum so effectively is that the phrase induces a mental picture. This image allows the reader or listener to experience the vision's strength through the words, which makes the message more memorable—a bit like Allstate's catchphrase "you're in good hands," which prompts the visualization of caring hands.

   The Three Pillars graphic creates an even stronger impression because the visual reinforces the words, similar to the way Allstate's logo reflects its tagline.

   The more people read, hear, and "see" our message, the greater the chances they will retain it.

9. *Ask a question.* Why is asking a question so effective? A question varies the pace and tone of your presentation or writing piece, adding appeal. Most importantly, questions involve your listeners, prompting them to think.

10. *Context and relevance.* It is important that your audience understand why your message is applicable to a point you are making. In addition, to be most effective, tailor your terminology so that your message speaks to your specific audience (e.g., elected officials, seniors, teens).

    To illustrate, engaging teens requires a multi-focused approach. It is necessary to appeal both to teens, and to their parents and teachers who encourage them to use the library, as teens and adults often have very different ideas when it comes to what is appealing.

At Howard County Library System (HCLS), we have found that the most effective focus for teens is "fun," and so we actually say the word fun regularly. All of our classes, events, workshops, and initiatives (what we once called programs) have educational value, but since teens place a higher value on fun, we describe them with sensational titles and highlight creative, daring, or high-tech elements involved, such as:

- "Tech Chicks"—A technology club for girls! Department of Defense robotics engineer Dr. Terri Kamm leads hands-on activities in the latest technology.
- "Food Fear Factor"—We dare you to taste Madagascar hissing cockroaches and delectable fried grasshoppers.

Adults place a higher value on education, so when we speak to parents and teachers of teens we emphasize the fun and educational nature of these classes and events.

You may be wondering what happened to Rule 7! Intentionally skipped, this lucky-numbered rule delivers such sage advice it needed its own section.

Speak Aspirationally (Rule 7)

Ours is a profession that tends to project a "woe is me" outlook. Open almost any library journal and you'll see something relating to our being undervalued and underappreciated. Examples include:

- "If we're not careful, the notion that the public library has no value or relevance to modern life (you know you've heard it before) could become the majority view . . . People who don't know much about libraries often predict that libraries will be dead and gone within 20 years."[4]
- "Will the public support (i.e., pay the salaries of) qualified librarians when it doesn't know what they do?"[5]
- "Libraries' relevance has been shrinking over the past decade."[6]
- "Libraries Challenged to Prove Their Value."[7]
- "Losing Libraries. Public libraries in the U.S. are in trouble. A LOT of trouble."[8]
- "Public libraries are doomed"[9]

Similarly, here's what we said about ourselves in a recent *Daily Herald* (Provo, Utah) article headlined, "Budget Cuts Force Libraries to Re-Examine Their Purpose"[10] (emphasis added):

- "Librarians concede that it's not always easy to demonstrate their value."
- "People think the library is dead because of the Internet."
- "We can't depend solely on tax dollars anymore."
- "A 2010 survey by *Library Journal* showed that 72 percent of surveyed libraries said they faced budget cuts in the previous year, while 43 percent said they had made cuts to staffing. *Nearly one in five respondents expressed pessimism about the future of libraries.*"

If this is how we talk about ourselves, how can we blame the newspaper for choosing the article's inflammatory headline, or the reporter for injecting the following:

- "There's no question libraries face an uncertain future."
- "Public libraries are under siege: plunging tax revenues are forcing closures and staff cutbacks, while e-readers and the Internet can make a library seem quaint."
- "Budget cuts in Denver threaten to shut . . . half the city's library branches."
- "Almost all public libraries rely on city and county governments to pay for staff, material and maintenance. Some communities have decided it's an expense they no longer can afford."

Negativity will get us nowhere. Such comments even set us back. By expressing pessimistic views about ourselves, we are, in essence, sealing our own fate.

If you were making funding decisions, would these types of comments convince you to bolster funding for public libraries? Likely not. This is because people invest in what they are confident will be *successful*.

We would therefore be wise to embrace exuberant optimism instead.

Optimism Is Contagious

One of the benefits of the Three Pillars is that the approach by its nature speaks aspirationally, teaching our audience our value in an upbeat, confident fashion—and everyone loves optimism.

So let's do away with gloom. Copying late comedian George Carlin's famous "seven words you can't say on TV," let's agree as a profession to purge the following phrases from our lexicon:

- We must remain relevant.
- Our future is uncertain.
- Nobody values our jobs.
- No one knows what we do; we're misunderstood.
- The library's relevance is shrinking.
- People think the Internet has replaced the library.
- We might be extinct in 20 years.

Any of these can be replaced with the following confident message:

A major component of our nation's strong education system, we deliver high quality *public education for all* through a curriculum that comprises three pillars: Self-Directed Education, Research Assistance & Instruction, and Instructive & Enlightening Experiences.

For extra emphasis, we can add:

And . . . we continuously aspire to reach new heights.

If your budget has been trimmed, resist all temptations to speak in dispirited, resigned terms when speaking to reporters. Also, never repeat a negative others assert. Instead, declare something positive, such as:

While the budget we have been allocated will present major challenges, we will maximize the funding we have received to continue delivering excellence in public education for all under each of our Three Pillars: Self-Directed Education, Research Assistance & Instruction, and Instructive & Enlightening Experiences. Why is this our obligation to the community? Because education drives economic advancement, enhancing quality of life.

This type of commanding language will begin teaching those who decided to cut your budget why they shouldn't have. You will also already be on your way to fewer cuts next time, and maybe even funding restoration.

Survey Language

We would also benefit from eliminating the negative undertones we inadvertently send our customers through the surveys we compile. For instance, common survey questions include:

- Do you think libraries are an amenity?
- Are libraries still relevant?
- With everything available on the Internet, do you still think libraries are important?

These types of questions foster thoughts we do not wish our customers to ever have—so why include them at all? Perhaps some people do not even think in these terms until we ask the question. Consider that the schools would never ask questions like this.

Instead, let's assume—like the schools—that it's an established fact that libraries *are* an economic imperative. We can then turn our surveys into teaching opportunities. For instance, a survey could begin:

> A major component of our state's strong education system, libraries deliver *public education for all* through a curriculum that comprises three pillars: Self-Directed Education, Research Assistance & Instruction, and Instructive & Enlightening Experiences. For each item/category noted, please indicate its importance to you using a scale from 1 to 5, with one being the least important, and five the most.

The pillars would then be listed, with various items and boxes to check under each. To illustrate, here's what Pillar II might look like:

Pillar II: Research Assistance & Instruction

___ Research assistance for children

___ Research assistance for teens

___ Research assistance for adults

___ Individualized instruction (e.g., creating a Gmail account, downloading e-books, completing an online job application)

___ Classes for infants through prekindergarten students (e.g., Baby Sign, Play Partners, Bilingual Banter, Go Figure!)

___ Classes for kindergarten through fifth-grade students (e.g., Chemistry in the Library, Everyday Engineering, Great Composers)

___ Classes for middle school students (e.g., Science Club, Movin' up to Middle School, Teen Iron Chef)

___ Classes for high school students (e.g., College Bound, Understanding the SAT)

___ Classes for adults (e.g., Are You e-Ready?, Your Inner Innovator, Rain Barrels and Rain Gardens, English Conversation Club)

In which categories should library instructors deliver more individualized instruction?

☐ Navigating the Internet

☐ E-mail

☐ Social media (e.g., Facebook, Twitter)

☐ E-books/downloadable audiobooks

☐ E-readers

☐ Word processing

☐ Adult basic education (e.g., English, basic math skills)

☐ Genealogy research

☐ Other _____

In which subject areas should library instructors assign curriculum priority during the next three years, and for which age group(s)?

☐ Science	☐ Children	☐ Teens	☐ Adults	☐ All
☐ Technology	☐ Children	☐ Teens	☐ Adults	☐ All
☐ Engineering	☐ Children	☐ Teens	☐ Adults	☐ All
☐ Math	☐ Children	☐ Teens	☐ Adults	☐ All
☐ Environment	☐ Children	☐ Teens	☐ Adults	☐ All
☐ Health	☐ Children	☐ Teens	☐ Adults	☐ All
☐ History	☐ Children	☐ Teens	☐ Adults	☐ All
☐ Art	☐ Children	☐ Teens	☐ Adults	☐ All
☐ Music	☐ Children	☐ Teens	☐ Adults	☐ All
☐ Finance	☐ Children	☐ Teens	☐ Adults	☐ All
☐ Business (including building resumes, job interview skills, etc.)	☐ Children	☐ Teens	☐ Adults	☐ All
☐ Other _____	☐ Children	☐ Teens	☐ Adults	☐ All

Figure 6.1   Survey—strategic language.

This sample survey language cleverly asserts that public education is a necessity—a fact, rather than an opinion. In our case, it's public education for everyone.

FOCUS ON RESULTS

We can also enhance our investment value by emphasizing outcome. To illustrate, many of us like to say, "We promote the love of reading," or "We encourage reading." While these are not bad phrases, they do not indicate results of any kind. The message we intend to communicate gains strength when we focus on outcome, with phrases such as, "We increase reading," "We improve academic achievement," "We advance the economy," and "We enhance quality of life."

Merging two of the outcome-oriented phrases raises the perceived value bar even higher. For example, when describing the educational merits of Battle of the Books, a popular academic competition for fifth grade students, we could assert, "By increasing student reading, we enhance academic achievement."

Similarly, instead of saying, "Students used Live Homework Help 10,000 times last year," replacing "used" (which focuses on process) with "improved their grades using" (which underscores outcome) increases assigned worth.

Logic and Business Savvy

You may be wondering how, if challenged, we would prove that Battle of the Books elevates student academic achievement, or Live Homework Help improves grades.

One might look at it from the opposite angle. How can they not?

As to Battle of the Books, it stands to reason that the more one reads, the more one understands, the better one writes, the more subjects one knows, the smarter one becomes. From all of this, one can logically infer improved overall academic achievement.

In addition, students, parents, coaches, school faculty, and principals inform us of enhanced academic achievement, as well as social skills, leadership, and teamwork, which are also critically important to academic success.

Furthermore, we hear how avid readers devour the contest's 16 preselected books, enjoying the challenge of vying for first place. We hear how the competition transforms reluctant readers into avid ones, and how all participants take pride in achieving their personal best.

Similar logic can be applied to Live Homework Help. The more solidly students grasp a subject matter, the better grades they will receive. Students and parents relay instances where Live Homework Help saved the day by clarifying a challenging chemistry or calculus concept late in the evening, enabling the successful completion of homework, a better test score, or an aced final exam. In addition, grateful students write comments, such as:

- "I got an A on my Samuel Gompers report, which I never would have received had it not been for you."
- "AWESOME! I got a 100% grade—thank you!"
- "I don't have anyone to help me and I don't know what I'd do without this."
- "I was stressing out about these Algebra II problems, but now I can do them in a snap!"
- "You helped me re-understand geometry, which might just save me on the PSATs!"
- "You helped me receive an A on my project."
- "This is so cool. I'm actually passing math now."
- "Like really, no lie. I had a D in math but this heavenly website raised it to an 89.7%—B+.
- "You helped me and I finished my work with an A+."

Does every tutoring Live Homework Help session improve grades? Although perhaps not always directly, one can reason that indirect improvement occurs each time.

In addition, consider also that the government makes bold claims quite regularly that cannot be proven 100 percent, such as, "The XYZ initiative will save hundreds of millions of dollars." While this type of statement is reasonably accurate, tabulations include assumptions.

A final example that supports our making confident assertions within reason, for 31 years, BMW crowned each of its vehicles "The Ultimate Driving Machine." This type of bold advertising is perfectly acceptable—even though some people question how BMW can prove the statement. Note that BMW's annual U.S. sales increased from 15,000 vehicles to 266,300 in this same time period—a 1,675 percent increase![11]

The point is that while humility can be a virtue in some circumstances, we must set modesty aside when desiring to maximize our budget. To receive full credit for what we do, we must project, metaphorically speaking, that we are "the ultimate driving machine" deserving of Evian (and BMW) funding.

So let's be resolute and declare that our curriculum component, Live Homework Help, *improves* student grades (notice I didn't call it a service!).

Education, Economic Advancement, Quality of Life

Focusing on results also strengthens the strongest word of all.

When feasible, in addition to saying *education*, also accentuate the outcome of obtaining education (e.g., new opportunities for better jobs). Add that education drives economic advancement, enhancing quality of life.

DISTINCTIVE SENSE OF PURPOSE

There's one more reason the Three Pillars Philosophy works so effectively. It has to do with a positive ramification, mainly benefiting staff. The discovery surfaced at HCLS as we continued to see the positive results of our image transformation efforts.

We realized that our revised vision, *public education for all,* had established a distinctive sense of purpose in which our staff members took great pride. With staff being the most critical component of any organization, this was an especially significant and welcomed revelation.

To learn whether this same result occurred with strategic vocabulary efforts elsewhere, we turned to Southwest Airlines. Known for its unique terminology and enthusiastic employees, the company attributes its success to having "reimagined what it means to be an airline." In fact, Southwest claims it isn't in the airline business at all, but rather "in the freedom business."[12]

With freedom as its defined purpose, Southwest says to its customers, "You are now free to move about the country." To its staff, the company encourages, "You are now free to be your best." The airline's innovative vision resulted in "a genuine sense of purpose that animates the company."[13]

Regardless of their role, Southwest staff members see themselves in the vision. They do not view themselves as mere flight attendants serving drinks to passengers, or baggage handlers simply loading suitcases onto a plane. Through their contributions and efficiencies, they see themselves as critical team players who are "giving people the freedom to fly." Purpose makes the difference.[14]

In other words, it's not just a job. It's a cause.

This remarkable result is what the Three Pillars Philosophy can achieve for library employees everywhere. Our cause is *education*.

OUR WORDS DEFINE OUR DESTINY

We come to the conclusion of Part I of this book, which has outlined the "what" and "why" of the Three Pillars approach. Implementing the vision will be the focus of Part II.

The power of language is invaluable. By first recognizing that we are what the world values most, we can then speak in strong, self-explanatory terms that unequivocally establish and convey our raison d'être and true value.

Freeman A. Hrabowski, III, President of UMBC (The University of Maryland, Baltimore County) who has propelled the school to unbelievable heights (*U.S. News & World Report*, ranks UMBC the #1 "Up and Coming" university in the nation and among the top colleges and universities[15]), incorporates strategic vocabulary in every facet of his leadership.

Dr. Hrabowski frequently ends his speeches with this anonymous quote:

Be careful what you think . . .

Your thoughts become your words,

Your words become your actions,

Your actions become your habits,

Your habits become your character,

Your character becomes your destiny.

Such is the power of language.

NOTES

1. Frank Luntz, *Words that Work: It's Not What You Say, It's What People Hear* (New York: Hyperion, 2007), p. 4.

2. Luntz, *Words that Work*, p. 8.

3. Luntz, *Words that Work*, p. 12.

4. Eli Neiburger, "Gamers . . . in the Library?," *American Libraries* 38, no. 5 (May 2007), p. 60.

5. Regina Powers, "A Plea for Respect," *American Libraries* 38, no. 7 (August 2007), p. 46.

6. Will Manley, "A Child Shall Lead Them," *American Libraries* 39, no. 11 (December 2008), p. 72.

7. "Libraries Challenged to Prove Their Value," LibraryJournal.com, http://www.libraryjournal.com/lj/community/buildingandfacilities/884026-266/libraries_challenged_to_prove_their.html.csp.

8. "Losing Libraries," http://www.losinglibraries.org/about.

9. "Public Libraries Are Doomed," *Library Hotline* 40, no. 38 (September 26, 2011), p. 3.

10. Kristen Wyatt, "Budget cuts force libraries to re-examine roles," *Daily Herald*, June 22, 2011, http://www.heraldextra.com/news/national/article_e63f09e5-cf3d-5108-b265-7d8e550fe34a.html.

11. John Neff, "BMW Drops 'Ultimate Driving Machine,'" *Autoblog*, August 7, 2006, http://www.autoblog.com/2006/08/07/bmw-drops-ultimate-driving-machine/.

12. William C. Taylor and Polly LaBarre, *Mavericks at Work: Why the Most Original Minds in Business Win* (New York: HarperCollins Publishers, 2006), p. 11.

13. Taylor and LaBarre, *Mavericks at Work*.

14. Taylor and LaBarre, *Mavericks at Work*.

15. See http://www.umbc.edu/aboutumbc/president/index.php.

PART II

IMPLEMENTATION—THE HOW

7

A+ PARTNERS IN
EDUCATION

Assuming you're convinced that this simple rebranding solution to our perception problems can work wonders and are ready to give it a try, where's a good place to start?

A smart first step involves further aligning ourselves with the *commonly understood* definition of education—"formal" education that leads to a degree. Fostering this connection causes our communities to view us as partners in education. Once such a visible partnership is in place, positioning *all* that we do under the *complete* definition of education as defined by the Three Pillars becomes a logical next phase, resulting in our being viewed as educational institutions in our own right.

You may already have established a trademark partnership with the schools in your jurisdiction. If this is the case, you are ideally poised to adopt the entire Three Pillars approach. If your relations with the schools are less formal or minimal, as you begin to introduce strategic vocabulary and our new education brand, you may also wish to strengthen your ties with the schools. Any efforts invested in augmenting your curriculum for this crucial customer base will reap innumerable rewards, one of which is an immediate association with education.

Note, however, that curriculum changes are not necessary to achieve heightened visibility. If you prefer to continue with what you already have in place, you can still elevate the prominence of your connection with the schools simply by implementing smart terminology and a savvy marketing twist.

Consolidate all of your existing school-related components—essentially everything for K-12 and college students. Examples include any research materials in your collection; specialized online research tools to which you subscribe; classes you teach, including book promotions (which you might call booktalks); reading lists you compile; films you show; Summer Reading Clubs you coordinate, and events you hold. You'll be surprised by how much you find.

Using strategic vocabulary to describe these components and activities (e.g., *research*, *class*, *instructors*, *teach*, *events*, *initiative*), repackage them by placing them under a catchy umbrella partnership name, and, preferably, a logo. (You are welcome to use "A+ Partners in Education," the name and logo coined for Howard County's comprehensive partnership between and among Howard County Library System [HCLS], Howard County Public School System [HCPSS], and Howard Community College [HCC].[1]) These actions alone will result in a visible connection to formal education.

Alternatively, you may wish to expand your relations and curriculum with the schools. Why might you want to do this? Because the stronger your alliance with the schools, the more powerful and enduring your link to formal education, and the more seamless your move to the complete definition of education. Moreover, strengthening ties between libraries and schools generates greater appreciation for public libraries, as the schools experience firsthand our full value.

Regardless of the partnership scope you aspire to achieve, you may glean some ideas from A+ Partners in Education in Howard County, Maryland. For simplification, most examples that follow represent the partnership component between HCPSS and HCLS. A+ began with these two entities, with HCC joining in several years later.

A+ PARTNERS IN EDUCATION

A+ Partners in Education put HCLS on the "education map." The partnership enabled us to be nominated for (and win!) the Howard County Chamber of Commerce Educator of the Year Award just one year after the partnership's inception. It also played a major role in our convincing Howard County to reclassify HCLS from the "Community Services" category in the county's operating and capital budget documents, to "Education," along with HCC and HCPSS.

Figure 7.1   A+ Partners in Education—logo.

Also known as "the A+ Partnership" or simply "A+", A+ Partners in Education has become an established element of Howard County's culture. Because the name is self-explanatory and incorporates a number of Luntz's "Ten Rules," it is highly effective.

Tailored for Any Jurisdiction

A comprehensive, unified approach to working with the schools, A+ can be tailored for any jurisdiction. The partnership was fully embraced by the schools, our library system, and the community in short order. One principal said it best when introduced to the plan: "It just makes sense!"

To give you a glimpse of the partnership's power, during the 10 years since its launch in 2002, A+ has facilitated:

- more than 652,000 interactions between HCLS Instructors and HCPSS and HCC students, parents, and faculty;
- the dissemination of 58,000 student A+ library cards; and
- nearly 4,000 school faculty members receiving educator cards with extended borrowing privileges.

For some perspective on these statistics, Howard County's population totals 282,000, HCLS comprises six branches, and HCPSS consists of 73 schools and 50,000 students.

Note that if you are aiming for a partnership that also includes a college or university and private schools, consider beginning with the public school system, then subsequently adding other educational institutions. We have found that a gradual progression of added partners allows for a successful expansion in terms of staffing, curriculum development, and publicity.

A+ Vision/Mission

The A+ vision expands the educational opportunities and enhances the academic achievement of each student. Working collaboratively, we leverage our expertise and funding to accomplish results we could not otherwise readily achieve. We take the library into the schools, and bring the schools—students, faculty, and staff—into the library.

Our mission includes ensuring every student has and uses a library card to borrow materials and access specialized online research tools. To increase scholarship, we assist with research assignments, develop and teach A+ Curriculum Classes, and organize A+ signature events and academic competitions.

In short, we provide our students the best possible chance of overall academic success.

Extraordinary Gains

The benefits of A+ to the schools include:

- Optimizing student academic achievement, including improved research, completed assignments, better grades, and expanded intellectual horizons.
- Bridging student achievement gaps.
- Expanding their team of educators with "adjunct faculty" (i.e., library Instructor & Research Specialists).
- Augmenting their print research materials and specialized online research tools.
- Adding online tutors through online homework assistance.
- Gaining access to numerous A+ Curriculum Classes taught by library Instructors in the schools and at the library.
- Extending student studying venues, as the library is open after school, evenings, weekends, and during school vacations and certain school holidays.
- Enabling online homework completion via the library's public access computers, each with word processing and printing capabilities.
- Participating in A+ signature events.
- Organizing A+ academic competitions.

The previously noted benefits also apply to the library. Additional gains for us include:

- Connecting with students, their parents, and school faculty in unprecedented ways.
- Increasing the number of cardholders, items borrowed, physical visits, and virtual visits.
- Increasing Summer Reading enrollment.
- Building a future generation of library customers and supporters.
- Heightening the visibility and importance of the library and school media centers.
- Shaping the role of library Instructors as educators.
- Linking libraries to the commonly understood definition of education.

Lastly, our funders love A+ because, in addition to leveraging expertise when we work together, we leverage public funding to deliver excellence in education.

"Joey"

The partnership can be summarized with an illustration of "Joey," a rising kindergartner. When Joey's parents register him for school in March, they will be asked to complete a library card application along with school forms through a joint letter from the superintendent of schools and the library's president and CEO. This same letter also invites Joey to "Kindergarten, Here We Come!," where he will learn what to expect in kindergarten and practice boarding a school bus. Joey will receive his new library card in the mail, along with an incentive to enroll in Summer Reading.

Joey and his parents will hear library instructors speak at Joey's back-to-school night. In October, Joey and his classmates will take a field trip to the library as part of the school system's kindergarten curriculum. Throughout the year, Joey will experience A+ Curriculum Classes taught by library instructors in his classroom. He will also return to the library for additional curriculum-related field trips arranged by his teacher. He will feel welcomed because he will recognize many of the instructors as he attends more classes at the library, uses our computers, and borrows books.

Joey, his parents, and siblings will have an opportunity to attend family night at the library hosted by his school's Parent Teacher Association. And, through the schools, Joey and his family will learn about the library's entire lineup of classes and events.

As years progress and homework mounts, Joey will learn that, in addition to guidance from his school's media specialist, he can receive additional assistance from instructors at the library, who will be able to plan ahead for Joey's projects thanks to A+ Assignment Alerts his teachers will have forwarded. Joey will learn that his library card provides him access to specialized online research tools available from school, home, or the library. He will learn that he has access to a personal online tutor—for free—from 2 P.M. to midnight, seven days a week, in the core subjects of math, science, social studies, and English. If Joey does not have Internet access at home, he will learn that he has access from any of the library's public access computers after school, evenings, Saturdays, and Sundays, and that word processing is available at each computer.

Joey will also be able to participate in A+ academic competitions jointly organized by the library and school system, including the BumbleBee, HCLS Spelling Bee, Battle of the Books, and Rube Goldberg Challenge.

History

Prior to A+, HCLS worked with 12 of Howard County's then 69 public schools (there are now 73). While some schools worked with us to set up library tables at back-to-school nights and hold periodic library card drives, communications and efforts were sporadic at best.

We began imagining a countywide partnership where outstanding working relations with media specialists (in Howard County, school librarians are called media specialists, and school libraries, media centers), principals, faculty, and staff would be the norm. We envisioned students receiving library cards through the schools, and HCLS Instructors being viewed by the schools as educators and "adjunct faculty."

A+ in the Making

We realized that we would need to convince the schools that this initiative would *supplement* and enhance the school system's curriculum and assist them in their jobs. Similarly, we recognized the importance of involving our staff to convey the partnership's benefits and include their ideas, and keeping our Board informed.

After securing the support of the superintendent of schools, HCLS staff, school media specialists, and key school administrators met to outline plans. To our pleasant surprise, everyone at this first meeting saw merit in a partnership of this nature. We scheduled monthly planning meetings that would culminate in a launch date the following year.

We invited the media specialists to hold their spring 2002 professional departmental meeting at our Central Branch. The day's agenda included reviewing and shaping goals for A+. Their experiences that day prompted them to add "HCPSS will hold media specialist, principal, and faculty meetings at HCLS" to the list of partnership objectives.

HCLS staff also shaped A+ objectives. We scheduled meetings systemwide so that everyone could attend. We discussed the partnership benefits for all parties, adding how it would make their jobs easier in some ways, such as knowing student assignments ahead of time. Staff offered new ideas at this meeting, suggesting, for example, that the school system could show a jointly created Summer Reading promotional video at all schools (which it did!).

We kept our Board apprised as the development stages unfolded. Indeed, many parties refined the A+ vision, mission and objectives, resulting in the commitment from our respective boards and top leaders of our organizations. In addition, we received full support from school administrators, media specialists, and library staff, establishing exemplary working relations among all parties.

Key Components

In addition to securing strong support from top leadership, the following key components contribute to the partnership's success.

- A strong communication network
- Library cards through school registration
- A+ Assignment Alerts
- Compulsory kindergarten field trips to the library
- A+ Curriculum Classes
- A+ signature events and academic competitions

Strong Communication Network

Of highest priority, establishing a strong network for effective communication to develop, coordinate, and promote the partnership is crucial. This can be accomplished by:

- designating a specific library branch for each elementary, middle, and high school— their "A+ branch";
- assigning each school and its A+ branch corresponding "A+ liaisons"; and
- establishing an A+ Advisory Committee.

A+ Branches

Assigning a library branch to each school facilitates communication and personalizes the partnership. Proximity typically dictates which branch is assigned to a particular school, although available staffing levels can also play a role in "districting" decisions when two branches are nearly equidistant.

Since HCC's campus is located at a single site, each department (e.g., Mathematics, Science and Technology, Arts and Humanities, English and World Languages, and Business and Computer Systems) is assigned a branch.

A+ Liaisons

A+ liaisons assume responsibility for regular communication between individual schools and their A+ branches. School liaisons include media center staff, as well as department coordinators and assistant principals. Library liaisons comprise Children's and Teens' Instructors.

To foster communications with HCC, Adult Instructors serve as liaisons for HCLS, while HCC department chiefs represent college departments.

In addition to communicating with library liaisons, school liaisons disseminate A+-related information to the school's faculty and administration, who, in turn, forward the details to students and parents through school newsletters, websites, meetings, and classroom announcements. Numerous principals e-mail their entire faculty, emphasizing the importance of students capitalizing on the partnership, especially online tutoring assistance and A+ signature events.

A+ Advisory Committee

The A+ Advisory Committee meets monthly to cultivate close working relations, review progress, and develop curriculum.

Library representation includes the systemwide positions of Community Education & Partnerships Coordinator, Head of Children's & Teens' Curriculum, Head of Materials Management, and Director of Public Relations. Children's and Teens' Instructors represent the branches.

From the school system, systemwide administrators include the Coordinator of Media and Educational Technology, and the English Language Learners Family Liaison Coordinator. In addition, media specialists, reading teachers, and elementary, middle, and high school teachers represent individual schools.

Library Cards through School Registration

Structuring a systematic, collaborative method for getting library cards into the hands of all students is a primary partnership goal. This win-win proposition facilitates future interactions at the library for school assignments. It also enables student access to specialized online research tools and online homework tutoring assistance. To achieve this goal, all kindergartners and new students receive library cards through the school system's registration process.

School personnel include library card applications with the other forms in school registration packets. Parents also find the letter shown in Figure 7.2 attached to the application—signed by the superintendent of schools and library president and CEO—introducing A+ and asking them to complete and return the application along with the school forms.

Schools forward the completed applications to the library for processing and mailing out of cards. Students receive their library cards at their home address, as do the students' family members (we have adapted the A+ application so that family members living at the same home address may receive library cards in the same manner).

A+ Assignment Alerts

Teachers communicate with library instructors about upcoming assignments through A+ Assignment Alert Forms, available from both the library and school system's websites for easy and quick communication (see Figure 7.3). Advance notice allows us to prepare for research needs ahead of time.

To illustrate, elementary school Assignment Alerts include an annual historical fiction project called "Asian Voices." Working from a list provided by the teacher, we gather books on the subject from all branches, directing them to the school's A+ branch. Broadening the selections available to students at the school's media center, the books are displayed, ready for the students to browse and borrow.

Other Assignment Alerts have included the study of leaves, and topics such as Cinderella from Around the World, Earth Day, and World War II.

Kindergarten, Here We Come!

An A+ class whose popularity has catapulted to the stratosphere since its pilot four years back, "Kindergarten, Here We Come!" eases the transition to kindergarten. Held in August, the class has come to be viewed as a "must do" experience for rising kindergarteners. Demand is such that we held 28 sessions this year at our six branches, with 1,400 students in attendance.

What is so valued about this class? Students meet new classmates and learn what to expect in kindergarten through books, music, and movement. They also practice boarding a real school bus.

Parents and students predictably shed a few tears, but since the goal is for less drama on the first day of school, this is a good thing!

A⁺ Partners in Education ^SM
a collaboration between libraries and schools
HOWARD COUNTY LIBRARY
HOWARD COUNTY PUBLIC SCHOOLS

Our goal is your child's academic success!

Dear Parents:

Through the A+ Partners in Education[SM] initiative, Howard County Library System (HCLS) and the Howard County Public School System are working together to provide for all students the best possible chances of overall academic success.

Attached is a library card application. Please fill it out and turn it in with your other registration forms. This will enable your child to get an HCLS card, good at all six branches, or allow HCLS to update your child's record. New cards will be mailed to your home.

For new students entering kindergarten this fall, please check your local HCLS branch this summer for information on *Kindergarten, Here We Come*, a class with stories and activities to help prepare for that all important first day. Students even get to practice boarding a real school bus. If your child will be entering middle school this fall, please check your local HCLS branch this summer for details on *Movin' Up To Middle School*, a workshop on making the big move to sixth grade. Students learn survival skills, pick up study secrets, and meet new friends.

We look forward to seeing you and your child at Howard County Library System!

Sydney L. Cousin
Superintendent
Howard County Public School System

Valerie J. Gross
President & CEO
Howard County Library System

Figure 7.2   A+ letter—Our goal is your child's academic success!

Here is some sample feedback we received from parents:

- "My daughter was a little apprehensive about starting kindergarten, but now she's so excited after this class."
- "It was great to have the opportunity for the kids to practice entering and exiting the bus. The teacher and bus driver were fabulous, and made my little girl comfortable with the experience. Thank you so much!"
- "My son was a bit nervous beforehand, but the class calmed his fears and made the whole process fun."

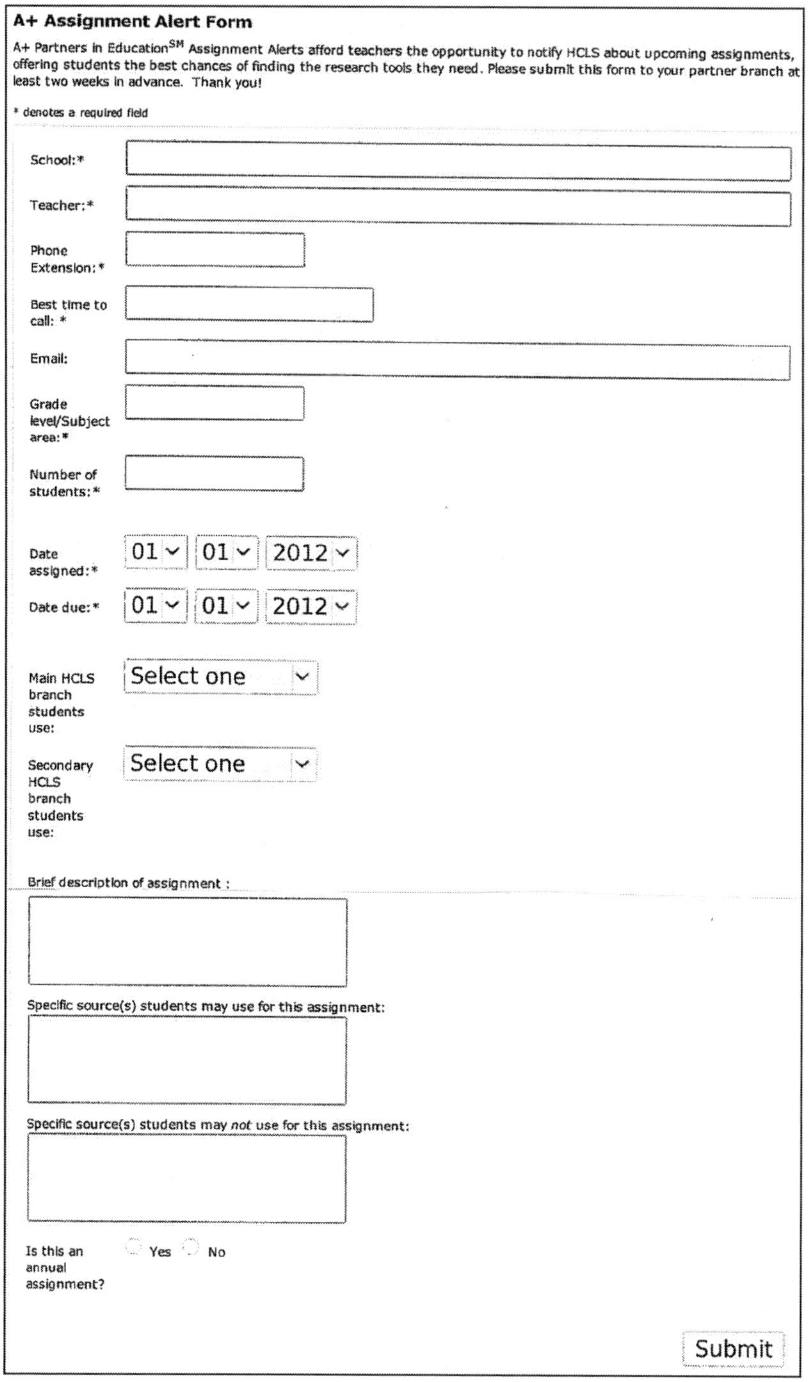

A+ Assignment Alert Form

A+ Partners in Education[SM] Assignment Alerts afford teachers the opportunity to notify HCLS about upcoming assignments, offering students the best chances of finding the research tools they need. Please submit this form to your partner branch at least two weeks in advance. Thank you!

* denotes a required field

School:*	
Teacher:*	
Phone Extension:*	
Best time to call: *	
Email:	
Grade level/Subject area:*	
Number of students:*	
Date assigned:*	01 ∨ 01 ∨ 2012 ∨
Date due:*	01 ∨ 01 ∨ 2012 ∨
Main HCLS branch students use:	Select one ∨
Secondary HCLS branch students use:	Select one ∨

Brief description of assignment :

Specific source(s) students may use for this assignment:

Specific source(s) students may *not* use for this assignment:

Is this an annual assignment?   ○ Yes ○ No

Submit

Figure 7.3   A+ Assignment Alert.

- "My daughter cried after the class because she didn't want to go home."
- "Unlike some other children who didn't want to leave their parents to go on the bus, my daughter didn't want to leave the bus!"

To view a video clip of the class, visit Youtube.com and key in "Kindergarten Here We Come Howard County."

Movin' Up to Middle School

We've added "Movin' Up to Middle School" to our lineup of A+ classes for students entering sixth grade. Students meet at the library to hear study tips, learn about their specific school, and meet other students attending their new school. More than 100 students attended our six classes this year.

The class includes student guest speakers, who present "lessons learned" and provide sound advice from veterans. We have also added a combination lock timed race so that students learn how to open their lockers under pressure. At one of our branches one attendee struggled with the combination lock during the race, refusing to leave until she was able to get the hang of it. She finally did it, and her mom thanked the staff for the extra coaching.

Kindergarten Field Trips to the Library

To establish an academic connection with the library at the beginning of each child's school experience, in addition to receiving library cards, all prekindergarten and kindergarten students participate in a field trip to the library as part of the school system's curriculum.

School teachers explain to the students beforehand what they will learn during their visit to their A+ branch. The day's lesson includes how to navigate with a simple map. Noted on the map are various collection areas, as well as the location of computers, study tables, and classrooms.

The day of the field trip, the students follow their maps as the tour progresses through the building. They then participate in an A+ class, and borrow books with their new library cards.

You have likely guessed the field trip's grand finale and inevitable highlight: experiencing the behind-the-scenes workings of the book drop. (Now that our RFID [radio-frequency identification] sorters are installed, we've doubled the time allocated for this concluding segment!)

Lastly, a post-trip survey assesses what the children remember from the field trip, and whether any subsequent family visits to the library occurred.

A+ Curriculum Classes

Library instructors teach A+ Curriculum Classes at our branches and, at the invitation of teachers, in the schools.

Kindergarten through fifth grade A+ classes include "Have Suitcase, Will Travel," "Splash into Art," "Ocean-in-a-Bottle," "Kindness Counts," "Weather or Not," "A Night Under the Stars," "Lemonade Science," and "H_2O, Away We Go!" Classes for teens include "Having a Ball with Chemistry," "Fallingwater," "Book Camp," "Anime Club," "Locker L.E.D.," "Maximize Your History Day Research," and "Tech Tools for Your Brain."

To best complement the school system's curriculum, we review our classes each year and adjust accordingly. For instance, with STEM (science, technology, engineering, and math) rising to higher priority levels in our increasingly knowledge-based and global economy, we have fortified classes in STEM subject areas, developing "Candy Science," "Wiggly Giggly Gelatin," "Snowflake Science," "Go Figure," "Robotics Fair," "Everyday Engineering," and "Chemistry in the Library" (this one sometimes requires a parent release form). We also added "Science Fair Starters."

Seasonal and specialized classes are outlined in our quarterly classes and events publication, *source* (PDFs are available at http://issuu.com/hoco_library). Regularly scheduled A+ classes we take into the schools are described in our *A+ Curriculum* guide (posted at hclibrary.org), which also includes details about online homework assistance and academic competitions. Disseminating this guide to all teachers at the beginning of each school year allows for optimal planning.

A+ Signature Initiatives

The A+ Partnership has grown to include an impressive lineup of signature initiatives that showcase student achievement and the partnership in dynamic ways. School media specialists and faculty routinely volunteer, alongside library staff.

Having developed these events over time, we would recommend implementing them incrementally to allow for schedule adjustments and the additional first-year efforts required for any new undertaking. We also suggest staggering these events for adequate preparation and promotion time.

An added benefit of the A+ competitions is that they provide opportunities outside of athletics for students to shine. Winners of these academic competitions receive beautiful trophies. We present equally stunning (and sizeable) trophies to the students' schools as well, which principals proudly display alongside those awarded for football triumphs.

Elected officials—many of whom determine our budgets—and community leaders attend these events, often serving as judges for the academic competitions. We take numerous photos for publicity and lobbying efforts, creating photo sheets to convey—at a glance—the importance of the second and third pillars of our curriculum.

Event examples include the following:

HCLS Spelling Bee

Registered with Scripps National Spelling Bee as an official Regional Bee, the HCLS Spelling Bee launched in 2005. Immediately a hit, this event established an avenue that guarantees representation at the National Bee each year.

Participation has grown to 64 contestants—winners of Howard County's public school, private school, and homeschool association bees. Attracting audiences of 1,000 people, the event has gained staunch community support. Local television stations cover the bee, which is rebroadcast numerous times. Newspapers also report on the event in a prominent fashion.

Thanks to presenting sponsor BB&T, the champion and finalist win $1,000 and $750 in college scholarships, respectively. The champion advances to the National Bee, complete with an all-expenses-paid trip to the competition in Washington, DC.

Comments from elected officials have included:

- "The Spelling Bee is one of my favorite annual events. I am honored to have the chance to speak and look forward to it every year." (Howard County Executive Ken Ulman[2])
- "When I am no longer serving on the Board of Education, I will have many fond memories, and my Spelling Bee Judgeship will be at the top of the list. Thanks again for the opportunity to serve, and please extend my appreciation to all Howard County Library staff who spent many long hours organizing yet another fantastic event." (Board of Education Chair Frank Aquino[3])

The County Executive and County Council present a joint proclamation. Last year's proclamation read as shown in Figure 7.4 (notice the second "whereas," which includes the Third Pillar of our educational mission!).

In addition to BB&T, the Friends of Howard County Library sponsors the HCLS Spelling Bee, along with in-kind support from HCLS and HCPSS.

BumbleBee

A companion initiative to the HCLS Spelling Bee, the cleverly and aptly named BumbleBee motivates students in grades one through three to improve their spelling, build their vocabularies, and develop the self-confidence needed to speak effectively in front of an audience. Added to our A+ curriculum in 2006, the BumbleBee also prepares students for the HCLS Spelling Bee.

School classrooms hold BumbleBees, whose winners progress to grade level bees at each school. Grade level champions from all schools are celebrated at the BumbleBee Awards Ceremony.

Howard County, Maryland
Joint Proclamation

Whereas... *Spelling bees instill confidence, improve students' spelling, increase their vocabularies and teach correct English usage thereby enhancing academic achievement; and*

Whereas... *Sponsored by BB&T and the Friends of Howard County Library, the 8th Annual Howard County Library System Spelling Bee delivers these benefits, while exemplifying the Third Pillar of the Library System's educational mission: Instructive & Enlightening Experiences; and*

Whereas... *We applaud this year's 64 contestants and 64 alternates, each of whom is already a champion in their own right, and wish them good luck as they vie for the honor to represent Howard County in Washington, D.C. at the Scripps National Spelling Bee.*

Now therefore, we ...
The Howard County Executive and the Howard County Council, do hereby proclaim

March 9, 2012
Howard County Library Spelling Bee Day
in Howard County, Maryland

IN WITNESS WHEREOF, we have hereby set our hands and affixed the seal of Howard County, Maryland on this 9th day of March, 2012

Howard County Executive

Ken Ulman

Howard County Council

Mary Kay Sigaty, Chairperson

Courtney Watson, Vice Chairperson

Calvin Ball, Member

Greg Fox, Member

Jennifer Terrasa, Member

Figure 7.4   HCLS Spelling Bee—proclamation.

Sponsored by the Howard County Rotary Clubs, the BumbleBee has grown to 50 award winners.

At the event, students shake hands with elected officials and key community leaders as they are called forward to accept their trophy, certificate of achievement, and dictionary. (Following last year's BumbleBee Awards Ceremony, one parent informed us that her son had asked later that evening, "Am I famous now?")

BumbleBee winners are acknowledged yet again when they take a bow on stage at the HCLS Spelling Bee.

Battle of the Books

A number of library systems throughout the country organize Battle of the Books (BOB), a reading exam with bells on. Held on a Friday night, the event improves reading and writing, and builds vocabularies. In addition, it's great fun.

HCLS thanks the public libraries in Michigan for bringing BOB to our attention. If you don't yet organize BOB at your library, perhaps this summary will inspire you to start one.

Launched in 2008, BOB has become such a favorite A+ event that it is viewed almost as a rite of passage for fifth grade students. Guided by a coach, BOB teams consist of five students plus alternates. The students read 16 preselected books that cover a range of interests, including adventure, folk tale, memoir, poetry, biography, science, and civics. Reading difficulty varies as well. The intent is to challenge both avid and reluctant readers while providing an enjoyable experience for all.

Teams dream up names (e.g., Book Bugs, Oompa Loompas, Litte Einsteins, Cheer Readers, Super Awesome Reading Warriors, and Pickerel's Page-Turning Penguins) then dress the part. The evening of the "Battle," students file into the gymnasium Olympic style as their team is announced. Energized by upbeat music, they parade around the perimeter, showing off their costumes and waving to the crowd before finding their assigned spots on the floor.

The Battle comprises 50 questions, with 30 seconds allocated to answering each one. High school student members of Future Educators of America volunteer as "runners." They entertain students and spectators alike as they hustle up the aisles to gather the teams' written answers after each question.

Elected officials clamor to be the judges who bestow first-, second-, and third-place awards in the following areas: Best Score, Best Costume, Best Team Name, Best Team Spirit, and Best Civility. The winning teams' schools receive a trophy. All students receive certificates of participation and a memento from the library.

Anticipating the sign-up of 60 teams in 2011, we had to scramble when 94 registered. Although we ended up being able to accept all teams (470 students), accomplishing this was no small feat. Working with the schools, we determined that the only way to adequately seat the crowd of 2,000 participants and spectators would be to divide the teams and hold two simultaneous events. This required doubling up on emcees, judges, volunteers, and sponsorships. The school system canceled an athletic event to reserve the requisite second high school gymnasium. In 2012, three high school gymnasiums were needed to accommodate the 140 participating teams (700 students) and their fans. And for 2013? We've reserved four venues—just in case!

Students love BOB. They also value the competition's educational value, as evidenced by these e-mail excerpts:

- I enjoyed the Battle of the Books so much that it was the topic of my personal narrative for sixth grade English class!
- I would never have chosen to read a poetry book until the Battle of the Books competition, but I got interested in John Grandit's book, *Technically, It's Not My Fault.* I've actually found a poetry book that I like! The Battle of the Books was such a memorable experience that I included it on my Life Road Map at the beginning of this school year. It was a life-shaping event for sure.
- Not only did the Battle of the Books pep me up to more reading, but it got me into art! When I went to the National Gallery of Art, I saw the very painting that Blue Balliett's book, *Chasing Vermeer,* is based upon.
- I would not likely have chosen to read books about a funeral home or the Great Fire in Chicago, but it turned out that both books were quite fun to read. The final and winning question happened to be about one of these books.

Equally enthusiastic, parents, and coaches have written:

- The kids I coached worked hard from December through April and they persevered. While not placing in the award categories, they did walk away winners in my book. They met weekly from January. We got to read and explore books they may have never picked up. I am very proud of them as you should be as well. The kids were motivated the entire time! I loved this event.

- The experience gained by the members of my team is absolutely priceless. I'm happy to say that the second grade sibling of one of our team members, and the son of our co-coach, participated in all of our meetings, read two of the books, and has since moved up to an Above Grade Level Reading Group—needless to say, he is anxiously awaiting fifth grade so he can participate. Also, our team members are now working out the details to start their own book club.

- I was not familiar with the event until our daughter competed in it this year. The selection of books was great. She was exposed to so many books and genres that she might not have looked at otherwise. I appreciated all the prizes given out. It made the night a win-win for all the students.

- An enormous thanks to you and all the sponsors of Battle of the Books. It was truly one of the most worthwhile programs in which my kids have participated. Our team, the Cheetah Readers, worked hard and had so much enthusiasm over the past five months—they are truly disappointed it has all come to an end!

To provide equal opportunity in education for all students, the Friends of Howard County Library and numerous additional contributors sponsor BOB, allowing each team to receive a complimentary set of books (approximately $100 per set). Both the library and school system contribute in-kind staffing and arrange for volunteers. The school system contributes the venues.

Teen Time

A popular after-school initiative begun in 2005 to address the challenges presented by at-risk middle school students, Teen Time improves student academics and life skills in a fun, welcoming, after-school environment. Library Instructors develop a curriculum that delivers a daily structured setting featuring guest speakers and activities. In addition to receiving homework assistance, Teen Time's 30 students participate in nutrition seminars, book clubs, stress management workshops, art classes, antismoking and antidrug workshops, movie screenings, and field trips. The year culminates with a Teen Time Showcase, where we acknowledge student achievement and Teen Time graduates.

A side benefit for HCLS, Teen Time has positively influenced overall teen behavior at the branch where the initiative is convened, resulting in an enjoyable library experience for everyone visiting this branch after school.

HCLS Rube Goldberg Challenge

A new STEM-related competition added to A+ in 2011, the HCLS Rube Goldberg Challenge prompted more than 100 fourth and fifth grade students (19 teams) to submit entries that pilot year. In 2012, nearly 400 students participated (75 teams).

Named after the Pulitzer Prize–winning cartoonist, sculptor, and author, the contest challenges students to transform everyday materials into wacky, complex machines that perform a simple task. The first assignment involved watering a plant in a convoluted fashion. The charge for 2012 was to pop a balloon. And the mission for 2013? Students are already strategizing how they will extract juice from an orange.

Working under the guidance of HCPSS teachers and HCLS instructors, students must incorporate science, technology, engineering, and math precepts into their inventions. They must also exhibit leadership and teambuilding skills. The teams create videos of their machines in action, which are posted on YouTube (the 2011 entries can be viewed at youtube.com/user/HCLRube Goldberg, and the 2012 entries at hclibrary.org/rubegoldberg/).

At our HCLS Rube Goldberg Challenge Celebration, we announce first-, second-, and third-place winners in the following categories: Most Green, Most Scientific, Most Humorous, Most Complex, and Community Favorite (the community votes online).

Howard County Library System and Howard County Public School System present

RUBE GOLDBERG

CHALLENGE

Who?

All fourth and fifth grade students in Howard County (under the direction of a Teacher Advisor).

What?

Pop a balloon! Named after the Pulitzer Prize winning cartoon, sculptor, and author, the contest challenges students to find the most complicated and convoluted way to solve the problem.

Why?

Students incorporate science, technology, engineering, and math (STEM) concepts along with everyday materials to create a wacky, innovative machine. Winning teams are awarded trophies and certificates in four categories: Most Green, Scientific, Humorous, and Complex.

How?

Teams of students incorporate at least three simple machines into a more complicated contraption that will pop a balloon. They will video the invention solving the task and document in writing how they developed their machine. Details available at hclibrary.org/rubegoldberg.

When?

Teacher Advisors must return an Intent to Participate form between October 31 to November 11. Entries (videos and documentation) are due by 9 pm on March 28, 2012.

an

A+

Partners
IN Education
initiative

Sponsored by Friends of Howard County Library.

Figure 7.5   HCLS Rube Goldberg Challenge—flyer.

Summer Reading Kickoff

Nearly 4,000 people attend our Summer Reading Kickoff each year. We know that Summer Reading increases student achievement, serving as an educational bridge between the end of the school year and the beginning of the next, so why not create a big splash with a kickoff? The HCLS event has featured Celebrity Readers (including our County Executive and County Council members), dancing dragons, reptile petting zoos, edible insects, the Bubble Lady, and folk dancing from around the globe—along with music, face painting, and animal balloons—drawing record audiences.

Bookmark Contest

Growing in popularity each summer, our fourth annual bookmark contest in 2012 garnered 1,700 entries from Howard County students, ranging from kindergarteners to rising high school seniors. The caliber of submissions continues to be incredibly impressive, making the job of our judges difficult. Enhancing the art education component of our curriculum, the bookmark contest concludes at the end of July. Judged on originality and design, winning bookmarks are printed and distributed at our branches and posted on our website (hclibrary.org). The winners are invited to the A+ Partners in Education Celebration held each fall, where they are recognized and receive a framed copy of their bookmark. All contest entries are displayed in the branches in September.

DEAR

A winning combination of kids, dogs, and books, DEAR (Dogs Educating and Assisting Readers) raises the reading levels of 50 third grade students each year. Our partners include HCPSS, with whom we work to enroll students whose reading proficiencies fall below target levels. Fidos for Freedom provides 21 therapy dogs and volunteer handlers for the heartwarming, highly effective initiative.

Sponsored by the Friends of Howard County Library, DEAR creates a relaxed, loving, nonjudgmental atmosphere where struggling readers quickly forget all fears. Students gain self-confidence while improving their reading skills by reading aloud to therapy dogs. Virtually all students read at or above their targeted level at the completion of the 9-week Saturday morning sessions.

The year culminates with a DEAR Graduation Ceremony, attracting crowds exceeding 200 people to celebrate the students' successes. Attendees include students, parents, instructors, dog handlers, supporters, and dignitaries—as well as the dogs. Students receive certificates and book bags. Onyx—an ironically named big, fluffy snow-white dog—always wears a tux for the occasion.

STEPS YOU MAY FIND USEFUL

We learned some lessons along the way which you may find useful as you work toward strengthening relations with the schools. If numerous school systems fall within your jurisdiction, establish relations with each—with the vision of eventually unifying all school systems under one partnership.

Staff and Board Involvement

Involve the library staff from the start. Explain why the partnership is important to the future success of the library, and how it fits into the library's broader education vision. Library staff must understand that positioning the library within the commonly understood definition of education assists with conveying the library's full value to the community. You'll not only obtain support this way, but also scads of great ideas.

Introduce the idea of placing certain curriculum components under a partnership name for added visibility. Engage staff members by asking them for suggestions, including the name you will assign your partnership, and which components of your curriculum can readily be repackaged under the partnership.

Simultaneously, introduce these same concepts to your Board, explaining the extraordinary gains made possible through a strengthened alliance with the schools.

Sell the Vision to the School System

Arrange to meet with key administrative leaders at the school system to present the partnership concept and details. Outline the vision for the partnership, speaking in terms of how collaboration will benefit the schools—students, faculty, and staff. Explain how the library can complement and advance the school's curriculum, and how working together leverages funding and expertise to improve student academic achievement. Provide a few examples of specific goals. Do underscore that this is meant to augment (as opposed to replace) existing resources at the school.

Since top leadership's involvement and support lends authority and credibility to the partnership, if at all possible this meeting should include the school system's superintendent, the library system's president and CEO, along with both organizations' chief operating officers, as well as other key administrative staff. From the school system, include the person who oversees the media specialists.

Planning

Once you have received a nod of support from the school system, formulate a planning committee (which can turn into your A+ Advisory Committee once the partnership has been launched). During the planning stages, both the school and library systems must mutually agree upon specific partnership objectives.

Here are a few sample clauses from our agreement you may wish to consider:

Howard County Library System Objectives

Howard County Library System will:

- Register HCPSS students for HCLS cards with the assistance of school faculty and staff.
- Share costs with HCPSS to provide access to Live Homework Help, an online tutoring service for students with Howard County Library cards.
- Teach A+ classes at HCPSS and HCLS to support HCPSS curriculum, promote HCLS resources, teach research skills, and increase reading.
- Organize classes and deliver tours for kindergarten classes who visit HCLS on field trips.
- Sponsor and coordinate the annual HCLS Spelling Bee.
- Provide HCPSS teachers an educator card with extended loan privileges to encourage borrowing HCLS materials for the classroom.
- Host HCPSS staff development sessions providing information on HCLS's curriculum.
- Communicate information about HCLS classes and events for school, principal, and PTA/PTSA newsletters.
- Encourage HCLS staff to participate on HCPSS committees.
- Designate a liaison at each HCLS branch to coordinate the partnership.

Howard County Public School System Objectives

Howard County Public School System will:

- Distribute HCLS card registration materials and information: through kindergarten and new student registration packets, media specialists, school site visits, and field trips to HCLS branches.
- Fund and schedule field trips to HCLS branches for all full-day kindergarten classes.

- Communicate information on HCPSS's curriculum, extracurricular projects, and homework assignments with HCLS liaisons to assist HCLS in meeting the research needs of students and their parents.
- Feature HCLS classes and events in school, principal, and PTA newsletters.
- Share costs with HCLS to provide access to Live Homework Help, an online tutoring service for students with Howard County Library cards.
- Promote the annual HCLS Spelling Bee and encourage participation from students in grades four through eight.
- Work collaboratively with HCLS staff to produce Summer Reading lists.
- Encourage staff to serve on HCLS committees.
- Designate an A+ liaison at each school to coordinate the partnership.
- Promote A+ to HCPSS in joint presentations with HCLS staff.

In addition to committing to in-kind contributions, each party should agree to financial contributions. For instance HCPSS agreed to pay for one half the cost of an online tutoring service (e.g., Live Homework Help or Brainfuse), with HCLS paying equally. Similarly, HCPSS pays for one half of the cost of the bus component for Kindergarten, Here We Come!, with the Friends of Howard County Library sponsoring the other 50 percent. Furthermore, HCPSS pays for any additional janitorial services required prior to and following major A+ events held at its locations.

You might prefer to begin with committing to in-kind contributions, persuading the school system to commit financially once they see for themselves the partnership's incredible power. For us, BOB evolved in this manner. While HCPSS initially provided only in-kind assistance for the reading competition, the school system now contributes financially as well. Work to convince the school system to sign an official partnership agreement. School system signatories should include the Board chair and superintendent. From the library, include the Board chair, and president and CEO. In addition, upper level management positions from both parties should sign the agreement.

Implementation—Kickoff and Signing

Begin promoting your chosen partnership name and/or emblem. Hold a partnership launch event, inviting school administrators, everyone in leadership positions at the schools, school teachers and media specialists, your Board, the Friends/Foundation Boards, your staff, elected officials, community leaders, and the entire community.

Invite your county executive/mayor to speak, as well as the state superintendent of schools, state superintendent of libraries, and the chairs of the board of education and library board. We have found that videotaping such events can be advantageous, as quotes can be used later for publicity pieces.

Mail letters to all principals, which will serve to inform them (1) about the partnership, (2) about the partnership launch, and (3) that you will be calling them to set up individual meetings at each school after the kickoff event. You will be pleasantly surprised. After one HCPSS principal received the letter in early August, she requested an A+ meeting as soon as possible. She wanted to include library card applications in packets that all students received the first day of school.

Consider holding an elaborate signing ceremony at the kickoff event. Here's how it works. All signatories receive a pen and an "original" partnership agreement that has yet to be signed. All parties sign the copy in front of them, then pass it to the next person, repeating this process until the copy they receive to be signed requires only their signature. Once the final signature is in place, that copy belongs to the signer. Each signatory thus leaves with a signed original.

In short, make as big of a deal out of the partnership kickoff as possible! You'll get some terrific press coverage.

Meet with Each Principal

Following the kickoff event, meet individually with each school. From the schools, include principals, assistant principals, media specialists, reading specialists, and, if possible, a representative teacher. From the library, include the A+ branch liaison (e.g., a Children's or Teens' Instructor), the A+ branch manager, and at least one systemwide position. At this meeting, explain how the partnership will supplement school resources, complement school curriculum, assist with bridging achievement gaps, and improve overall academic achievement for all students.

While time consuming, these meetings are well worth the investment. In Howard County, one harried principal, who said she had only 30 minutes for the meeting, was still envisioning ideas two hours later. Another principal, who initially did not want to meet, requested 1,000 library card applications for her school. She also said she would require students to use the library for certain assignments.

In Howard County, the meetings resulted in library staff being invited to speak at back-to-school nights, and to contribute additional ideas for A+ Curriculum Classes—including book clubs for boys at several middle schools. (Note that rather than being perceived as a possible threat, we were seen as a welcomed partner to their team.)

We were invited to highlight A+ at new teacher orientations and teacher professional development days, and to serve on the school system's District Planning Team, Media Advisory Committee, and Technology Advisory Committee. In addition, we were invited to participate in a joint committee with the County, the schools, and the community college to collaborate on the future direction of technology. We also had the privilege of serving on a panel for the school's Triple A Community Partners Conference for Accelerated Academic Achievement, which highlighted A+. Additionally, the superintendent of schools included A+ on the agenda for a statewide principal meeting.

Lastly, the school system offered to promote our bilingual children's classes (Spanish/English, Chinese/English, Korean/English, and American Sign Language/English), held at each of our branches, and to translate our library card applications and selected other materials into the top five foreign languages spoken by students and their families.

A+ Educator Card

In response to teacher requests, we initiated the A+ Educator Card, which we highly recommend. It was an immediate success. The card gives teachers and college professors who are employed in your jurisdiction extended borrowing privileges. Instructional items may be borrowed for twice the usual checkout period, and are given a 10-day grace period for fines.

Ongoing Publicity

Promote the partnership through press releases, public speaking, television segments, newspaper articles, library publications, school newsletters, and conference presentations. PTA Council presentations are especially effective. In addition, include impressive A+ components in your "What's New at the Library" kinds of presentations you deliver (e.g., for the Chamber of Commerce and Rotary Clubs).

Don't forget to promote the partnership internally. Your library system's staff newsletter is a great way to inform staff about partnership accomplishments on a regular basis. It is also a highly visible way to recognize staff, praising them for their outstanding contributions. Ideally, convince A+ liaisons to contribute, as frontline staff communications are especially effective.

The partnership also provides an excellent opportunity to promote the library's entire curriculum to faculty, students, and parents. Send press releases to the school system for inclusion in their various newsletters, and to media specialists for promotion to students through the media centers.

A+ PARTNERS IN EDUCATION CELEBRATION

Each fall, we organize the A+ Partners in Education Celebration, an event that highlights the successes of the past year and looks ahead to the next. Elected officials and community leaders attend to hear school faculty and library staff relate examples of how A+ benefits students.

Initially, we worked with the school system to produce a video that included interviews with principals, teachers, and administrators. The video served as a powerful marketing tool to explain and promote the partnership. In 2010 we began producing three-minute videos summarizing the past year's signature initiatives with both HCPSS and HCC, which we show at the celebration (e.g., "A+ Signature Events with HCPSS" and "A+ Signature Initiatives with HCC," which can be viewed at hclibrary.org, or youtube.com/howardcountylibrary).

MEASURING SUCCESS

At least five measurable goals can determine the partnership's success—increases in:

- Use of the library's specialized online research tools
- Student use of online homework assistance
- Research assistance interactions at library branches
- The number of students holding library cards
- Attendance at library classes and events

An additional measurement tool, surveys ascertain perceived value of the partnership. For instance, teacher feedback obtained through surveys distributed at the end of each A+ class at the schools assists with continuous improvement for both class content and teaching effectiveness.

Other measurement methods include tracking the compelling testimonials from parents, teachers, and students.

Lastly, revenue increases will reflect the partnership's success, most importantly in the crucial area of public funding, and also in sponsorships for your signature events (e.g., the Rotary Clubs have joined forces to sponsor the HCLS BumbleBee each year).

Linked to formal education in this heightened way, the library's perceived value will automatically increase and funding will follow.

WHAT'S NEXT FOR A+?

What else is envisioned for A+? As part of our new Charles E. Miller Branch & Historical Center that opened in December 2011, we are "bringing history to life" in an unprecedented way through a more comprehensive local history curriculum.

The new Miller Branch is also an ideal place to focus on students' environmental education, as the building is designed to achieve LEED Silver Certification, complete with a green, vegetative roof.[4] In addition, the adjacent Enchanted Garden, an outdoor teaching venue, centers not only on environmental education—including a rain garden, bioswale, rain barrels, porous surfaces, and compost bins—but also science and health education (e.g., the garden features 65 native species of plants, a Peter Rabbit Patch, and a Pizza Garden). Our collection and A+ Curriculum Classes will be further developed for these areas.

LAUNCHING "A+" IN YOUR AREA

In addition to aligning ourselves with formal education in a highly visible way, partnerships with schools make our jobs more rewarding by opening up unparalleled opportunities to market and deliver our curriculum to the student population. Assignment Alerts are a godsend, allowing our staff to prepare beforehand for the inevitable rush of students working on a particular project.

By incorporating library card applications into school registration, schools alleviate the need for library card drives while ensuring that their students have the ability to borrow library materials, conduct online research, and benefit from online tutoring.

Staff members also enjoy connecting with students in more meaningful ways. Having visited their schools, we know their principals, teachers, and media specialists. And, we know—before they ask—which project they need to work on, all of which astonishes students!

Other library systems, such as Wadsworth Ella M. Everhard Public Library in Wadsworth, Ohio, have elected to capitalize on the branded "A+" initiative. Wadsworth's adaptation includes the outstanding brochure shown in Figure 7.6.[5]

If you are interested in further pursuing A+, please visit hclibrary.org to read more about the partnership. The posted "Toolkit" includes the logo.

A+ Partners in Education is invaluable in and of itself. It is also a stepping stone to implement the larger vision of positioning everything that we do under the complete definition of education.

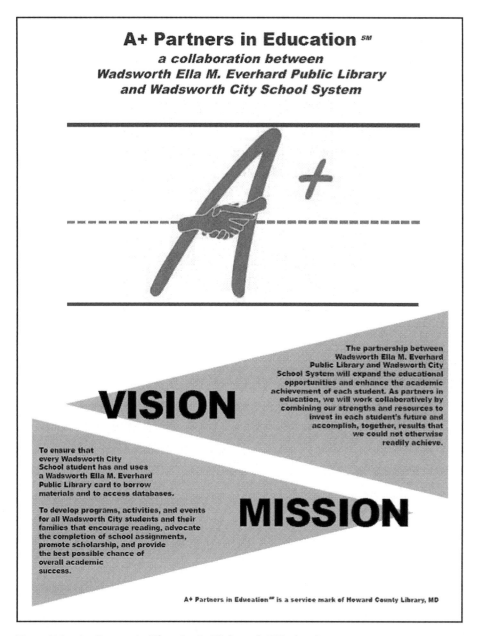

Figure 7.6   A+ Partners in Education in Wadsworth OH—brochure.

NOTES

1. The A+ logo is available at www.hclibrary.org (A+ Partners in Education Toolkit).

2. Excerpt from County Executive Ken Ulman's March 17, 2009, e-mail to the author.

3. Excerpt from the 2009 Chair of the Board of Education and Head Judge's March 23, 2009, e-mail to the author.

4. LEED stands for "Leadership in Energy and Environmental Design."

5. *A+ Partners in Education: A collaboration between Wadsworth Ella M. Everhard Public Library and Wadsworth City School System.* Brochure reprinted with permission of the Wadsworth Ella M. Everhard Public Library, Wadsworth, Ohio, www.wadsworthlibrary.com.

8

INTERNAL STEPS

As you develop or augment a version of A+ Partners in Education, begin embracing the broader vision of "education for all."

Consider that this approach maximizes assigned respect and allocated funding through the intelligent application of language. It is therefore of paramount importance that everyone on staff care deeply about both respect and funding.

On its face, this sounds obvious—and for respect, it is. Employees do care about the level of respect assigned to them, whether by customers or elected officials.

However, surprisingly enough, not everyone on the team makes the connection between their need to care about funding and their jobs. Some staff members think that worrying about funding is someone else's job. Replace this erroneous assumption by underscoring that everyone plays a vital role in the success of the organization because each staff member influences funding decisions through what they do, how they do it, and how they talk about what they do.

STRATEGIC VOCABULARY = JOB SECURITY

Once staff members recognize that funding is actually everyone's concern, they must then make the connection between the use of strategic vocabulary and increased funding, and, ultimately, job security. If these links are understood, they will be more willing to modify terminology. A side benefit, once staff members view themselves as influential in elevating our value, they will take more pride in the organization's funding successes that enable the system to flourish.

Whether you choose to implement this new approach in whole or in part, it is beneficial to explain the concepts to the entire staff—in every pay grade and classification—so that everyone understands how the language we use influences maximum funding increases in times of economic growth, and minimizes cuts in times of hardship.

LEADERSHIP TEAM

Start by introducing the "what" and the "why" of the Three Pillars Philosophy to your Leadership Team. Provide examples of how the vision is timeless, such as how it does not matter what format books take in the future for Pillar I to stand strong. Outline how the concept attains for us the credit we deserve without needing to constantly explain what we do, creating a distinctive sense of purpose that *no other organization or company can claim*: we are public education for all.

ALL STAFF

Once the Leadership Team understands the philosophy, everyone can be introduced to the vision through a series of systemwide meetings.

At Howard County Library System (HCLS), we called them Outlook Forums—not bad, but not the clever idea the Citrus County Library System staff came up with to inspire everyone to get on board. What was their tongue-in-cheek title? They called them "Drink the KoolAid" meetings (where they served KoolAid).

Whatever you choose to call these gatherings, describe for staff how strategic language shapes perceived value and thus funding decisions (bottled Evian and generic water as props work well to make this point).

Engage your audience in a discussion of how your entire curriculum falls under the Three Pillars, and how the pillars represent the complete definition of the word *education*. Explain how this vision repositions your library as an educational institution, along with the schools and colleges in your area, and the many benefits of being viewed as such. Describe the enhanced respect, meaning, pride, and fun that accompany this approach, the result of people finally understanding who we are, what we do, and why it matters—from the very words we use.

BOARDS

Convey the philosophy to the library board in a similar, albeit slightly broader, fashion.

If the term *education* is not in your vision or mission statements, propose to your board that the word be included. Explain that the recommendation represents an interim, immediate improvement until the next round of strategic planning can take place.

For example, suggest editing *lifelong learning* to *lifelong education*. Alternatively, *information* can be replaced with *education*. If possible, avoid adding *education* while retaining *information*, as doing so is redundant and dilutes the statement's power. Further, retaining both could send the wrong message to the reader that your use of the term *education* pertains to "formal" education.

Lastly, if you spot those dangerous *recreation* and *entertainment* red flags anywhere in the statements, propose deleting those.

At a later date, propose edits to board policies, including your materials selection policy. For instance, references to *information* would be replaced with *education*. *Programs and services* would become *curriculum*. *Reference* would become *research*, and phrases such as "access to information" would gain strength as "equal opportunity in education."

As to friends and foundation boards, since they exist to support the library, introduce members to the concepts. Their fundraising efforts will produce greater results as they begin to incorporate the stronger, more persuasive language in their correspondence, publications, and promotions.

PROUD SUPPORTER OF **Choose Civility**

Friends of Howard County Library supports Howard County Library System in its mission to deliver high-quality PUBLIC EDUCATION for all ages. The Friends financially support initiatives and events such as:

- DEAR (Dogs Educating & Assisting Readers) for third grade students
- Battle of the Books for fifth grade students
- Teen Time for middle school students
- Word Up poetry contest for middle and high school students

- HCLS Teen Idol for middle and high school students
- Summer Reading Club for children, teens, and adults
- Money Matters fair for all ages
- Family film series
- Author events

*To join Friends of Howard County Library, visit **jointhefriends.org.***

Figure 8.1 Friends support. Used with permission from Howard County Library System and also Friends of Howard County Library.

SMART STARTERS

Where to start? Consider retiring *storytime* (or *story hour*) and *program*. These terms are recommended due to their prevalence. Exchange them for *class, seminar, workshop, event*, and *initiative*—and *children's class* for *storytime*. Once phased out, you and your staff will experience instant elevation in stature.

Also eliminate any associated terms, such as *programming*, which is not as strong as *class content, curriculum development*, and *classes and events*, depending on the intent of your meaning. Similarly, the phrase *programs and services* strengthens tenfold when transformed into *curriculum*, as does *storytime room* when the space becomes *children's classroom*.

BABY STEPS

You might prefer a more gradual progression for what can be a sea change for so many.

To illustrate, *storytime* and *storytime room* can initially migrate to *storytime class* and *storytime classroom*. Although unintended, this was our first step at HCLS. At the time, we did not realize that the stronger *children's class* and *children's classroom* would come to light.

Were we to start over, we would probably jump straight to *children's class*. This is because each move takes time. Understandably, remnants of *storytime class* still linger in conversations among staff two years after we subsequently shifted to *children's class*. It's just human nature. Since habits die hard, electing a direct move eliminates a hurdle.

Nevertheless, if you think your staff would be more amenable to first moving to *storytime class* to get used to saying the word *class*, then the two-step process is a good idea.

JOB TITLES

As to position titles, exchanging *Circulation Clerk* (or *Library Aide* at some libraries) for *Customer Service Specialist* is a recommended first step. Why start with this one? Because everyone will love it. They (especially your Customer Service Specialists) will see how the new title describes the role accurately while elevating the level of respect assigned to the position. (Ideally, replace *Circulation Desk* with *Customer Service Desk*—or a combined *Customer Service & Research Desk*—simultaneously.)

As a next step, elevate the perceived value of *Library Associate* and *Librarian* by replacing the titles with *Instructor & Research Specialist*. Pay differentials can reward staff with greater education and experience.

If you have not yet invested in name badges for all staff members, consider doing so. Your staff will wear their new titles with pride.

KEY ADMINISTRATIVE POSITIONS

Introduce your board to the more intuitive titles for key administrative positions that heighten the stature of the entire organization. Note that in the academic and business worlds, positions such as *COO, CFO,* and *Director of Human Relations* are immediately understood, whereas (assuming this is the case) your current ones can puzzle people who do not know much about libraries.

Summarize why *President & CEO* (or, just *President*) is a model title for the top post, citing New York and Boston as public libraries whose lead we can all follow. If your title is *Director*, explain that director positions tend be mid-level management positions in many corporate and academic organizational charts.

If *City Librarian* or *County Librarian* happens to be your library's top position, explain how these titles have likely lingered over time, and the many advantages of updating them to *President & CEO*.

If your board chair is currently called *president* (as ours was), propose that the board rename that position to *chair*, the first enabling step for the cascading edits to follow, beginning with *President & CEO*.

DEPARTMENT NAMES

Department name changes can occur as titles are modified. For example, once you change job titles to *Instructor & Research Specialist*, the department can be renamed *Instruction & Research*, with the supervisor's title changed to *Instruction & Research Supervisor*.

INVOLVE STAFF

Involving staff in various ways as your education brand unfolds is critically important. The "power of us" will improve whatever you are implementing and will achieve staff buy-in.

For certain word choice decisions, you will likely opt for input from only a select few before moving forward, then informing everyone, explaining why. The word *education* and the Three Pillars language may fall under this category after you have introduced everyone to the broad vision.

Sometimes, expediency will necessitate on-the-spot decisions. For example, as the Director of Public Relations and I were making final edits to a publication recently, she said, "What if we said '30,000 students *enrolled in* Summer Reading,' instead of *registered for*?" We made the edit, and began using the more strategic word *enroll* when suitable.

Delegating Decisions

For other terminology, consider delegating decision-making authority to staff. For instance, thinking we could improve on the sought-after A+ class, *Booktalks*, we formed committees to come up with a better substitute.

Staff bantered ideas about, including *Book Previews* and *Book Trailers*, ultimately recommending *Book Promotions*, which we adopted. Now we say:

> We teach an A+ class called Book Promotions, where students experience snippets of 20+ books summarized and performed by HCLS Instructors. Inevitably, students persuade their parents to take them to the library shortly thereafter to borrow titles to which they were introduced that day in school.

Ongoing Communication

Say and write the new vocabulary often to infuse it into your culture. Capitalize on conversations, e-mails, newsletters, and intranet posts to communicate with staff, keeping the vision front and center.

To illustrate, here's an excerpt from my opening of the September 2010 HCLS *Team Update*, which served two purposes. The piece updated staff as to the status of the language transition underway, while also emphasizing how staff opinions contributed to the process:

> To further convey staff expertise, we have begun analyzing the job title *Information Specialist & Instructor*. Discussion at the September Leadership Team meeting (which included feedback from many of you), and subsequent conversations have concluded:
>
> - *Research Specialist & Instructor* (or reversing the order as some of you have suggested—*Instructor & Research Specialist*) enhances the role's value
> - Unlike *Information*, the term *Research* conveys:
>   - Action (verb and noun)
>   - Staff expertise
>   - Heightened value
>   - Empowerment
>   - Clarity (minimizes confusion with IT)
>
> If you haven't already, you will have an opportunity to discuss this modification at departmental staff meetings. We will gather and assess all feedback, and plan to implement a modified job title for this position in the near future.
> Thank you for all you do.
> Sincerely,
> Valerie

Other communications can reiterate the philosophy's importance, as did this excerpt from my October 2010 *Team Update* message to the staff ("Strategic Vocabulary" is one of the seven "internal pillars" in our strategic plan, which explains the title case):

> Strategic Vocabulary heightens our image by conveying what we do in terms people understand. The more we convey that Howard County Library delivers public education for all, the higher our perceived value will climb.
> Your continued efforts to incorporate Strategic Vocabulary into everyday language is of tremendous assistance, especially now, when lobbying efforts to maximize the funds we are allocated in the next fiscal year shift into high gear. (As you likely know, we must present a persuasive case to Howard County Government each year. Everyone competes for the same dollars: the library system, school system, community college, police and fire departments, etc.) So thank you to everyone for using our value-enhanced terminology at every opportunity.
> There are two reasons to convey our true value. The first? Maximized funding, which enables all that we do. The second reason is equally important: greater pride in being part of our spectacular Howard County Library team.
> I wish you an enjoyable rest of October, and Happy Halloween!
> Sincerely,
> Valerie

Professional Development Day

Another modification easily made, consider changing the name of your *Staff Day* or *Staff Development Day* to *Professional Development Day*. This edit conveys that continuing education takes place at the event, clarifying that the day is not just an excuse for a day off, a common misperception held by staff and customers alike. (If such a day is not yet an annual event at your library, consider that similar types of events take place regularly in schools and businesses.)

Our most recent Professional Development Day at HCLS included a major focus on strategic vocabulary. The team responsible for breakout sessions dreamed up the following Strategic Vocabulary Word Search, adding some fun to our systemwide language alignment goals. This exercise awarded nominal prizes to those who found the most words in the allotted time. It also served as another step in familiarizing staff to the preferred terminology.

Strategic Vocabulary Word Search

Name: _____

M	U	L	U	C	I	R	R	U	C	L	I	A	C	D	D	B	F	N
B	E	D	Z	G	F	I	T	G	Q	E	D	K	K	Q	A	N	A	V
J	W	L	A	F	L	C	G	V	U	W	A	S	T	G	Z	S	I	W
N	O	I	T	A	C	U	D	E	G	N	I	U	N	I	T	N	O	C
L	Q	F	W	V	S	R	A	L	L	I	P	E	E	R	H	T	D	F
L	S	E	M	I	N	A	R	S	F	W	U	Z	H	S	L	E	S	K
N	O	E	X	P	L	A	N	A	T	I	O	N	N	E	E	D	E	D
H	C	N	T	C	U	R	T	S	N	I	O	R	O	H	R	U	R	N
C	L	R	U	V	W	K	T	E	H	T	A	L	K	V	C	C	K	P
R	A	I	E	C	N	A	H	N	E	M	U	A	R	S	Q	A	B	H
A	S	C	S	E	L	F	D	I	R	E	C	T	E	D	H	T	E	Y
E	S	H	S	H	I	V	K	Q	K	I	U	I	S	O	Z	O	W	T
S	E	I	W	P	V	P	X	R	B	X	L	V	Z	O	H	R	P	Z
E	S	N	V	A	B	N	X	A	T	N	S	N	V	V	K	P	J	S
R	E	G	I	N	N	O	V	A	T	I	V	E	V	I	J	N	R	C

CLASSES	CONTINUINGEDUCATION	CURRICULUM
EDUCATOR	ENHANCE	INNOVATIVE
INSTRUCT	NOEXPLANATIONNEEDED	WORKSHOPS
RESEARCH	SELFDIRECTED	SEMINARS
TEACH	THREEPILLARS	VITAL
LIFEENRICHING		

Figure 8.2 Strategic vocabulary word search.

AWARDS

Staff awards can also strengthen desired language. For example, several years back, the title Instructor had not yet achieved commonplace status at HCLS. We recognized an opportunity to further weave the term into our lexicon in a staff "Bonus Award" given to all Children's Instructors at one of our branches.

Having originally drafted the wording on the plaque to read *Children's Department*, we edited the language to *Children's Instructors* once we realized they made up the entire department.

The recipients display these awards proudly on their desks—a preferred language reinforcement opportunity for staff and office guests who admire the award.

Figure 8.3 Before edits—Children's Department.

Figure 8.4 After edits—Children's Instructors.

SIGNAGE

Signage can be of immense assistance with bringing about the vocabulary shift you desire. These visual reminders showcase certain terms you would like your staff to use.

Signs displayed in public areas can guide staff and customer word choices alike. Figures 8.5 and 8.6 are two signage examples from the HCLS Charles E. Miller Branch & Historical Center that depict how strategic vocabulary prominently displayed can serve as teaching opportunities.[1]

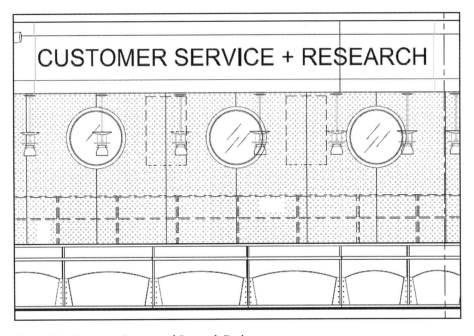

Figure 8.5 Customer Service and Research Desk.

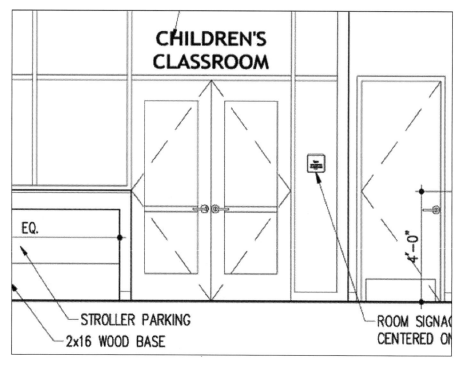

Figure 8.6 Children's Classroom.

All who see this signage will eventually call these two areas the Customer Service and Research desk, and the Children's Classroom.

Also, hang a poster-size rendering of the Three Pillars image in a central location at each of your facilities where it will be highly visible to both staff and customers.

FILE NAMES AND REPORT HEADINGS

Edit folder and file names in your computer, as well as account headings on financial reports to reflect the vocabulary you aspire to use.

For example, a *Programs* folder could be changed to *Initiatives* or *Classes and Events*, and a budget account heading called *Children's Programming* can be edited to *Children's Classes and Events*.

Also edit your statistical reports. We suggest changing:

- *Circulation* to *Items Borrowed* (see "Before" and "After" examples in Figures 8.7 and 8.8, respectively)
- *Program Attendance* to *Class and Event Attendance,* and
- *Information Questions* to *Research Assistance Interactions.*

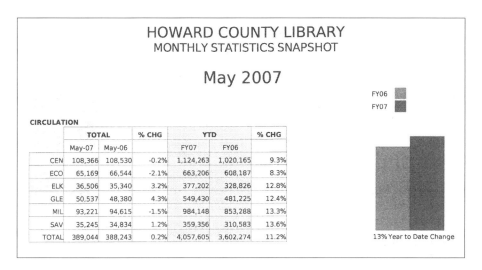

Figure 8.7 Before edits—*Circulation.*

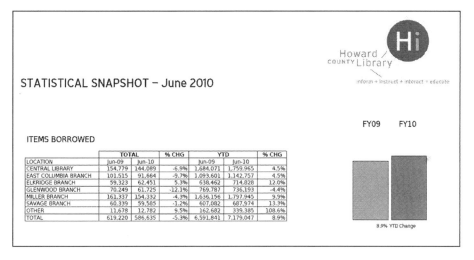

Figure 8.8 After edits—*Items Borrowed.*

OPERATING BUDGET CATEGORIES

You may even wish to incorporate strategic vocabulary into your Operating Budget categories. While still in the experimental state, included here is Figure 8.9, the current HCLS Operating Budget expense categories for fiscal year 2012, and Figure 8.10, which depicts precisely the same numbers recategorized (we plan to propose the modified presentation with our fiscal year 2013 request).

Note that Education and Training for staff has been relabeled Professional Development, and Salaries and Benefits has been classified into the descriptive areas of Instruction, Customer Service, Administration, Operations, and IT. We will also propose trading the heading *Expenses* for *Expenditures,* as the latter term conveys an investment that brings value over time. Which do you find more compelling?

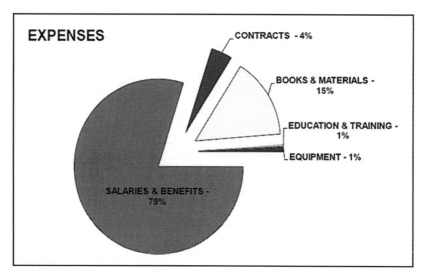

Figure 8.9   Current chart—HCLS Operating Budget Expenses.

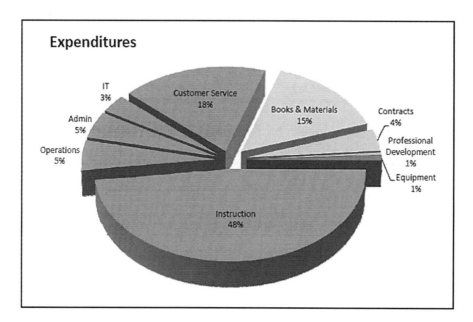

Figure 8.10   Proposed chart—HCLS Operating Budget Expenditures.

THE HIRING PROCESS

The hiring process presents an optimal opportunity to advertise our education brand. Even if never brought in for an interview, applicants can be introduced to who we are, what we do, and why it matters, through well-crafted position descriptions and employment applications that incorporate the Three Pillars Philosophy.

Employment Application

In addition to asking the basic questions, consider crafting an opening paragraph for your employment application that conveys your vision. Figure 8.11 shows a sample. Note the

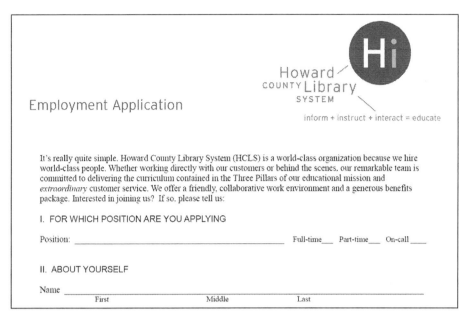

Figure 8.11   HCLS Employment Application.

use of smart terminology, including *world-class*, *curriculum*, *Three Pillars*, and *educational mission*.

Position Descriptions

Position descriptions are also useful teaching tools. Hundreds of people read these every day on your website, so seize the marketing opportunity.

The excerpts in Figure 8.12 from our Adult Instructor position description show how we've incorporated our mission and strategic vocabulary into the role's responsibilities. Note the use of the words *education, curriculum, Three Pillars, teach, classes, seminars, instruction, A+ Partners in Education*, and *research*.

Ads

We also incorporate our strategic vocabulary into any accompanying advertisement text. For instance, where we formerly would have said that we hire great "library associates/librarians/programmers" to "do" our "storytimes," we now say that we hire great "Instructors" to "teach" our "children's classes." Space permitting, we add, ". . . that teach the foundations of reading, and any subject matter—including math and science—through children's literature."

Interview Questions

Likewise, job interviews can teach candidates our philosophy. Candidate responses disclose their level of understanding, and whether they think innovatively or traditionally.

When internal candidates apply for a promotion, their responses to the questions reveal the extent to which the employees are familiar and aligned with the vision.

Here are some sample questions we have found to be effective at HCLS for our Instructor positions:

- Our mission is to provide high-quality public education for all ages. Why do you believe it is important for libraries to include the word education in their mission statements?
- Tell us what you know about our classes and events.

POSITION DESCRIPTION
Instructor & Research Specialist

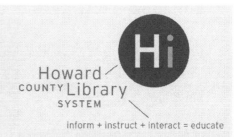

Howard
COUNTY Library
SYSTEM

inform + instruct + interact = educate

RESPONSIBILITY

- Positions Howard County Library System (HCLS) as a major component of public education for all ages
- Effectively lives the Seven Pillars of HCLS's strategic plan (Authentic Values, Strategic Vocabulary, Everyone a Leader, Winning Teamwork, Community Partnerships, The Power of Us, and Fiercely Loyal Customers), motivating others to do so as well
- Fully embraces HCLS's educational mission, effectively communicating our curriculum, which comprises Three Pillars (Self-Directed Education, Research Assistance & Instruction, Instructive & Enlightening Experiences)

ESSENTIAL FUNCTIONS

- Delivers research assistance to the public
- Plans, teaches, and facilitates public events, classes, seminars, and workshops, which reflect the educational goals of the system
- Visits schools to teach A+ Partners in Education classes, including book promotions, and provide instruction resources for high school and college students and staff
- Works at any HCLS Customer Service or Research Desk
- A+ Partnership Liaison as assigned
- Participates in special events in the community as assigned
- Enchanted Garden facilitator as assigned

EDUCATION*, EXPERIENCE AND SKILLS

- Four-year college degree
- People skills – ability to work effectively with others and enjoy it
- Extraordinary customer service skills
- Demonstrated ability to develop and maintain effective, collaborative working relationships
- Demonstrated interest in working with the public
- Demonstrated ability to handle multiple projects and meet deadlines
- Excellent communication skills, both written and oral
- Tech savvy

* The President & CEO may substitute demonstrated work-related experience or skills for the specific degree requirement of any position.

Figure 8.12 HCLS Position Description—Instructor & Research Specialist.

- As part of your responsibilities as an Instructor & Research Specialist, you will teach classes, lead book discussions, and introduce guest speakers. Tell us about your experience in each of these areas.

- What is your experience with electronic resources, such as specialized online research tools, smart phone apps, and social networking sites?

- Describe a time when you delivered outstanding research assistance to a customer.

- (For Children's Instructor) You now have an opportunity to teach a portion of a children's class that you have prepared.

- (For Teens' Instructor) You now have an opportunity to teach a portion of a class for teens that you have prepared.

- (For Adult Instructor) You now have an opportunity to present the Author Event Introduction that you have prepared.

HCLS INSTITUTE

Infusing professional language into your staff continuing education program will heighten its perceived value. Staff will take greater pride in participating. Outsiders will be duly impressed.

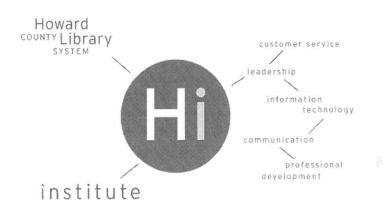

Figure 8.13 HCLS Institute (logo).

We decided to toss aside our lackluster-sounding *Staff Development Program* in favor of *HCLS Institute*, a curriculum comprising courses categorized in "tracks."

For example, staff may enroll in the "Customer Service is Personal" track. We even created a logo.

Traditions

Our newest Institute track is called "Traditions." All new staff members are automatically enrolled when hired. The six-month track begins on the first day of employment, replacing New Employee Orientation.

The idea is to immerse new employees into the culture of our organization on their first day of work with a day-long agenda that centers on the "why" of our existence. Focusing on our distinctive sense of purpose, the day also expresses our gratitude for the value staff members bring to our organization.

My role in Traditions is to greet the new employees when they arrive. We discuss our vision and mission. To introduce our strategic language I say, "Five years ago, your titles would have been *Circulation Clerk*. Which would you rather be? A *Circulation Clerk*, or a *Customer Service Specialist*?"

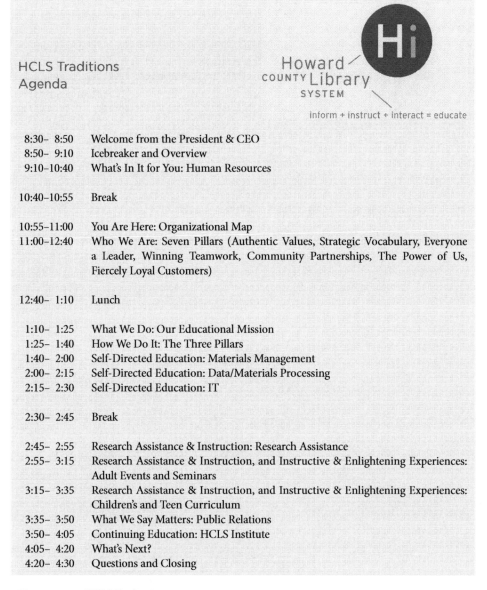

HCLS Traditions
Agenda

Howard
COUNTY Library
SYSTEM
inform + instruct + interact = educate

8:30– 8:50	Welcome from the President & CEO
8:50– 9:10	Icebreaker and Overview
9:10–10:40	What's In It for You: Human Resources
10:40–10:55	Break
10:55–11:00	You Are Here: Organizational Map
11:00–12:40	Who We Are: Seven Pillars (Authentic Values, Strategic Vocabulary, Everyone a Leader, Winning Teamwork, Community Partnerships, The Power of Us, Fiercely Loyal Customers)
12:40– 1:10	Lunch
1:10– 1:25	What We Do: Our Educational Mission
1:25– 1:40	How We Do It: The Three Pillars
1:40– 2:00	Self-Directed Education: Materials Management
2:00– 2:15	Self-Directed Education: Data/Materials Processing
2:15– 2:30	Self-Directed Education: IT
2:30– 2:45	Break
2:45– 2:55	Research Assistance & Instruction: Research Assistance
2:55– 3:15	Research Assistance & Instruction, and Instructive & Enlightening Experiences: Adult Events and Seminars
3:15– 3:35	Research Assistance & Instruction, and Instructive & Enlightening Experiences: Children's and Teen Curriculum
3:35– 3:50	What We Say Matters: Public Relations
3:50– 4:05	Continuing Education: HCLS Institute
4:05– 4:20	What's Next?
4:20– 4:30	Questions and Closing

Figure 8.14   HCLS Traditions.

ACHIEVING EXCELLENCE

As a concluding example, staff evaluations serve to highlight the importance of everyone's participation in living the vision. Capitalizing on yet another strategic vocabulary opportunity, we renamed our form *Achieving Excellence*.

Achieving Excellence includes a section that reads, "Please discuss the degree to which the employee enhances or advances the Three Pillars of HCLS' educational mission and curriculum." This part provides an opportunity for staff members and supervisors to discuss the team member's contributions to our education brand.

We can also assess the extent to which supervisors understand the concepts by how an evaluation is written. For instance, the sentence, "Sharon ran a program at the East Columbia Branch called 'I Just Got a Dog. Now What Do I Do?'" indicates the need to further convey the many benefits of the far stronger "Sharon taught a class at the East Columbia Branch . . ."

DID YOU CHANGE YOUR STAFFING TO EMBRACE THIS NEW PHILOSOPHY?

Some workshop participants were curious to know how long it took to convince staff to join in on the Three Pillars vision, and whether we experienced any staff resistance.

Persuading current staff members to embrace this new way of looking at ourselves evolved gradually over time. While some staff members immediately grasped the benefits, others raised the questions you might expect, such as, "Does it really matter?" By first informing the staff of the rationale behind the change—enhanced respect and funding—and then through staff involvement, we gained a growing number of advocates. As we continued to experience successes with the approach (especially funding successes during challenging economic times), more and more doubters became convinced of the power of language.

Our employees now take great pride in being part of an organization that has a distinctive sense of purpose and is highly regarded in the community as a major component of education. This pride was perhaps most evident in 2010 as we worked together to compile our current strategic plan.

As to new staff members, our language updates have provided the advantage of being able to hire from a broader, highly qualified candidate pool.

Instead of placing ads with traditional titles that convey little to those who know nothing about libraries (e.g., *Circulation Clerk, Library Associate, Librarian, Associate Director*), we advertise with no-explanation-needed titles (e.g., *Customer Service Specialist, Instructor & Research Specialist, Chief Operating Officer*).

We also emphasize education and business in the wording of our ads, which we place under the categories of "Education," and also "Business" for positions such as *Customer Service Specialist* and *Chief Operating Officer*.

The result? Those who would not have seen themselves in the mysteriously worded traditional job titles suddenly do! They now apply because the jobs are self-explanatory. They know what an Instructor and Chief Operating Officer do. They understand what classes are and what research is. In addition to "librarians," applicants now include public and private school teachers, as well as people with business backgrounds. People now view us as a professionally run educational institution.

Nothing has changed with regard to job expectations. All we did was alter our language, which now fully conveys the job with just the title.

Our overall team has evolved into an effective, focused unit that delivers on our educational mission with extraordinary customer service.

"COMMUNITY SERVICES" TO "EDUCATION"

While some library systems are already categorized as "Education" by their governing entities for budget purposes, many fall under a classification similar to "Community Services." For example, HCLS had been part of the Community Services section of Howard County government's Operating and Capital budgets, along with Recreation and Parks and Citizen Services.

Although Community Services is clearly important, the classification is incorrect for public libraries. If your library is under a similar category, unless the school system is also classified where you are, consider requesting a reclassification to Education.

At HCLS, we began such an endeavor in 2006 once A+ Partners in Education was firmly established. We had also phased in some smart terminology by that time.

To give you a sense of the argument we set forth, Figure 8.15 is the memorandum I sent to then County Executive Jim Robey (now a State Senator). Even without the benefit of the Three Pillars (which had yet to be developed) and the full strategic vocabulary spectrum we use now (missing from this document is *Instructor* and *curriculum*), the case is not too

Proposal

Howard / COUNTY Library

inform + inspire + interact = educate

To: Howard County Executive James N. Robey
From: Valerie J. Gross, Director, Howard County Library
Date: February 28, 2006
Subject: Reclassification of Howard County Library

Howard County Library takes pride in being one of the premier library systems in the country. Along with the Howard County Public School System and Howard Community College, we serve the educational needs of literally everyone in the county, regardless of age, means or background.

Howard County Library's core mission—education—is evidenced by the following:

- "Public library resources and services are essential components of the educational system." (Annotated Code of Maryland Education in Volume §23–101)
- A+ Partners in Education positions Howard County as a state and national leader in education
    - Live Homework Help and research databases – available 24/7
    - Interactive practice tests (LearnATest) for the GED and SAT – available 24/7
    - HCL Spelling Bee
    - Teen Time (academic enrichment program for at-risk teens)
    - Dogs Educating and Assisting Readers (struggling third graders dramatically improve reading skills by reading to therapy dogs)
    - Summer Reading Clubs (reading has been shown to be the most important factor in avoiding the student "summer learning loss")
- Adult Literacy (HCL Project Literacy sets the standard for adult literacy classes in the state)
- "Play Partners" and "Three, Two, Fun!" (classes that teach the foundations of reading to infants and toddlers, including letter recognition, rhyme, alliteration, etc.)
- "You Can Count on Mother Goose" and "Spring into Science" (classes that teach math and science concepts to pre-K and elementary school students through children's literature)
- HCL won Educator of the Year Award (2003)
- Participation in Maryland Teachers Pension (Library staff participate in the same pension plan as Maryland's public school teachers)

The above examples position the Library squarely under education. In fact, Howard County Library's overall program is lifelong education. For these reasons, I propose that Howard County Library be moved from the "Community Services" section of the County's Operating and Capital budgets to the "Education" category.

Categorizing the Library in the Education component of the budget will further elevate Howard County as a leader in education. Such a visible connection with education will benefit the County long-term economically, as Howard County takes great pride in its exceptional educational system, which includes a top rated school system, community college and public library system. Thank you for considering this proposal.

Figure 8.15 Community Services to Education—Reclassification Proposal.

bad! You'll see my title was *Director* at the time, and you'll spot a few words we would no longer use.

Always open minded, Mr. Robey was convinced. He supported the reclassification, which was ratified and implemented the following year under a new, equally forward-thinking County Executive, Ken Ulman.

The result for us was symbolic as well as tangible. The new category, which grouped us with the school system and community college, elevated our value while serving as an endorsement that the library system is education.

At the annual County Executive and County Council budget hearings, we now testify alongside the school system and community college. These hearings are well attended, covered by newspaper reporters, televised live, and are rebroadcast numerous times.

If you aren't already classified under education (and kudos to those of you who are already there), do consider requesting a meeting with your mayor or county executive to discuss the many reasons to move the library into the correct category. Show up prepared with a succinct summary of your impressive curriculum categorized under each of the Three Pillars. Take copies of the Three Pillars visual, and incorporate your smartest terminology. A recipe for success.

NOTE

1. Grimm+Parker Architects. August 2, 2011, renderings of the first floor Customer Service + Research Desk and Children's Classroom signage for the first floor of the new HCLS Charles E. Miller Branch & Historical Center in Ellicott City, MD, opened December 2011. http://www.grimmandparker.com/.

9

KNOCK THEIR SOCKS OFF

If you haven't yet experienced how applying the Three Pillars Philosophy to everything you write and say captivates audiences, you are in for a pleasant surprise. Try it and you'll see!

Your publications, presentations, budget testimony, and correspondence will rivet the attention of any reader or listener when they are filled with strong vocabulary and the education brand. You'll also discover that your use of this refashioned language will teach others to use our revised lexicon—for the benefit of libraries nationwide. This is because people repeat what they hear and read.

EDIT, EDIT, EDIT

Armed with your strategic vocabulary, start by making simple edits. Comb your website and publications for generic terms and phrases, and then transform them into powerful vehicles to convey your true value.

For instance, if you discover a traditional sentence like the following, you can quickly turn it into a commanding teaching opportunity:

Traditional:	"We have STEM programs for children and teens."
Transformed:	"ABC Public Library Instructors teach STEM classes for pre-K through high school students."

You may wish to elaborate further. To illustrate, you might write:

A launching point in the science, technology, engineering, and math (STEM) pipeline of future scientists, mathematicians, and engineers to fill high-tech jobs in this global economy, ABC Public Library delivers an impressive line-up of STEM-related classes for pre-K through high school students. Developed and taught by Library Instructors, examples include Fall into Science, Chemistry in the Kitchen, Roller Coaster Physics, Go Figure, Robotics Fair, and Everyday Engineering.

The words *instructor*, *teach*, *classes*, and *students* (and, in the longer version, *STEM pipeline*, *high-tech jobs*, and *global economy*) will astound readers. They'll also begin repeating the terms.

Be on the lookout for any and all potential enhancements. To illustrate, as we were working on our fiscal year 2011 Annual Report, we spotted a way to upgrade the following sentence:

Draft: "HCLS offered 'Can We Build It? Yes We Can!' and 'Today You Get to be an Architect' in partnership with Grimm + Parker Architects."

Revised: "HCLS Instructors partnered with Grimm + Parker Architects to teach 'Can We Build It? Yes We Can!' and 'Today You Get To be an Architect,' classes for pre-school and elementary school students."

Offered was the weaker word in the first round of writing, which we improved with the term *teach* in the final text. You also likely noticed that we wove in *instructors, classes,* and *students.*

Headings

Edits to publication headings rank among the smartest. Highly visible, great headings can impress readers at a glance, while also teaching them our language.

To achieve this desired effect, Madison (WI) Public Library recently changed its *Programs* banner on its website to *Events and Classes.*[1]

Figure 9.1   Madison (WI) Public Library website image: Events and Classes.

Similarly Palm Springs (CA) Public Library edited the title of its *Events and Programs* brochure to *Events and Classes.*[2]

As one more example, at HCLS, we include text on the front cover of our quarterly classes and events guide, *source*[3] that highlights our most popular children's classes. The heading that used to say *Ongoing Storytimes* now reads *Ongoing Classes.*

While seemingly inconsequential, these edits represent key teaching opportunities. Anyone who sees the revised headings will unconsciously begin kicking the habit of saying *programs.* They'll be calling them *classes* in no time! They'll also start to view the library as education.

ONGOING CLASSES
Details inside

Play Partners
Tuesdays @ Elkridge
Fridays @ Central
Saturdays @ Elkridge

Picture Book Parade
Thursdays @ Savage
Fridays @ Glenwood

All Together Now
Mondays @ East Columbia
Thursdays @ East Columbia
Saturdays @ Central

Pajama Time
Tuesdays @ Savage

Figure 9.2 Palm Springs (CA) Events and Classes.

Figure 9.3 HCLS Ongoing Classes.

Keys

Referenced frequently by parents when registering their children for our classes, "keys" (or "legends") can be influential when updated with strategic vocabulary. Figures 9.4 and 9.5 show a "before" and "after" view of a key we include in *source* to denote whether a class is drop-in, requires registration, or involves obtaining a ticket beforehand. Each occurrence of the word *program* was replaced with *class*.

Surveys

If you seek feedback from customers through surveys, you may find language similar to this:

Your feedback is important to us and will assist us in identifying areas where we can improve services and better understand the needs in our community.

Replacing *services* with *curriculum*, and *needs in our community* with *excellence in education* as follows can greatly strengthen the message:

Your feedback is important to us and will assist us in identifying areas where we can improve our curriculum to continue delivering excellence in education under each of our Three

Pillars: Self-Directed Education, Research Assistance & Instruction, and Instructive & Enlightening Experiences.

A simple revision such as this teaches our value and terminology to anyone who takes our surveys.

Other surveys you distribute may include attendee evaluations following a class or event. In those, eliminate all references to the word *programs*, exchanging it for *classes* and *events*.

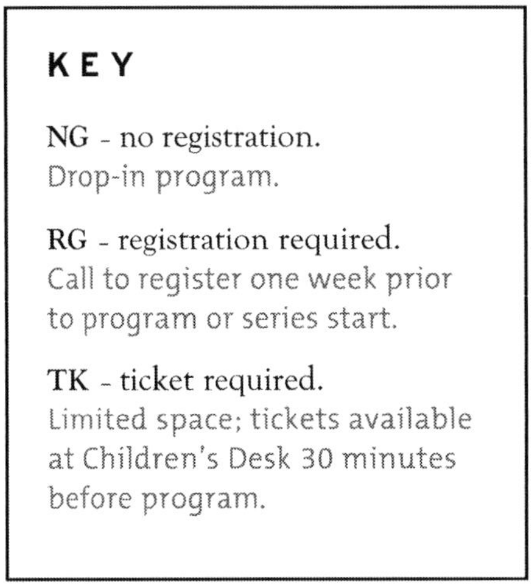

KEY

NG - no registration.
Drop-in program.

RG - registration required.
Call to register one week prior to program or series start.

TK - ticket required.
Limited space; tickets available at Children's Desk 30 minutes before program.

Figure 9.4 HCLS children's classes key—before edits.

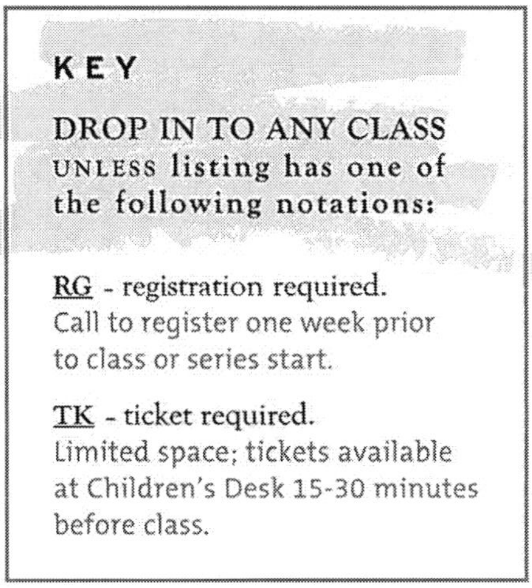

KEY

DROP IN TO ANY CLASS UNLESS listing has one of the following notations:

RG - registration required.
Call to register one week prior to class or series start.

TK - ticket required.
Limited space; tickets available at Children's Desk 15-30 minutes before class.

Figure 9.5 HCLS children's classes key—after edits.

URLs

Even URLs can serve as teaching opportunities. To illustrate, several years back, we were about to launch a monthly e-newsletter. Out of habit, our first thought was to assign it the address:

info-news@hclibrary.org

It then occurred to us that *info* in the address made it nondescript. We edited it to:

education-news@hclibrary.org

This edit serves as a subtle teaching tool every time we send the newsletter to our growing list of subscribers.

Signage

Signage is king when it comes to teaching opportunities. Look for existing signage throughout your buildings that could benefit from a makeover. Start with the most visible and influential edits, revising prominent identification signage: *Circulation* to *Customer Service*; *Reference* (or *Information*) to *Research*; and *Storytime Room* to *Children's Classroom*.

Other improvements may be less obvious. For instance, we discovered an opportunity about a year ago on a free-standing sign that trumpets our Health Education Center located at our Central Branch. Previously called our Health *Information* Center, we renamed it Health *Education* Center. We also traded the term *project* for *partnership*. The "before" and "after" examples in Figures 9.6 and 9.7 demonstrate the effect of the edits.

Figure 9.6   HCLS Health Education Center—   **Figure 9.7**   HCLS Health Education Center—
before edits.   after edits.

In addition, consider displaying key signage that promotes your educational mission. To illustrate, at our newest branch, the Public Education for All sign[4] (see Figure 9.8) greets visitors in the lobby area (the blank screens are LCD panels).

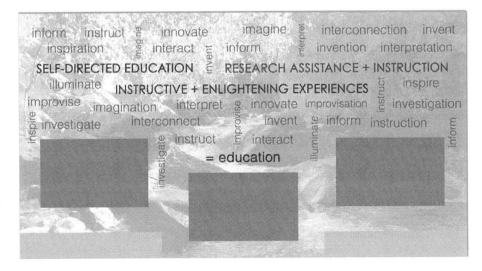

Figure 9.8   HCLS Miller Branch "Public Education for All" mural.

PERSUASIVE PUBLIC SPEAKING

Public speaking presents that optimal opportunity to connect with an audience at a more personal level. By presenting to community leaders and organizations, you can win advocates and sponsors.

Agree to as many speaking invitations as you can. Seek out opportunities as well. For instance, speak before your city or county council, state and federal legislators, Chamber of Commerce, Rotary and Kiwanis clubs, Parent Teacher Associations, and Leadership groups.

Offer to present an overview of how the library advances education, economic development, and quality of life. For repeat addresses, focus on "What's New." Either way, organize your speech under the Three Pillars.

Electronic presentations capitalize on the power of visualization. Incorporate them whenever possible. Show the Three Pillars image in the beginning, and again as you transition from one pillar to the next. Include compelling photos and images that represent your classes, events, and partnerships. If you find yourself in a low-tech venue, bring folders for everyone that include an agenda and various handouts (e.g., the Three Pillars image, compelling photo sheets capturing your classes and events). Even better—do both!

Introduction

Right out of the gate, you will astound audiences when you introduce yourself. Whether you are President and CEO; COO; Director of a department; or have Instructor, Research, Curriculum, Education, Classes, Seminars, Specialist, or Customer Service anywhere in your title, they'll pay attention because they won't be expecting the title they hear.

So you begin. "I am John Doe, Chief Operating Officer at ABC Public Library. It's an honor to be here. Thank you for the invitation to be part of your esteemed group this morning."

You will have captured their attention, as they will be thinking, "Wow! Chief Operating Officer! I didn't know they had Chief Operating Officers at libraries."

If it's a new group, include how you are governed, emphasizing any similarities to the school system and community college.

Then explain your operating budget and its categories. Display a pie chart that includes impressive categories (e.g., Instruction). You'll have their full attention as they ponder, "Interesting . . . Fifty percent of their budget goes to *instruction* . . . in a library."

Vision/Mission

Convey your vision and mission by saying something like, "Who are we? We're a major component of ABC's strong education system, along with the school system and community college. While the schools are key customers—and we certainly work closely with them through A+ Partners in Education—our customer base is much broader. We deliver high-quality public education for everyone—from infants through our wisest seniors—through a curriculum that comprises Three Pillars: Self-Directed Education, Research Assistance & Instruction, and Instructive & Enlightening Experiences."

I propose to you that no one will be wandering to the back for a second cup of coffee. Attendees will stay glued to their seats as they hear the words *school system, college, A+ Partners in Education, public education,* and *curriculum.*

Steer clear from the commonly heard phrase "cradle to grave," as neither *cradle* nor *grave* conjures up ideal images. Also, consider that *birth* means a number of things, so it's not the best term to use. Try *infant.* The word brings to mind a positive picture of a bright-eyed, inquisitive, very small person.

As a quick review, don't say "we serve," which is not very strong. Say "we develop and deliver a quality curriculum"—that's knock-their-socks-off Evian.

Also, avoid the phrase, "We meet the needs of the community." Whenever you find it, replace it with authoritative language that positions your library as a visionary leader—something like:

We regularly assess our curriculum, bolstering the most critical subjects, such as health, science, technology, financial, and environmental education.

You may wish to add, "For example, in this economy, we've strengthened our collection and classes in the areas of resume writing and job interview skills."

Fantastic Facts

Continuing your presentation, feature some fantastic facts about your library—number of annual visits, items borrowed, research assistance interactions, and attendance at your classes and events. People will be paying attention for two reasons—your notable statistics and the categories under which you placed them.

The Three Pillars

Next, transition to your curriculum, advancing to a slide with the Three Pillars image as you state something like, "Applying sound business principles, our academic and support team delivers educational excellence through a three-pronged curriculum. Everything we do falls under these Three Pillars."

Your audience will follow right along with you because not only will they be looking at the pillars themselves, but they will also hear the words *business principles*, *academic*, *educational*, and *curriculum*. Each of these terms will have an arresting effect on your listener.

At this point, walk your audience through each pillar, providing examples for each.

Pillar I

You might begin with,

Our first pillar, Self-Directed Education, includes everything each of *you* finds on your own—whether at our six branches or online—thanks to our experts. This pillar includes our vast collection of items in all genres and formats, thousands of specialized online research tools, and the 'shortcuts' we compile—brochures that set forth easy steps to, for instance, download an e-book or audiobook onto your Kindle. Our extraordinary customer service makes finding what you need a breeze.

Note the use of the words *education*, *experts*, and *specialized online research tools*, and also *extraordinary customer service*—terms that ensure continued audience engagement.

Your presentation can include a variety of photos of people browsing the stacks, conducting research at the computer, using Wi-Fi on their laptops, and borrowing books.

If you loan e-readers, include a slide depicting your collection, and bring a show and tell as a prop. In addition, include visuals of any specialized collections you might have, such as a World Languages Collection.

Pillar II

Show the Three Pillars slide again as you move to Pillar II. Your commentary here can be something like, "Our second pillar, Research Assistance & Instruction, includes personalized research assistance, as well as instruction for individuals and groups."

Provide some concrete examples of research assistance you and your team deliver, and a sampling of *classes*, *seminars*, and *workshops* for all ages, along with slides capturing the essence of each. Feature plenty of hot-topic classes in the areas of math, science, health, and environmental education, and those that are especially endearing (i.e., pictures of children and dogs).

Your use of the self-explanatory title, Instructor & Research Specialist, and the words *classes*, *seminars*, *workshops*, *teach*, and *education* will have your listeners spellbound.

If, like us, your library handles U.S. passport applications, include this curriculum component here as well. It fits because research assistance is involved in the processing of the forms, especially for more complex passport situations.

Pillar III

One last time, show the Three Pillars slide as you transition to Pillar III while you explain, "And the third pillar of our curriculum, Instructive & Enlightening Experiences, comprises the community and cultural center concepts, as well as partnerships. We bring people together to experience and discuss ideas."

Again, provide examples, such as A+ Partners in Education, and any other partnerships you have established. Include author events and cinema viewings you host, as well as any type of fair or big event in which you are involved—even if off site.

Include slides representing your partnerships, and your past year's events. Here are some images we use (Events:[5] HCLS BumbleBee, HCLS Spelling Bee, Battle of the Books, DEAR, Alexander McCall Smith, 5K & Family Fun Run, Summer Reading Kickoff, Bookmark Contest; Partnerships: Choose Civility,[6] Choose Civility Symposium,[7] and Well & Wise[8]).

More Than One

When a curriculum component crosses several pillars, place it under the pillar that describes it best. For instance, A+ Partners in Education crosses all three. A slide of A+ under Pillar III works well because the partnership itself falls there. As you describe the initiative, refer back to Pillars I and II, summarizing those elements as well.

Similarly, the education we deliver for job seekers crosses at least two pillars. For the strongest impression, place this segment under Pillar II, also referring back to Pillar I. Say something like,

We've strengthened our workforce development curriculum this past year due to high demand in our current economy.

- To enhance Self-Directed Education, we've bolstered our collection of books and specialized online research tools in the subject areas of resume writing and successful job interviews.
- For Research Assistance & Instruction, we have augmented our line-up of classes on these same topics. In addition, our instructors teach more personalized research sessions—including the completion of online job applications for those seeking employment.

Notice that when spoken this way, when the job market recovers, our timeless pillars still stand firm, with only subject matter shifting focus.

Closing Segment

If any capital projects are underway, you may wish to insert a few slides of those (emphasize how the projects will enable the enhancement of your curriculum), then close with:

Why does all this matter? Because *education* drives *economic advancement*, enhancing *quality of life*.

This dramatic ending will leave them speechless.

By conveying your true and complete value in this to-the-point fashion, you will have strengthened ties with your audience, generated more fiercely loyal customers, and garnered financial support—for future operating and capital budget needs, and also for sponsorships and donations to your Friends groups and foundations.

The Ultimate Compliment

I'll never forget my first speech framed and spoken in this manner. It was for a Rotary Club, and it was rather exhilarating. I had not, until that time, spoken words like *curriculum*, *class*, or *instructor* in front of an audience. In fact, the words didn't roll off my tongue very easily yet. I still had to consciously think about what I was saying (a transition stage that lasts only a short while!).

After my concluding comment, nobody moved. People sat still, entranced.

Up until then, they had assumed we were generic, loaning books and "doing" storytimes (language we had taught them by using it ourselves). They were not expecting Evian.

Eventually, someone raised a hand, asking in awe, "How much do you charge?" (This was quite the compliment, as the question indicated heightened perceived value.)

I smiled, "Equal opportunity in education. No charge. Your taxes, well invested."

A burst of questions ensued, followed by animated accolades and applause all around. Then, the perfect ending: "What can we sponsor?"

Music to anyone's ears, this question resulted in all seven Howard County Rotary Clubs joining forces to sponsor the HCLS BumbleBee. One club also sponsors Battle of the Books.

Presentation Outline

Rotary Club of Columbia
March 22, 2011 ♦ 6:30 pm

I. Thank You!

II. Fantastic Facts
- Vision: A major component of Howard County's strong education system, we advance the economy, enhancing quality of life.
- Mission: We deliver high-quality public education for all ages.
- Statistics: Borrowing, Visits, Research Assistance Interactions, Classes and Events Attendance

III. Curriculum Updates
- Pillar I: **Self-Directed Education** – E-readers
- Pillar II: **Research Assistance & Instruction** – Classes for all ages
- Pillar III: **Instructive & Enlightening Experiences** – A+ Partners in Education, HCLS Project Literacy, Choose Civility, Evening in the Stacks, BumbleBee/HCLS Spelling Bee, Battle of the Books, HCLS Rube Goldberg Challenge, 5K & Family Fun Run, Summer Reading Kickoff

IV. Capital Projects

V. Invitation
- Sat., March 26   **DEAR Graduation**, *East Columbia Branch (11 am–12 pm)*
- Sat., April 2   **Money Matters Fair**, *East Columbia Branch (10 am–1 pm)*
- Fri., April 8   **Battle of the Books**, *Atholton HS; Marriotts Ridge HS (7–10 pm)*
- Sat., April 9   **Children's Discovery Fair**, *East Columbia Branch (10 am–1 pm)*
- Sun., April 10   **Alexander McCall Smith** (*The No. 1 Ladies' Detective Agency Series*), *East Columbia Branch (6–10 pm)*
- Tues., April 12   **College Fair**, *Centennial High School (6:30–8:30 pm)*
- Thurs., May 5   **Rube Goldberg Contest**, *East Columbia Branch (TBD)*
- Sat., June 4   **5K & Family Fun Run**, *East Columbia Branch (8 am)*
- Sat., June 4   **Summer Reading Celebration**, *East Columbia Branch (9:30 am–1 pm)*
- Fri., June 10   **Teen Time Celebration**, *East Columbia Branch (6:30–9 pm)*

VI. Questions?

Figure 9.9   Presentation outline.

A number of our staff members speak regularly at Rotary Club meetings. Figure 9.9 shows a recent agenda I used.

NOTEWORTHY INTERVIEWS

Whether for television, radio, or print, remarkable interviews framed around the Three Pillars will enthrall reporters and journalists.

Whenever possible, weave the phrase *public education for all* into your answers. Also, link your answers to the pillar under which the subject matter of the question falls, making a direct connection to education. And, of course, use your most effective strategic vocabulary!

It's easy. It's impressive. It's also a teaching opportunity for the audience—and the reporter. Don't be surprised if the reporter reiterates your language as the interview progresses.

As with presentations, when a question pertains to all three pillars, walk the reporter through each one, categorizing details accordingly. For instance, for a general question related to A+ Partners in Education, you might say something like, "The A+ Partnership with the schools crosses all three pillars of our educational mission. Under Self-Directed Education, all students and faculty receive library cards and borrow materials from our collection that supplement items found in the school libraries. Their cards also give them access to the thousands of specialized online research tools to which we subscribe—such as *Access Science*, the *Wall Street Journal*, and *Groves Dictionary of Art*. Under Pillar II, Research Assistance & Instruction, Library Instructors . . ."

You get the idea!

Even details relating to a new Integrated Library System can be placed under the pillars. To illustrate, instead of saying, "We have a new ILS to meet the needs of customers," say, "Our new ILS enhances the manner in which we deliver Self-Directed Education, greatly improving convenience, effectiveness, and efficiency."

For in-person interviews, take props (e.g., an e-reader, A+ related materials, professional-looking publications). Television reporters may decide to zoom in on items, incorporating the shots into the story for added interest. Props are effective, even for radio if you're there in person. They can animate a conversation.

E-mail photos of your classes and events, along with an image of the Three Pillars, to interviewers. These will occasionally be incorporated after the fact. If it's radio, while clearly less applicable, sometimes a podcast includes an accompanying image.

REMARKABLE REMARKS

Use similar tactics for opening remarks. Mention the pillars when possible. For example, at author events, after a gracious welcome, inform the crowd, "It's events like this that exemplify the third pillar of our educational mission, Instructive & Enlightening Experiences."

Likewise, at groundbreaking and opening day ceremonies for new branches, don't say merely that you now have more space for books and computers, say that you now have more space to enhance public education for all—more space for Self-Directed Education, including books and computers, more classroom space for Research Assistance & Instruction, and ample meeting room space to enhance Instructive & Enlightening Experiences. If you speak in these terms, reporters in attendance will pick up on what you say.

To illustrate this concept, here were the remarks I delivered at a 2010 groundbreaking ceremony for a new branch. As you read it, put yourself in the shoes of the many elected officials present that morning—local, state, and federal. Consider the influential power of the language used and its potential favorable effect on future funding decisions for public libraries.

Good morning, and welcome! It is with great enthusiasm and gratitude that I welcome you to today's Groundbreaking Ceremony for Howard County Library's new Charles E. Miller Branch & Historical Center.

When I joined this fabulous Howard County Library team back in July 2001, I recall my first visit to the Miller Branch. It was packed! The shelves needed continuous replenishing.

Children, teens and adults were waiting in long lines to borrow books. It was standing room only for the Picture Book Parade preschool class I had the privilege of attending. Registration for Summer Science exceeded available seats in the class. All computers were in use. The meeting room was booked in the afternoon for a Master Gardener workshop, and a Potter Pizza Party event sponsored by the Friends of Howard County Library was scheduled that evening.

Noting both the cramped quarters and the "needing-renovation" feel to the building, I took a tour of the outside. There, off to the side was a vast corn field! Intrigued, I wondered, "What's over there?"

And here we are today, simply ecstatic that we are actually breaking ground in that very corn field for a spacious, grand venue that will match the exceptional education we deliver for all ages.

What will be unique about the new Miller Branch?

To support our first educational pillar, Self-Directed Education, there will be three times the space for books and materials in all formats, and for computers.

As to our second pillar, Research Assistance & Instruction, room for the personalized research assistance our instructors deliver will triple, as will the children and teen classroom space.

And for our third pillar, Instructive & Enlightening Experiences, ample meeting rooms will afford us the opportunity to enhance our role as a community and cultural center, bringing people together to discuss ideas through our many signature events and partnerships.

The new branch will bring a new focus to our County and State's history, with a Historical Center on the second floor. The building itself will reflect Historic Ellicott City. The stone bridge running through the building will connect the past to present and the present to the future. And, hints of the Enchanted Forest will be incorporated into the Children's Area design.

We will capitalize on the new building's projected LEED Silver Certification to focus on Environmental Education, and the Enchanted Garden on the quarter-acre parcel next to the Children's Area will further enhance Health and Nutrition Education. A teaching garden that will "grow healthy habits" and a whimsical, fantastical place to visit time and again, the Enchanted Garden will include a Peter Rabbit Patch (where we will grow cabbage, carrots, turnips, lettuce), a Pizza Garden (growing tomatoes, basil, oregano, green peppers), learning stations, a sun dial, water features, and a picnic and reading area. Our partners include the Master Gardeners, HCPSS, PTAs, HCC, the County, Horizon Foundation, Nature Conservancy, Economic Development Authority, and the University of Maryland—to name a few.

The new Charles E. Miller Branch & Historical Center will be a beautiful, state-of-the-art, inspiring destination.

Our first thank you goes to a true visionary—someone who recognizes that high-quality public education for everyone is vital to our economy and quality of life, and deserves a venue that matches that quality. We express our sincere appreciation for the top priority he has placed in funding this project. Please join me in thanking, and welcoming, County Executive Ken Ulman.

How did the media report on this? The opening paragraph from reporter Sarah Breitenbach's February 22, 2010, article in *The Columbia Flier*, "New, improved Miller Library taking shape: Ellicott City branch, due to open next year, will have triple the space,"[9] began:

A much-anticipated county library, designed to ease demand, maximize public education and enhance research opportunities, is under construction in Ellicott City after years of planning.

The reporter repeated what she had heard, further enhancing our image.

RIVETING WRITING AND PUBLICATIONS

Publications and writing pieces are also greatly enhanced when organized by the Three Pillars and infused with strong language. Your readership will find your publications more fascinating. Just as important, customers will begin repeating what they read.

Annual Reports

Annual reports and any accompanying letters you write can incorporate the Three Pillars. To illustrate, following are examples from the 2011 HCLS Annual Report, along with the document's

2011 Annual Report

Howard
COUNTY Library
SYSTEM

inform + instruct + interact = educate

Dear Community Leader,

We are pleased to present Howard County Library System's 2011 Annual Report.

We hope you take pride knowing that HCLS has become synonymous with high-quality public education for all.

Our customer base encompasses people of all ages, means and backgrounds, who visited our six branches nearly **3 million** times last year. Our team of educators and support staff delivers excellence through a curriculum that comprises three pillars:

I.   **Self-Directed Education** reached <u>7 million</u> items borrowed—*the highest per capita in the state* (and ninth highest in the nation)!

II.   **Research Assistance & Instruction** expanded dramatically, with the expertise of HCLS instructors tapped <u>1.6 million</u> times—*a 15 percent increase* over the previous year.

III. **Instructive & Enlightening Experiences** benefited nearly <u>a quarter of a million students of all ages</u> who attended and participated in our award-winning classes and events, reflecting a *20 percent* increase from the prior year.

We aim to earn our top national ranking each and every time you connect with us, whether in person, by phone, by mail, or online. So please continue telling us where we excel, and how we might shine even brighter. We always appreciate hearing your thoughts and suggestions.

In addition to thanking our innovative staff for another year of remarkable accomplishments, we are grateful to the Howard County Executive, Howard County Council, Maryland State Legislators, HCLS Board of Trustees, Friends of Howard County Library, philanthropic partners, devoted volunteers, and, most importantly, our dynamic community.

Thank you for your tremendously gratifying support.

Sincerely,

Charles H. McLaughlin
Chair (2011)
HCLS Board of Trustees

Valerie J. Gross
President & CEO

Figure 9.10   HCLS 2011 Annual Report cover letter.

accompanying letter to community leaders. We'll start with the letter (see Figure 9.10), since that is typically read first by those to whom we send the report. I should point out that we figured out only last year that we could assign statistics to each of the pillars. See what you think!

Did the letter impress you? Note that, while you were paying attention to the language, recipients of the letter will simply read it. The idea is to get their heads nodding with approval.

As to the Annual Report itself, the document is completely organized under the Three Pillars. Figure 9.11 shows the report's first page, which proclaims "Education. Everyone." This headline is intended to grab attention, elevate perceived value, and teach anyone in a flash who we are, what we do, and why it matters—from the title alone.

Figure 9.11   HCLS 2011 Annual Report—Self-Directed Education.

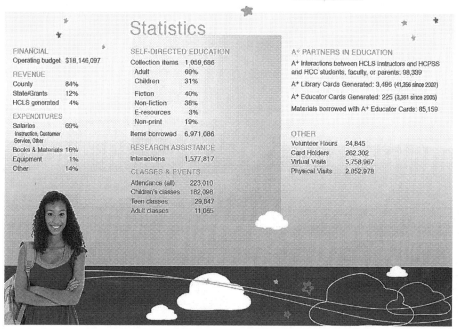

Figure 9.12 HCLS 2011 Annual Report—Research Assistance & Instruction.

Figures 9.12 and 9.13 are pages two and three of the document's six pages,[10] included to show the effectiveness of organizing everything under the pillars (the full document can be viewed at hclibrary.org):

Note that even the statistics have been assigned headings that nearly match the pillars. Figures 9.14 and 9.15 are the statistics enlarged so that you can read the categories.

Website Welcome

Some of you may already include a "Welcome" piece on your website. If so, enliven it with strategic vocabulary. If you summarize your curriculum, try categorizing the various components under the Three Pillars.

Instructive & Enlightening Experiences

HCLS Rube Goldberg Challenge. Nineteen teams of fourth and fifth grade students (100 students) submitted entries for this new STEM component of A+ Partners in Education. An academic competition named after the Pulitzer Prize winning cartoonist, sculptor, and author, the Rube Goldberg Challenge charges students with transforming everyday materials into wacky, convoluted, innovative machines that perform a simple task. This year's assignment? Water a plant. Congratulations to the award recipients: The Green Jelly Beans from Hollifield Station ES for Most Scientific Award; Trident of Poseidon from Hollifield Station ES for Most Humorous Award; The Mechanical Machine Masters from Hollifield Station ES for Most Complex Award; Pointers Run Inventionistas from Pointers Run ES for Most Green Award; and Trident of Poseidon from Hollifield Station ES for Community Favorite Award.

HCLS Spelling Bee. Setting a grand champion two-years-running record by correctly spelling the word "deleterious," Clarksville Middle School student Sam Osheroff won a $1,000 college scholarship and the opportunity to represent Howard County

Meet the Author. HCLS hosted a number of bestselling author events, including Maryland's Poet Laureate Stanley Plumly; Warren St. John, author of *Outcasts United*; and former CNN correspondent Kathleen Koch, author of *Rising from Katrina*. As part of Money Matters, bestselling author and nationally syndicated *Washington Post* columnist Michelle Singletary spoke to a packed audience about managing money in today's difficult economy. The highlight of the year, Alexander McCall Smith appeared in April. Internationally acclaimed and bestselling author of The No. 1 Ladies' Detective Agency series, McCall Smith charmed an audience of nearly 400 with his talk, "The Very Small Things of Life." County Council Chair Dr. Calvin Ball delivered a joint proclamation from the County Executive and County Council, declaring April 10, 2011 to be Alexander McCall Smith Day in Howard County.

Howard County Book Connection. This highly visible component of the A+ Partnership between HCLS and Howard Community College (HCC) brings people together through the reading and discussion of a selected book. The 2010-11 selection featured *Listening is an Act of Love: A Celebration of American Life from the StoryCorps Project*, edited by Dave Isay. Throughout the year, HCC and HCLS showcased a variety of educational events and activities including presentations by writer and radio commentator David Greenberger, Native American storyteller Joseph Stands with Many, local history authors Ali Kahn and Peggy Fox, and slam poets Gayle Danley and Twain Dooley.

at the 2011 National Spelling Bee. Wilde Lake Middle School eighth grade student Andrew Johnson won second place and a $750 scholarship. A total of 62 students from public and private schools and homeschool associations competed this year. FY 11 set new

records in the history of the initiative in terms of student performance.

BumbleBee. A companion initiative to the HCLS Spelling Bee for younger students, the BumbleBee ceremony celebrated 43 students with a trophy. The students were recognized again on stage at the HCLS Spelling Bee.

Battle of the Books. Due to the unprecedented and overwhelming enrollment response for this academic competition, Battle of the Books was held simultaneously at two

separate venues this year. Ninety teams of fifth grade students (600 students) read 15 preselected books then vied for first place in the 50-question exam. Congratulations to the Nuclear Panther Bookworms from Northfield ES and Wizard of Books from Lisbon ES who took first place at Atholton and Marriotts Ridge, respectively. First place winners for Best Civility were Marshmallow Mayhem (Stevens Forest ES) and Mythical Readers (Deep Run ES). Best Costume winners were Oompa-Loompas (St. John's Lane ES) and Reading Up a Storm (Thunder Hill ES). Readers of the Round Table (St. John's Lane ES) and Sherlock Holmies (Lisbon ES) won Best Team Name, and Pump It Up Pajama Party Girls (Clemens Crossing ES) and Next Generation Nerds (Triadelphia Ridge ES) won Best Team Spirit.

Money Matters Fair. This financial education event presented in partnership with Howard County Council Chair Calvin Ball, HCC, HCPSS, makingCHANGE, and Friends of HCL attracted 900 people. The fifth annual event featured financial education activities for children, as well as advice for teens and adults related to college savings plans, credit reports, identity theft, affordable insurance, and tax returns.

Evening in the Stacks: The Roaring 20s. Lauded by many as "the best ever," HCLS' annual gala attracted 500 guests and raised a record $67,000 for its educational

Figure 9.13 HCLS 2011 Annual Report—Instructive & Enlightening Experiences.

If you have yet to write one, Figure 9.16 is an example from our website that incorporates the above concepts.

Strong phrases to point out include: *extraordinary customer service, educators, major component of our strong education system, high-quality public education for all*, and *unparalleled curriculum*.

Convincing Budget Testimony

As you lobby for funding at the local, state, and federal levels, use only strategic vocabulary, incorporate the Three Pillars, and apply as many tricks of the trade as you can.

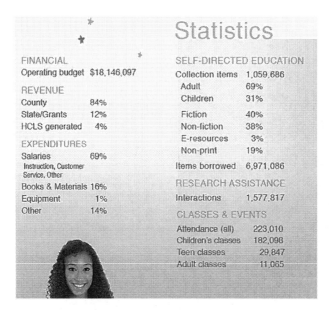

Figure 9.14   HCLS 2011 Annual Report statistics.

A+ PARTNERS IN EDUCATION

A+ Interactions between HCLS instructors and HCPSS and HCC students, faculty, or parents: 98,339

A+ Library Cards Generated: 3,496 (41,356 since 2002)

A+ Educator Cards Generated: 225 (3,361 since 2005)

Materials borrowed with A+ Educator Cards: 85,159

OTHER

Volunteer Hours	24,845
Card Holders	262,302
Virtual Visits	5,758,967
Physical Visits	2,852,978

Figure 9.15   HCLS 2011 Annual Report A+ statistics.

Figures 9.17 and 9.18 provide two examples from 2011—oral testimony I presented at a Howard County Executive's Budget Hearing, and a letter submitted to the Senate Budget and Taxation committee at the State level.

What do you think we printed on the reverse side of each of these documents? You likely guessed it: the Three Pillars image!

Engaging E-mails

The most frequent business communication, e-mails present opportunities to teach people our revised language. Since many are forwarded, our precise words frequently benefit more than one person.

Welcome!

At Howard County Library System, we aim to delight you with extraordinary customer service – whether in person, by telephone, or online. An academic and business-oriented team that is second to none, we are here for you.

A major component of Howard County's strong education system, Howard County Library System (HCLS) is a nationally recognized leader among the great public libraries that delivers high-quality public education for all ages. We invite you to peruse our web site for all three pillars of our unparalleled curriculum:

I. *Self-Directed Education*: Find books and materials in all formats from a collection of one million items housed at our six branches, and a vast array of e-resources - all made conveniently available to you by our experts.

II. *Research Assistance & Instruction*: Sign up for our exceptional line-up of classes, seminars, and workshops for infants, toddlers, children, teens, and adults taught by HCLS instructors; and learn about our adult basic education initiative, HCLS Project Literacy, where instructors and volunteer tutors have taught English, basic math, and life skills to 6,500 students from 33 countries. As part of Cultural Connections, we also process passport applications at our East Columbia Branch.

III. *Instructive & Enlightening Experiences*: Discover our community partnerships, including A+ Partners in Education, Choose Civility, and Well & Wise, as well as our many signature events, such as the HCLS Spelling Bee, BumbleBee, Battle of the Books, DEAR (Dogs Educating and Assisting Readers), HCLS Rube Goldberg Challenge, Summer Reading Kickoff, best-selling author events, and Evening in the Stacks.

In addition, our web site connects you with our staff and Board of Trustees, as well as volunteer opportunities, donation options, and the Friends of HCLS. We love hearing from you, so please feel free to provide us with feedback. We want to know what you like and what you would like.

It is our hope that you will drop by frequently, both in person and online. One way or another, we look forward to your visit!

Sincerely,
Valerie J. Gross
President & CEO

Figure 9.16   HCLS website "Welcome" letter.

Howard County Executive's Budget Hearing
March 16, 2011

Testimony in support of Howard County Library System
Valerie J. Gross
President & CEO, Howard County Library System

Good evening. I am Valerie Gross, President & CEO of Howard County Library System. Thank you for the opportunity to testify. Thank you for your tremendous support of Howard County Library System's first-rate curriculum that benefits <u>students of all ages</u> who visit our six branches nearly **3 million times** each year.

Now, more than ever, Howard County residents young and old value excellence in education for *everyone*, as evidenced by last year's statistics—which also point to a <u>major return on funds invested</u>:

- **Self-Directed Education** achieved a record *7.2 million items borrowed*—a 9 percent increase.
- **Research Assistance & Instruction** rose 16 percent, with *1.4 million interactions*.
- **Instructive & Enlightening Experiences** saw a 15 percent increase, with *200,000 participants* at our award-winning classes and signature events.

Statistics continue to escalate, and are guaranteed to soar when the new Miller Branch opens. In addition to elevating history, the new branch will be the location of Howard County Library System's Enchanted Garden—a teaching garden that will enhance **environmental** and **health education** for children and adults alike.

We have submitted a proposed **status quo budget** for FY 12 that, as always, places a high priority on our team of incredibly talented educators and support staff. Also included are additional positions to adequately staff the new larger and undoubtedly much busier Miller Branch, which features <u>six times more classroom space</u> than the current venue to accommodate customer demand.

How many additional positions are we requesting? Only 12. To maximize funding, we have proposed a cost-effective, staggered approach to hire the necessary <u>Instructors</u> and <u>Specialists</u> for the new Miller Branch.

A nationally recognized leader among the great public library systems, we take pride in our contributions to Howard County's economy, and exceptional quality of life. We recognize and appreciate the difficult decisions you will be making as you compile your FY 12 Countywide budget. It is our sincere hope that you will find our proposal to be prudent under the circumstances—and **a wise investment**. Thank you for your consideration, and for the many ways you demonstrate your support of Howard County Library System.

Respectfully submitted,

Valerie J. Gross

Valerie J. Gross

Figure 9.17　Public hearing testimony—local.

March 15, 2011

Senate Budget and Taxation
Miller Senate Office Building, 3 West Wing
11 Bladen St.
Annapolis, MD 21401-1991

RE: Testimony in support of the $5 million in the Governor's proposed FY12 Budget for
     public library capital projects—Hearings before the Capital Budget Subcommittee,
     3/21/2011.

Dear Chair DeGrange and Distinguished Senators:

I write to emphasize the importance of (1) *fully funding the $5 million* in Governor O'Malley's
FY12 budget for public library capital projects, and (2) *maintaining the funding as mandatory*.
Your investment **enhances high-quality public education for all ages while leveraging funding**.

HIGH-QUALITY PUBLIC EDUCATION FOR ALL AGES

Along with our award-winning public schools, colleges and universities, Maryland's 24 public
library systems are a <u>key component of Maryland's strong education system</u>, driving economic
advancement and improving quality of life. In our unique educational role, libraries deliver *high-
quality public education* for everyone in the state, and **like the schools, adequate class space is
vital to delivering our curriculum**, which comprises three pillars: Self-Directed Education, Research Assistance & Instruction, and Instructive & Enlightening Experiences.

MAJOR INCENTIVE FOR LOCAL FUNDING

Thank you for enacting §23–510 of the Education Article, Annotated Code of Maryland, authoriz-
ing $5 million in state funding annually for public library capital projects. While minimal when
compared to allocations for schools and colleges, the return on investment is immense. For example:

> HCLS is scheduled to receive $1M in FY12 toward construction of Phase II of the new Miller
> Branch & Historical Center campus, the first of a series of contingent projects that, combined, will
> gain 20,000 SF of public service space as follows: (1) The existing Branch will be renovated into
> HCLS business offices, and also critically needed classroom and community meeting room space;
> and (2) relocating our business offices will enable 16,000 SF of administrative space at our Central
> and East Columbia branches to be repurposed into public service areas, accommodating the need
> for more instructional spaces, as well as dedicated venues for Teen Time, HCLS' novel program
> for at-risk youth, and HCLS Project Literacy, our Adult Basic Education initiative with 500 stu-
> dents enrolled. *The $1M from the State is **a major incentive** for the County to fund these projects*.

With public education your top funding priority, it is critical that the *full $5 million be al-
located* to FY12 public library capital projects, and that such funding *remain mandatory*. Thank
you for considering our request for this wise investment in the future of education throughout
Maryland.

Respectfully submitted,

Valerie J. Gross
President & CEO

Figure 9.18 Public hearing testimony—state.

To illustrate, here's an e-mail I received several years back from a staff assistant in the County Executive's office, along with my response.

> From: Susan 9/22/08
>   Subject: Questions re programming
>   Hi Valerie! I attended Community Day this weekend with the County Executive. We received questions about programming at the Savage Library. Where should I direct those who asked?
>
> * * *
>
> Hi, Susan! All of our classes for infants through pre-K at our Savage Branch are listed in *source*, our quarterly classes and events guide.
>   Classes we have developed for the K-12 age group, which Library Instructors teach both at the Library and in school classrooms as part of A+ Partners in Education, are also in *source*—as well as in our *A+ Curriculum.*

In 2008, we had just begun migrating away from the term *programming*. Although old habits die hard, chances are good that Susan is now using our preferred term.

Thank-You Letters

You no doubt send thank-you notes to elected officials and community leaders for various reasons, such as attending your events and approving budgets.

The next time you hand write a note, or compose an e-mail or formal letter, instead of extending a thank you for your library, or for public libraries in general, consider ending with the following statement that encapsulates your mission and value:

"Thank you for your tremendous support of public education for all."

Similarly, thank-you letters to donors can incorporate your vision in a highly impressive way, with phrases such as:

Your company's generosity directly benefits students of all ages in our community. We are proud to have your support, and extend our heartfelt thanks for your contribution, which enables us to fulfill our mission of delivering exceptional education for all ages.

SOUND BITE SPEECH

You'll think I made up this final example, but it actually happened. Several years back, I was given the opportunity to speak "for one minute" about what the library does—twice in the same month.

The first occasion was for a group of real estate agents called the Million Dollar Club. The one-minute speech followed the acceptance of a Summer Reading Club donation (not a million dollars—maybe next time!).

The second opportunity occurred at a Rotary Club meeting. This particular club starts each meeting with a "Vocational Moment," a one-minute-or-less speech that summarizes the speaker's profession. Having forgotten to assign the task that morning, the club president asked me, their presenter, whether I would accept this charge as well.

Sound bite speech prepared, I readily agreed. Short as it was, the speech:

- Incorporated strategic vocabulary
- Used the most powerful word: education

- Asked a question
- Focused on results

Here's what I said:

Who are we? We are partners in education.

What do we do? We provide equal access to quality education for all—regardless of age, background, or means.

Why does it matter? Because education drives economic advancement, enhancing quality of life.

What happened both times? At first, astonishment. Then, a standing ovation.

NOTES

1. Madison Public Library, Madison, WI, www.madisonpubliclibrary.org/events-and-classes; image used with permission.

2. Palm Springs Public Library, Palm Springs, CA, www.palmspringsca.gov/index.aspx?page=78; image used with permission.

3. PDF issues of *source* can be viewed at http://issuu.com/hoco_library/docs.

4. Grimm+Parker Architects. August 2, 2011 renderings of the first floor lobby "Public Education for All" signage for the new HCLS Charles E. Miller Branch & Historical Center in Ellicott City, MD, opened December 2011, http://www.grimmandparker.com/.

5. To view HCLS event photos, visit hclibrary.org (click on the Flckr icon in the lower right-hand portion of the screen).

6. Valerie J. Gross, "Choose Civility: Public Libraries Take Center Stage," *Public Libraries* 50, no. 4 (July/August 2011), pp. 30–37.

7. For symposium details, visit choosecivility.org.

8. Well & Wise website: http://hocowellandwise.org/.

9. Sarah Breitenbach, "Officials Break Ground on New Miller Library," *The Columbia Flier*, February 25, 2010, p. 8.

10. The complete fiscal year 2011 Annual Report is available as a PDF at www.hclibrary.org.To illustrate, here's an e-mail I received several years back from a staff assistant in the County Executive's office, along with my response.

From: Susan 9/22/08

Subject: Questions re programming

Hi Valerie! I attended Community Day this weekend with the County Executive. We received questions about programming at the Savage Library. Where should I direct those who asked?

10

SENSATIONAL STRATEGIC PLANNING

Once the Three Pillars Philosophy has begun to transform your organization, consider trying a strategic planning process that is straightforward—and extraordinary. For our purposes, we'll call it Three Pillars Strategic Planning (3P Strategic Planning).

What makes 3P Strategic Planning so simple? For starters, it saves time, as it eliminates circuitous deliberations about purpose. Because the Three Pillars approach is grounded in the timeless, influential vision that we are public education for all, discussions center exclusively on the future of a library's curriculum and how it will be delivered.

For further simplification, 3P Strategic Planning poses three identical questions to all participants. Guided by these questions, staff members at all levels of the organization, the library board, community leaders, and customers advise on curriculum. In addition, staff members recommend the best ways to accomplish the goals that will be adopted.

Why is the experience so remarkable? 3P Strategic Planning creates unparalleled opportunities to enhance a library's curriculum while propelling the education vision and mission forward. The process involves a series of workshops that double as prime teaching opportunities for everyone involved. Each workshop begins with a presentation—the knock-their-socks-off kind described in Chapter 9, tailored somewhat for each audience.

Equally important, 3P Strategic Planning incorporates Appreciative Inquiry, a methodology that achieves comprehensive participation while channeling desirable outcomes through carefully crafted language. Combined, the Three Pillars and Appreciative Inquiry philosophies set the stage for ideal strategic planning that unleashes innovation, enthusiasm, and commitment.

The one-year process culminates with the publication of a plan that charts a five-year course. Adopted by the library board, the document then also serves as an official endorsement of the education brand.

VISION AND MISSION STATEMENTS

By virtue of having embraced education as your distinctive sense of purpose, discussions about your vision and mission statements will be minimal. Requiring only fine tuning, the statements should be set before your strategic planning begins.

Your vision statement needs to convey that you are education. It should also focus on results—an improved economy and quality of life.

Similarly, your mission statement should communicate that you deliver education, and to whom. Include language that means "everyone," such as *everyone, all,* or *all ages.* Adding a strong adjective describing the degree of the education delivered is also effective—terms like *quality, high-quality, high-caliber, first-rate, and world-class.*

Keep both statements short and concise. One sentence is best, as in the following examples:

- Our Vision: A major component of ABC's strong education system, we advance the economy, enhancing quality of life.
- Our Mission: We deliver high-quality public education for everyone.

If you prefer the phrase *excellence in education,* that would work well, as would any of the suggested phrases in Chapter 2 (p. 15).

Although *public* can convey *equal access,* you may wish to include *equal access,* or *equal opportunity* in the statements.

Including the Three Pillars language is also a possibility. For instance, the previous mission statement could continue, ". . . through a curriculum that comprises three pillars: Self-Directed Education, Research Assistance & Instruction, and Instructive & Enlightening Experiences." Although longer, the words serve as a teaching opportunity. Alternatively, the pillars can be introduced in text that follows the statements.

You may be tempted to include additional details, as these short, focused recommendations likely differ from your current, lengthier statements. If you feel compelled to include more, consider elaborating in a separate commentary section outlining how your vision and mission will be implemented.

Lastly, notice that saying "we" (e.g., "We deliver . . .") as opposed to speaking in the third person (e.g., "The mission of ABC Public Library is to deliver . . ."), shortens the sentences considerably and personalizes the message. The first-person "we" speaks to all members of the team, who will more readily see themselves in the statements. Similarly, perhaps you observed that the previous sample statements start with "our" (e.g., "Our Vision: . . ."), a unifying first-person pronoun you may wish to use.

APPRECIATIVE INQUIRY

Appreciative Inquiry is based on the belief that organizations are "constructions of the imagination and are, therefore, capable of change at the speed of imagination."[1] The approach involves staff members at all levels and integrates skillfully applied terminology to achieve positive results.

To illustrate, if employees are asked to pinpoint what is not working, one can predict that discussions will revolve around what is wrong about their organization, giving rise to stagnant, glass-half-empty staff outlooks.

By contrast, asking the team to identify what is working well will prompt positive, success-oriented conversations, producing a sense of pride that will translate into optimistic, glass-nearly-full views of their work environment.

Neil Samuels summarized the concepts concisely when he said that Appreciative Inquiry directs "questions away from deficits and gaps. We focus instead on what gives energy, and support leaders, their teams, and their organizations on remembering and re-discovering themselves at their best. As a result, a powerful vision for, and commitment to, an energizing future emerges."[2]

The concepts of harnessing the power of language to attain the most positive outcome correlate with the Three Pillars Philosophy.

At Howard County Library System (HCLS), we introduced Appreciative Inquiry into our strategic planning process in 2005. Involving literally everyone, the positive, inclusive approach contributed to our staff's pride in and commitment to attaining the goals set forth in the resulting document, *Strong Foundations, Enduring Success: Howard County Library's Strategic Plan, 2005–2010.*[3] This team "ownership" also garnered substantial support for the education and strategic vocabulary vision still under development at the time.

Five years later, recognizing the tremendous power of both the Three Pillars Philosophy and Appreciative Inquiry, we blended the two. This resulted in a dynamic, streamlined, participatory strategic planning process. It culminated not only with proud employees committed to achieving the aspirations outlined in *Public Education for All: Howard County Library's Strategic Plan, 2010–2015*,[4] but also with widespread support among staff for our education brand.

The details and sample communications included in the pages that follow[5] are intended to provide further explanation, and to save you some time should you choose to try 3P Strategic Planning.

TIMELINE

Allow one year for the entire process, which is organized by the Appreciative Inquiry categories:

- Discover—Identifying successes and strengths
- Dream—Envisioning a thriving future
- Design—Incorporating Discover and Dream components into a strategic plan
- Destiny—Implementing the strategic plan

Based on a fiscal year that begins July 1 and ends June 30, here is a general outline of the phases:

I. **Synopsis** (July–September)
   A. Overview for the Leadership Team
   B. Overview for the Library Board
   C. Overview for staff members
II. **Discover and Dream** (October–December)
   A. Leadership Summit
   B. Library Board—Mini-Summit
   C. Community Leadership Breakfast
   D. Outlook Forums: "From Today's Achievements Grow Tomorrow's Successes"
   E. Community Conversations
III. **Design** (January–May)
   A. Updates—Library Board and staff
   B. Strategic Plan—First draft
   C. Outlook Forums: "Polishing the Design Together"
   D. Strategic Plan—Revised draft
   E. Professional Development Day
   F. Strategic Plan—Final draft
   G. Review—Leadership Team
IV. **Destiny** (June)
   A. Library Board Approval
   B. Publication
   C. Dissemination

SYNOPSIS

The Synopsis phase introduces staff and library board members to the entire strategic planning process for the year. Overviews, which can take place as part of other regularly scheduled meetings, outline the merits of 3P Strategic Planning. Provide a summary of Appreciative Inquiry, which may be new to your audiences.

Distribute a timeline similar to the sample above, except with greater detail (e.g., include all dates and venues), explaining what will take place at each juncture. Emphasize elements that will be most relevant to those with whom you are communicating.

Summarize how community leaders and members of the general public will participate in the Community Leadership Breakfast and Community Conversations. Invite all library board members to the Community Leadership Breakfast.

Even though they might not understand it all (Appreciative Inquiry can sound a bit scholarly to the uninitiated), one thing is certain. Everyone will be duly impressed by the well-organized, participatory process you will have outlined.

DISCOVER AND DREAM

Since Discover and Dream discussions overlap somewhat, the two Appreciative Inquiry categories are combined in a "Discover and Dream" phase.

Reflective, Discover builds the foundation for Dream by assessing the best about the present and the past. Focusing on strengths, discussions among stakeholders center on who we are, what we do, and why it is important, capturing the exceptional public education that has taken place.

By comparison, Dream is forward thinking. Dream generates ideas for a thriving future curriculum, with already achieved successes as a starting point—a collective dream for each of the Three Pillars.

Workshop Components

Convening a series of similar workshops—labeled Summit, Forums, Breakfast, and Conversations—over the course of three months builds momentum, and generates the ideas and details needed for the Design phase.

Presentation

Begin each workshop with a compelling welcome and opening presentation similar to the one described in Chapter 9 that captures the highlights of the past five years under each of the pillars. The structure of your presentation, along with the strategic vocabulary used will leave staff audiences proud, and community members amazed.

While much of your presentation will be identical for all audiences (e.g., slides stating your *public education for all* vision), adapt certain slides according to your audience. At the Community Leadership Breakfast, for instance, include plenty of photos of elected officials and community leaders. Although staff members will also appreciate seeing photos of senators and CEOs, they'll be even more engaged when they see pictures of themselves, so when presenting to internal audiences, feature staff where possible. An easy way to do this is to follow the slide with the U.S. Congressman with one featuring staff at the same event. (If your archives lack photos, start taking them now! Take multiple shots that represent all three pillars.)

Your concluding slide should serve as a transition for the next segment of the workshop. A slide with the following two bullet points can accomplish this:

- Imagining our future
- Charting our course for the next five years

Workshop Materials

At all workshops, in addition to paper and pens, place numerous copies of impressive show-and-tell pieces on the tables for easy reference during discussions. Items should include:

- Flyers of the Three Pillars with brief explanatory text (see Chapter 2)
- Recent issues of your classes and events guide

- A "Fantastic Facts" sheet
- Impressive brochures related to your curriculum
- Photo sheets capturing classes and events
- Annual Reports

Also, at each venue, display several poster-sized images of the Three Pillars on easels. The more these items incorporate strategic vocabulary, the more effective they will be.

Both the presentation and these visuals will instill a sense of pride in staff, and will astonish community participants, who will be expecting the usual run-of-the-mill library phrases and meandering vision and mission. What will they get instead? Strong, self-explanatory language that depicts a crystal clear, impressive vision.

The Questions

At each workshop, participants answer the same three questions. When attendees divide into work groups, everyone analyzes and provides insights in response to the first question, which is broad in scope. Questions two and three, which are pillar specific, are assigned so that a group discusses only its assigned pillar.

For example, 72 attendees would be divided into 12 work groups, each with 6 people. The questions relating specifically to Pillar I would be assigned to four of the work groups. Pillar II questions would be assigned to another four, with questions focusing on Pillar III assigned to the remaining four work groups.

The questions are:

1. What makes the Library critical to education for people of all ages? Please identify the areas in which the Library excels.
2. Please identify the *economic, social,* and *technology* trends on the horizon in the region and beyond that the Library should consider as it plans for curriculum enhancements to [Self-Directed Education/Research Assistance & Instruction/Instructive & Enlightening Experiences].
3. In light of these trends, how might the Library strengthen, enhance, and expand its curriculum under [Self-Directed Education/Research Assistance & Instruction/Instructive & Enlightening Experiences] in the next five years?

Notice that all questions reinforce that everything we do is education. They also prompt participants to repeat the strategic language used in the questions in their answers—an especially effective teaching opportunity.

Allow time at the end of each workshop for all work groups to report key feedback or points to the entire group.

Figures 10.1–10.3 show how the questions can be presented.

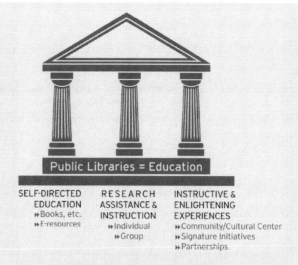

SELF-DIRECTED EDUCATION	RESEARCH ASSISTANCE & INSTRUCTION	INSTRUCTIVE & ENLIGHTENING EXPERIENCES
⟩ Books, etc. ⟩ E-resources	⟩ Individual ⟩ Group	⟩ Community/Cultural Center ⟩ Signature Initiatives ⟩ Partnerships

Work Group
Pillar I: Self-Directed Education

Includes everything customers find on their own:
books and materials in all formats, and specialized online research tools
(e.g., *Access Science, Wall Street Journal*)

Instructions: Discuss the following questions. Question one is general. Questions two and three relate specifically to Pillar I of the Library's curriculum: Self-Directed Education.

Summarize the group's answers on the sheets provided. Include specific examples that illustrate the main points. Capture words and phrases that are insightful and memorable, including metaphors, and other descriptive language. Please write legibly.

1. What makes the Library critical to education for people of all ages? Please identify the areas in which the Library excels.
2. Please identify the *economic, social,* and *technology* trends on the horizon in the region and beyond that the Library should consider as it plans for curriculum enhancements to Self-Directed Education.
3. In light of these trends, how might the Library strengthen, enhance, and expand its curriculum under Self-Directed Education in the next five years?

Figure 10.1   Work group questions: Pillar I.

PHOTOS

Take lots of photos at each workshop (be sure to obtain signed model releases). These photos will be used to personalize the process at a later juncture, and can also spice up the final strategic plan document.

LEADERSHIP SUMMIT

Begin your series of workshops by holding a half-day Leadership Summit for staff. Invite Leadership Team members, as well as other employees who represent departments and branches.

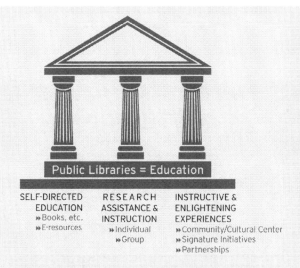

SELF-DIRECTED | RESEARCH | INSTRUCTIVE &
EDUCATION | ASSISTANCE & | ENLIGHTENING
» Books, etc. | INSTRUCTION | EXPERIENCES
» E-resources | » Individual | » Community/Cultural Center
| » Group | » Signature Initiatives
| | » Partnerships

Work Group
Pillar II: Research Assistance & Instruction

Includes individualized assistance and instruction, as well as classes, seminars, and workshops for all ages, taught by Library instructors.

Instructions: Discuss the following questions. Question one is general. Questions two and three relate specifically to Pillar II of the Library's curriculum: Research Assistance & Instruction.

Summarize the group's answers on the sheets provided. Include specific examples that illustrate the main points. Capture words and phrases that are insightful and memorable, including metaphors, and other descriptive language. Please write legibly.

1. What makes the Library critical to education for people of all ages? Please identify the areas in which the Library excels.
2. Please identify the *economic*, *social*, and *technology* trends on the horizon in the region and beyond that the Library should consider as it plans for curriculum enhancements to Research Assistance & Instruction.
3. In light of these trends, how might the Library strengthen, enhance, and expand its curriculum under Research Assistance & Instruction in the next five years?

Figure 10.2 Work group questions: Pillar II.

Choose an offsite venue if possible, as a conference-like environment is conducive to brainstorming, and more fun.

The Leadership Summit falls first in the timeline because participants are tapped to be facilitators and scribes at subsequent Discover and Dream phase workshops.

Issue an invitation to the staff you have selected to participate. Here is a sample introduction that conveys the event's purpose:

Dear Colleague,

Congratulations on being selected to participate in our Leadership Summit, the kick-off event of the Library's new strategic plan.

Our inclusive and participatory strategic planning process combines the Three Pillars Philosophy with the methods of Appreciative Inquiry, involving every staff member at all

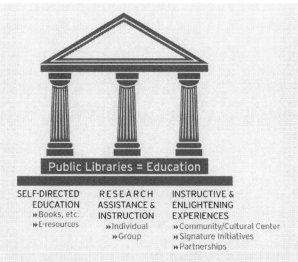

Public Libraries = Education

SELF-DIRECTED EDUCATION	RESEARCH ASSISTANCE &	INSTRUCTIVE & ENLIGHTENING
»Books, etc.	INSTRUCTION	EXPERIENCES
»E-resources	»Individual	»Community/Cultural Center
	»Group	»Signature Initiatives
		»Partnerships

Work Group
Pillar III: Instructive & Enlightening Experiences

Includes the cultural and community center concepts, events, partnerships, and signature initiatives.

Instructions: Discuss the following questions. Question one is general. Questions two and three relate specifically to Pillar III of the Library's curriculum: Instructive & Enlightening Experiences.

Summarize the group's answers on the sheets provided. Include specific examples that illustrate the main points. Capture words and phrases that are insightful and memorable, including metaphors, and other descriptive language. Please write legibly.

1. What makes the Library critical to education for people of all ages? Please identify the areas in which the Library excels.
2. Please identify the *economic*, *social*, and *technology* trends on the horizon in the city/county, region, and beyond that the Library should consider as it plans for curriculum enhancements to Instructive & Enlightening Experiences.
3. In light of these trends, how might the Library strengthen, enhance, and expand its curriculum under Instructive & Enlightening Experiences in the next five years?

Figure 10.3   Work group questions: Pillar III.

levels of the organization. The year-long process will be organized under Appreciative Inquiry's four phases: Discover, Dream, Design, and Destiny.

All staff members will have opportunities to share their success stories in the Discover phase, a critical first step that celebrates past accomplishments, establishing the foundation for future successes. Similarly, staff will envision the future we desire as part of the Dream phase.

We'll then enter the Design phase, setting forth specifics in a written draft. Our concluding phase, Destiny, will implement our new strategic plan that will describe who we are, our envisioned future, and how we will achieve that future.

Designing our future is really writing our collective autobiography. We will begin writing the next chapter of our history at the Leadership Summit. You will be one of 40 staff leaders to participate that day in a conversation about our future.

The day will include an opening presentation capturing present successes under each of our Three Pillars. Summit participants will then form teams to discuss assigned questions. We will then reconvene so that all teams can report back to all Summit participants.

The products of the Summit—visions for each of the Three Pillars and accompanying strategies—will formulate the first draft of our new strategic plan.

As the process continues, Summit participants, will be tapped to lead groups at the all-staff Outlook Forums, Library Board Mini-Summit, Community Leadership Breakfast, and Community Groups representing our broad customer base.

In addition, we'll tap you as leaders for Professional Development Day, where we'll celebrate the successes of the past five years and contribute finishing touches to the plan.

The Leadership Summit is scheduled for three hours, twice the time allotted for the Community Leadership Breakfast. This is because, in addition to the three curriculum-related questions, Leadership Summit participants discuss optimal internal focuses. At HCLS, we call them "internal pillars." We have adopted the internal pillars shown in Figure 10.4.

1.	Authentic Values	We subscribe to the core values of respect, inclusiveness, unity, communication, continuing education, exceptional customer service, progress.
2.	Strategic Vocabulary	Strategic language is part of our everyday vocabulary.
3.	Everyone a Leader	Every staff member is a leader.
4.	Winning Teamwork	We collaborate within and across departments and locations.
5.	Community Partnerships	We seek continuously to strengthen partnerships.
6.	The Power of Us	None of us is as smart as all of us together.
7.	Fiercely Loyal Customers	We transform customers into loyal customers for life.

Figure 10.4   HCLS's seven internal pillars.

LIBRARY BOARD—MINI-SUMMIT

Hold a Mini-Summit to engage your Board members. Scheduling an hour prior to a regularly scheduled Board meeting for this purpose offers convenience. Invite Leadership Summit participants to summarize staff member discussions to date.

Show the Board the opening presentation you'll be giving at the Community Leadership Breakfast. Since the Mini-Summit is an abbreviated workshop, Board members are not asked to form work groups, but rather to offer feedback on ideas generated from the Leadership Summit, with time allowed for them to add their thoughts and ideas to the mix.

COMMUNITY LEADERSHIP BREAKFAST

Invite key leaders from organizations and companies in your library's jurisdiction to a Community Leadership Breakfast. Include CEOs from the hospital, banks, chamber of commerce, tourism, and hotels; superintendents, presidents, and top administrative staff from schools, colleges, and universities; select elected officials, such as Board of Education members; and major players from your local governing body (e.g., the mayor's office). Also invite your library board, and board members from your Foundation and Friends groups.

Subject: ABC Public Library Strategic Plan | Invitation

Dear Community Leader,

As ABC Public Library enters the final year of its current strategic plan, we have initiated a year-long endeavor to create a new plan. The perspectives of community leaders are a key component of charting our course for the next five years.

We invite you to assist us in shaping the future direction of ABC Public Library's curriculum by attending a breakfast we have planned for this purpose:

What: Strategic Plan Community Leadership Breakfast
When: Tuesday, November 1, 7:45 to 9:30 am
Where: ABC Public Library, Central Branch (123 First St., ABC, Anystate 12345)

      AGENDA

      7:45 to 8   Continental Breakfast

      8 to 8:25   Welcome and Presentation
- Jane Doe, ABCPL President & CEO
- Sharon Smith, Chair, ABCPL Board of Trustees
- John Doe, Strategic Plan Project Leader and Facilitator

      8:25 to 9:10 Discussion

      9:10 to 9:30 Summary Reports

Please RSVP to Steve Jones (123.456.7890 or sjones@abcpl.org) by October 10. We hope you can join us!

Sincerely,

Figure 10.5   Strategic Plan Community Leadership Breakfast invitation.

A sample invitation is shown in Figure 10.5.

Arrange for participants from the Leadership Summit to be facilitators and scribes for this esteemed group of community leaders. Disseminate guidelines outlining the process, and provide a few tips—such as the following:

Strategic Plan Community Leadership Breakfast

FACILITATOR GUIDELINES

Purpose

The purpose of the Strategic Plan Community Leadership Breakfast is to solicit the thoughts and ideas of community leaders to advance the Three Pillars of the Library's educational mission.

There will be a total of 12 discussion groups: four groups for each pillar.

Your Role

Your role is to facilitate discussion within your assigned group. A scribe assigned to each group will take notes, allowing you to give your full attention to directing the discussion.

Your goal is to encourage all participants to answer three questions. Your tasks will be to keep the discussion focused on the particular pillar, to summarize points, and to conclude discussions.

Discussion Guidelines

The three questions for all groups are:

- What makes the Library critical to education for people of all ages? Please identify the areas in which the Library excels.
- Please identify the *economic, social,* and *technology* trends on the horizon in the region and beyond that the Library should consider as it plans for curriculum enhancements to [Self-Directed Education/Research Assistance & Instruction/Instructive & Enlightening Experiences].
- In light of these trends, how might the Library strengthen, enhance, and expand its curriculum under [Self-Directed Education/Research Assistance & Instruction/Instructive & Enlightening Experiences] in the next five years?

Approximately 45 minutes have been scheduled to answer these questions. It is important to keep the conversation moving.

Introduce yourself to your group and be approachable. Demonstrate interest and enthusiasm in what group members have to say. Do not evaluate any recommended strategies.

You will be seated at the table. It is important to speak clearly and loudly enough for all members of your group to hear you.

While participants will view a slide show before the discussions that will introduce them to our curriculum's Three Pillars, don't assume they will be able to generate ideas about future curriculum components without some coaxing from you. It will likely be necessary for you to explain and describe your respective pillar before you read questions two and three. Don't become anxious if there is silence after you make a statement or ask a question. Wait 10 to 20 seconds. If there is no response, it might be necessary to rephrase the question.

Information on the Three Pillars will also be found on the fact sheets, which will be placed on all tables the morning of the breakfast.

Effective facilitation techniques vary little from the active listening skills of customer service. Open-ended questions encourage discussion; closed-ended questions end discussions.

You can say to the group or a particular person:

- "Tell me what you think"
- "Please explain . . ."
- "What do you think about . . ."
- "Do you have any examples . . ."

"Why" questions are helpful in getting fuller explanations or more details.

Your reaction to comments, suggestions and ideas should be neutral (e.g., "Thank you for your suggestion" rather than "Wow, that's a great idea!").

Let everyone finish their statements and, if necessary, paraphrase or summarize to be sure the scribe can capture the main points.

Encourage participants to avoid talking over each other.

Questions like "Does anyone have anything to add?" or "Have we exhausted that topic?" will bring discussions to conclusion.

There are two goals to the discussion: (1) to elicit ideas, recommendations and insights useful in designing our future curriculum, and (2) to impress participants with our commitment to delivering high-quality public education to everyone in the community.

Your friendly and skillful facilitation of the discussions will contribute to achieving these goals.

Summary Reports

Given time constraints, plan to summarize only two to three highlights from your group during the Summary Reports portion of the breakfast.

You will undoubtedly receive glowing feedback from participants. At HCLS, comments we received following the Community Leadership Breakfast were overwhelmingly positive. One participant wrote, "Wow, that was as close to perfect as such an event can be! Our group generated a ton of great material. I imagine the others did too. Thanks."

OUTLOOK FORUMS: "FROM TODAY'S ACHIEVEMENTS GROW TOMORROW'S SUCCESSES"

Next in your series of workshops, hold Outlook Forum sessions for staff. Calling them a descriptive title, such as "From Today's Achievements Grow Tomorrow's Successes," adds distinction and intrigue.

The following phrases work well when communicating with all staff:

- When we vividly imagine our future—how our library will function, what it is likely to become—we bring the future powerfully into the present. These compelling images of the future will capture our attention, focus our energy, and direct our action. They function as self-fulfilling prophecies.
- Our goal is to take our success to new heights. Creating the future together strengthens relationships and commitment to the future, forging the unbreakable bonds of shared destiny.
- Our year-long strategic planning timeline will correspond to the Discover, Dream, Design, and Destiny phases of Appreciative Inquiry. Along the way, we will clarify or redefine crucial issues, challenges and opportunities, formulate strategies to manage these issues and establish an effective implementation plan.
- What does our future curriculum under each of our Three Pillars look like?

Schedule these workshops so that all staff can attend (at HCLS, we held eight sessions within a two-week period scheduling them at all six branches, adding a second session at our two largest branches). They should be at least one hour long.

Invite Leadership Summit participants to serve as group facilitators and to record the conversations, providing guidelines similar to the above sample for the Community Leadership Breakfast.

At the sessions, explain that creating your library's future begins by reviewing recent accomplishments, and then dreaming about possibilities. Tell them their input is instrumental to the process, and will be incorporated into the new strategic plan. Provide a brief verbal summary of the Community Leadership Breakfast, conveying the high regard in which the community holds them.

Once in their work groups, it may be helpful to start discussions with more probing questions, such as:

- How have we been successful in delivering our curriculum under all Three Pillars?
- What was the success?
- What factors contributed to the success?
- Why is it important?
- How does it make you feel?
- How has it contributed to the Library's overall success?
- How has it contributed to our customers valuing the Library?
- How does it enhance our educational mission?

COMMUNITY CONVERSATIONS

The concluding set of workshops, Community Conversations, solicits feedback and ideas from representatives of your broad customer base.

You may wish to convene teens, parents of children and teens, young adults, and retired persons. Aim for groups of 10 to 12 people, as these Conversations mirror the structure of the library board's Mini-Summit, with discussion taking place as an entire group.

Allow an hour for the entire workshop. Begin with an abbreviated presentation, followed by the three questions. For young children, the questions will need to be modified.

DESIGN

Entering into the Design phase marks the beginning of the writing process. Keep your library board and staff updated of progress during this time period.

Outlook Forums: "Polishing the Design Together"

Hold a second set of Outlook Forums called "Polishing the Design Together." This second round of systemwide discussions sends a strong message to staff members that their involvement is valued and their feedback is important.

At these meetings, update staff on progress and solicit feedback. Outline any internal pillar drafts that emerged from discussions held at the Leadership Summit and seek their input on those as well.

Combined, the two rounds of Outlook Forums foster a sense of ownership in both the process and the final document.

Professional Development Day

By May, document drafts will have progressed to finishing stages, which means that the new strategic plan can already be the focus of a Professional Development Day or similar assembly. In the best of all possible worlds, by this time, you will even have crafted a strategic plan title that reflects the education brand. If so, announce it.

Why might you want to celebrate with staff before the document is finalized and disseminated? To garner even more support and generate enthusiasm.

Open the day by thanking staff for being extraordinary. Show a slide presentation that celebrates your successes over the past five years, many of which staff will have highlighted during the first round of Outlook Forums. Photos should feature staff members as much as possible.

Then, cash in for the first time on all of those photos you took during the strategic planning workshops. Recap the stages with a slide show depicting each step. While the photos from the Community Leadership Breakfast can also show the community leaders in attendance, choose shots that also include the staff facilitators and scribes.

Introductory slides should include the Three Pillars image. Include a slide of any internal pillars that were decided upon.

Final Design Steps

Following Professional Development Day, incorporate any further edits to the strategic plan, then present the revised draft to your Leadership Team for final review. Make any finishing touches, then submit it to the library board for approval.

DESTINY

Present a summary of the year's process to the library board. Highlight select, especially impressive components of the plan.

Once the Board approves the plan, the 3P Strategic Planning process is complete. Post the document on your website as a PDF.

Print copies and disseminate them to your staff, Board members, and all who participated in the Community Leadership Breakfast and Community Conversations. In addition, send copies to your elected officials, especially if the plan's title conveys *public education for all*.

Once these steps are complete, you are ready for implementation.

NOTES

1. Jane Magruder Watkins and Bernard J. Mohr, *Appreciative Inquiry: Change at the Speed of Imagination* (San Francisco, CA: Jossey-Bass/Pfeiffer, 2001), p. xxxii.

2. Neil Samuels, "Appreciative Inquiry—A Summary," *Profound Conversations: Creating Conversations that Matter*, http://www.profoundconversations.com/index.php/appreciative-inquiry-a-summary/.

3. "Strong Foundations, Enduring Success: Howard County Library's Strategic Plan July 1, 2005–June 30, 2010," Howard County (MD) Library, http://www.hclibrary.org/index.php?page=119.

4. "Public Education for All: Howard County Library's Strategic Plan, 2010–2015," Howard County (MD) Library, http://www.hclibrary.org/index.php?page=119.

5. Many of the ideas and examples contained in this chapter reflect the work of Lew Belfont, HCLS Head of Customer Service. Mr. Belfont has spearheaded the efforts of our staff in the strategic planning process since 2005. Used with permission.

11

STRONG INVESTMENT

While the Three Pillars Philosophy gains respect for our profession, equally significant, this vision also delivers optimal public funding levels for our operating and capital budgets.

EQUAL FOOTING WITH THE SCHOOLS

Once solidly positioned as public education for all, we can achieve equal footing with the schools. In this context, equal footing means that:

- Percentage increases or decreases in your library's operating budget from one year to the next resemble those of the area's public schools.
- The percentage of your operating and capital budgets funded from public revenue matches the schools' percentages (e.g., if school capital projects are funded 100 percent from public sources, your library's capital projects are as well).

For those of you who have already established equal footing with the schools, the Three Pillars Philosophy will assist with continuation. If you are working toward this goal, the approach will help to make it a reality.

Would the Schools Do That?

Although vocabulary choices are key in conveying our full value, strategic budget decisions serve to reinforce the positive effects of our language.

A prudent question to keep in mind for funding-related decisions is, "Would the schools do that?" If the answer is, "Yes," then what is being considered is likely strategic. If the answer is, "Highly unlikely," consider analyzing short-term and long-term ramifications one last time before proceeding.

To illustrate, some libraries faced steep budget cuts last year. Confronted with tough decisions, they reduced staff and hours of operation. Would the schools do that?

Already positioned as education and therefore given the highest funding priority, the schools are far less likely to find themselves in such a situation—but if they did, the answer would be, "Yes."

Some of these same libraries then raised private funds to restore hours of operation, which means they now pay a portion of staff salaries with gifts. Would the schools do that? Highly unlikely.

Why not? Because, by definition, public education meets its operating budget expenses with public funding.

Although replacing publicly funded operating dollars with gift money may be charitable, the gesture fuels the misperceptions we are working to dispel, sending an unintended and misleading signal that we are discretionary. The action also sets an inappropriate precedent that may be difficult to reverse in subsequent years, regardless of the state of the economy.

Smarter would be to curtail operating hours in the short-term while working to restore lost public funding by establishing equal footing with the schools.

Donations as Supplemental Funding

It is important to note that both schools and libraries benefit from supplemental funding obtained through donations and fundraising efforts from foundations. The schools also benefit from the efforts of Parent Teacher Associations and booster clubs, while libraries are grateful to the fine work of their invaluable Friends groups.

This type of funding should augment—as opposed to replace—the public funding we receive.

What are some examples of appropriate gift applications for libraries? The "extras" that make us shine, such as contributions to receptions; Summer Reading prizes; trophies and college scholarships awarded to A+ academic competition champions; costs relating to notable author events; printing costs for full-color classes and events guides (which would otherwise be black and white); start-up costs for cutting-edge ideas; as well as artwork and other amenities that add a touch of class to your library's ambiance.

As a sideline, most library budgets include a "miscellaneous" revenue source that consists of funding from fines and ancillary services, including copiers, faxes, and passport applications. Unlike gifts and corporate sponsorships, this type of revenue is appropriate to include as a revenue source for your operating budget, as the funding results from our daily business and requires no solicitation.

EVERYONE EVIAN

We need to emphasize and broadcast that our educators deliver education for everyone. While an intuitive concept, and one which we all support, our profession's language does not always relay this message.

Some libraries focus on how our curriculum benefits customers with low incomes, even offering statements to the press along the lines of, "We serve the underserved," "We serve those who have no computers at home," or "We are the poor people's university."

While benevolent, this tactic tends to work to our disadvantage. Not only is it incomplete, it also equates us with social services, securing generic funding at best.

Does our curriculum benefit the economically disadvantaged? Of course. However, it also benefits the wealthiest in our community.

Although some people willingly pay taxes for the benefit of those less privileged, why not employ a comprehensive approach that speaks personally to people in all tax brackets—a strategy that focuses not only on *everyone*, but also on *Evian* (see Chapter 1).

Being viewed as Evian always works in our favor. This is because the enhanced prestige the Three Pillars Philosophy achieves is not construed as status, but rather, excellence and value, and everyone wants the best for their families and for themselves.

In other words, the image we aspire to project is based on quality and the delivery of a superior curriculum, or "product." Evian means being perceived as extraordinary. This impression of quality achieves optimal financial support because a first-rate education appeals to people of all means—from the economically disadvantaged to the most affluent.

Take, for instance, the computer access that libraries deliver. An Evian message conveys that we deliver state-of-the-art technology to everyone—including those whose home computer systems rival ours. We want everyone to visit the library to use our computers—not only for our cutting-edge technology, but also for our exceptional customer service, studious environment, and expert research assistance.

We would therefore be smart to eliminate "We serve the underserved" from our vocabulary, replacing these types of phrases with inclusive ones, such as "We deliver high-quality public education for all," and "We deliver equal opportunity in education for everyone."

PEOPLE EVERYWHERE FUND WHAT THEY VALUE

The Three Pillars Philosophy will work to our advantage in any jurisdiction because, regardless of a community's level of affluence, two things are certain:

- competition for available public funding is challenging (e.g., schools, libraries, and police vie for the same tax dollars[1]), and,
- that which is most valued will be funded at the highest level.

Consequently, as our value quotient increases in our respective communities, so will the resulting allocation of available operating and capital dollars.

To give you an example, back in 2001 I approached the Howard County Planning Board with the need for a new branch, one that would be three times the size of the obsolete branch it would replace. What was the Planning Board's response? They asked me how I was planning to pay for it.

Recall that, at the time, Howard County Library System (HCLS) was included in the Community Services sections of the County's budgets, and A+ Partners in Education and the Three Pillars Philosophy were only budding ideas. Even so, I responded with what was then a brand new concept: that, like the schools, we deliver public education—except our customer base is everyone in the county—and so the building should be funded in the same manner, with public funding.

While the project never made it "out of committee" that year, the response motivated us to begin branding ourselves as education.

Fast forward 10 years, and we have completed that project, fully funded with taxpayer money (except for the frog statues and water features donated by the Friends of Howard County Library). What influenced this result? *Accurately conveying our value*, which convinced the community and elected officials that a strong investment in public education for all is a strong investment in our future.

This account is intended to demonstrate that the more we join forces in the implementation of the Three Pillars Philosophy, the greater our chances of receiving not only optimal local funding, but also optimal state and federal funding.

WISE AND SMART

Although the Three Pillars Philosophy centers on our being recognized as education along with schools, colleges, and universities, the vision also blends the best of the academic and business worlds. Accentuating sound business practices is always a good idea, and especially advisable if education is a less than positive word in your area at this time.

Keep in mind that negative associations with education do not stem from people questioning the inherent value of education, but rather the perception that the quality of the education provided by the schools may be inadequate or that funding is being mismanaged.

To achieve positive associations, take preemptive action through prudent use of language. In all of your communications, speak to both the quality of your curriculum and the sound business practices to which you subscribe.

In addition to saying *high-quality public education*, weave in the terms *efficient*, *effective*, and *accountability*.

Also, highlight partnerships you have launched with other organizations (such as the schools), emphasizing how working together "leverages funding and expertise."

SMART, WISE—AND RETIRED

If your location happens to include a high population of retirees, it is possible that, in addition to questioning the effectiveness and efficiencies of the schools, resentment may be caused by the need to pay taxes for an institution from which this population will not benefit directly.

The Three Pillars Philosophy works successfully in this situation as well. The key is to teach retirees that education includes libraries—not just the schools. They must also comprehend our full curriculum under each of the Three Pillars, and recognize precisely what's in it for them.

Once these components are solidly in place, retirees will value and support libraries—because people fund what they value.

Why not position all public libraries as a major incentive for people to retire in any state? Although sunny locations with warm winter climates may be compelling for this customer base, above all, older adults desire a meaningful retirement that includes ample opportunities to engage their minds and connect with others. They long for exceptional continuing education—for intellectual stimulation and human interaction that enhances their quality of life.

Pillars II and III resonate particularly well with an aging population. Knowing this, convene classes in subject areas in which older adults are interested, such as health and history education. Capitalize on the growing demand for technology-related classes, including social networking. Organize free blood pressure checks, film screenings, author events, and book discussion groups.

Retirees also value scholarly seminars where they can contribute their views relating to subjects in which they are knowledgeable (e.g., at HCLS we held a three-part seminar series on Afghanistan last year, which was well attended by seniors).

Each of these classes and events will present an opportunity to develop fiercely local customers, and to also market Pillar I. Entice attendees to borrow from your collection before and after these classes and events by filling tables with topic-related books, audiobooks, and brochures promoting e-books, then placing the displays in prominent places.

◆ ◆ ◆

We've come to the concluding chapter, which rounds out themes already covered, centering on the foundational idea of the education advantage.

NOTE

1. For libraries funded through a dedicated tax, the philosophy's resulting effects on perceived value optimize your chances of levying the tax rate you seek.

12

A NEW ERA

Perhaps you've already tested the strategic vocabulary waters a bit and marveled at your words' powerful effects.

If you haven't yet experimented, try using some of the terms. You'll soon find yourself in conversations like I did on a recent Tuesday night.

After a yoga class, a few of us gym regulars chatted as we gathered our belongings and commiserated about the tough instructor. Someone in the group tossed a question my way.

"Hey, I hear you're opening a new library branch. Are you hiring?"

Somewhat distracted, I answered, "Yes, mainly Instructors. Also some Customer Service Specialists—and one IT position."

Surprised, my classmate Cindy interjected, "You have Instructors?"

"Yes!" I said, only then recognizing that I had inadvertently introduced some strategic vocabulary.

Puzzled, she asked, "What for?"

Guessing this might also be the first time Cindy would hear the words *research*, *classes*, and *teach* associated with a library, I said, matter-of-factly and in quick progression, "For any research assistance you might need. For the classes we teach for students of all ages."

Eyes widening, she pursued, "You teach classes?"

"Yes," I explained, "That's a key component of our curriculum. Our classes for infants through pre-K teach the foundations of reading—rhythm, rhyme, alliteration, sounds in words, letters, numbers and vocabulary—listening comprehension, creative skills, social skills, and any subject matter—including math and science—through children's literature—classes like Play Partners, Go Figure!, and Summer Science."

Assessing my audience, I continued, "Kindergarten through fifth grade classes include Great Composers, Splash into Art, and Lemonade Science. And for teens? Everyday Engineering (they build things like spaghetti bridges), Chemistry in the Library, and Tech Chicks. We teach those at our branches and in the schools through A+ Partners in Education."

Cindy's jaw had dropped.

I concluded, "And for adults, we teach classes in practical matters and all kinds of subjects—health, art, gardening, history, business—like I Just Got A Dog, Now What Do I Do?; Acupuncture; and Job Searching 101."

"Wow," she exhaled, "That's incredible." Reflecting for a moment, she lamented, "I wish all that had been available for my kids when they were growing up."

Cindy's children are in their 20s. All that *had* been there for them. She just hadn't understood the meaning of our language that was in place a decade ago. Consequently, she assumed all we did was loan books.

But not anymore! Cindy has joined the ranks of a growing segment of the population that has experienced our value-enhanced, self-explanatory language. As a result, she understands our curriculum more accurately, which means she now assigns us greater respect and worth.

Cindy will soon be repeating the same strategic terms without a second thought, offering remarks similar to "The class was awesome!" and "Loved the Instructor,"—comments that float past our ears and appear on Twitter and Facebook regularly at this point.

Although my conversation with Cindy occurred by chance, opportunities for intentional exchanges abound. For example, when someone says, "So tell me about ABC Public Library," try answering, "Our team of educators and support staff delivers public education for all through a curriculum that comprises three pillars: Self-Directed Education, Research Assistance & Instruction, and Instructive & Enlightening Experiences."

Most critically, say that magic word. When people ask what profession you are in, respond, "Education." When forms ask for "Occupation" or "Type of Business," write "Education."

While some of these efforts may seem inconsequential, combined, they all contribute to the building of a brand for our profession that broadcasts "indispensable."

STRONG, TIMELESS

The Three Pillars Philosophy works equally well whether a library consists of one location or 100. Other than modifying what we say, no changes are required to implement the vision.

At the same time, you may wish to strengthen your curriculum to the extent you are able—especially Pillars II and III, since the nonconnoisseur currently associates us exclusively with Pillar I.

An added advantage to augmenting your classes and events is that they provide for optimal marketing opportunities. Signature events (e.g., notable author events, Summer Reading kick-off, 5K and Family Fun Run, health fairs, financial education fairs, A+ academic competitions) can involve your entire staff, bolstered with volunteers. Invite the mayor or county executive to deliver opening remarks (or be the #1 runner in your Fun Run!). Arrange for a crew of elected officials and community leaders to serve as judges if you choose to orchestrate an academic competition.

For author events, if your meeting rooms seat smaller crowds, consider renting chairs to convene a bookstore-style seating configuration in the public area of the library during regular operating hours. This type of setup is ideal, as it delivers a spacious venue that showcases your library while also keeping the doors open to the general public. Customers who are not attending the event can still conduct research at your computers and mill about the stacks to borrow materials. Just post signs in the building and notices on your website beforehand to let people know what will be happening.

THE HUMAN CONNECTION

As technology further distances personal connections, Pillar III will become increasingly important over time. Public libraries are uniquely positioned to unite the community, bringing people together through events and partnerships.

The library is the natural lead organization for A+ Partners in Education and community-wide partnerships because literally everyone is our customer, including the organizations with whom we partner. We are the unifying hub for the spokes in the wheel—the common denominator.

Continuously balancing the pillars as years progress means that the allocation of space within our buildings will fluctuate. For instance, as more books are read electronically and demand for classes and events increases, less space may be required for bookshelves while far more will be necessary for classrooms and meeting rooms.

A number of newer library buildings include large meeting rooms as well as auditoriums. At Howard County Library System, our new 63,000 square-foot branch includes a 3,000 square-foot meeting room that can be partitioned into three classrooms, an 800 square-foot children's class-room, a 700 square-foot tech lab, and two 500 square-foot multipurpose classrooms. Varying in size, the spaces are conducive to teaching classes, seminars, and workshops, and organizing events. The venues are also ideal for community use.

TAILORING 3P

Modified slightly, the Three Pillars Philosophy also applies to specialized and academic libraries.

For example, libraries for the blind and physically handicapped can adopt much of the suggested terminology, narrowing the audience where needed. A modified mission statement could read, "We deliver high-quality public education for the blind and physically challenged."

Although school, college, and university libraries will want to omit the word *public* from the suggested phrases that include the term, much of the strategic vocabulary works for this category of libraries as well.

A mission statement for a university library could be worded, "We deliver high-quality education for ABC University students, faculty, and staff through a curriculum that comprises Three Pillars: Self-Directed Education, Research Assistance & Instruction, and Instructive & Enlightening Experiences."

IT'S LIKE GREEN OLIVES . . .

It's like green olives . . . or dry wine . . . or sharp cheddar cheese—or anything you love now but were hesitant at first to sample. Strategic vocabulary is an acquired taste.

Start by conscientiously making an effort to say the words. Once you get used to them, they'll soon become part of your everyday vocabulary. As you begin seeing the positive effects of your language, you'll be invigorated.

Also, don't be too hard on yourself. Old habits die hard.

At first, you'll find yourself thinking of the strategic word right after uttering a traditional one.

You'll advance to a point where you'll catch yourself, asking someone to "Please go to the Circula . . . I mean, Customer Service Desk."

You'll keep going, and before you know it, you will have arrived at a place where strategic vocabulary is second nature.

A GOOD START

A number of library systems have already begun to transform their image through smart use of language. Feedback following workshops and webinars included the following:

- Palm Springs (California) Public Library Director Barbara L. Roberts wrote, "We have used what we learned to great advantage when planning our fall schedule of events and *classes*. We are also in the process of designing training for staff that will emphasize the evolution of their roles into pro-active educators rather than the historically more passive public service workers."[1]

- Citrus County (Florida) Library System Communications Facilitator Sabrina Smith wrote, "We are excited to try out some of these ideas. Everyone has especially gotten on board with altering *programs* to *classes* and focusing on promoting *education* to the community. We're revamping our reference librarian's job duties, including introducing new things like research appointments in an effort to take us from 'generic to Evian.' Transitioning away from the term *reference librarian* to *instructor & research specialist* is a great way to showcase our librarians' value."[2]

In addition to more of us embracing the strategic vocabulary in our everyday communications, we see enlightenment on other fronts as well.

For example, the Supreme Court of Suffolk County in New York recently held that libraries are "educational institutions" on equal footing with the schools for zoning purposes. In response, New York Library Association Executive Director Micheal Borges is quoted in *Library Journal* as saying that the ruling "'recognizes libraries as educational institutions and librarians as educators.'"[3]

JUST THINK

Imagine if, across our entire profession:

- *Education, Instruction*, and *Research* replaced Information and Reference.
- *Instructor & Research Specialist* replaced Librarian and Library Associate.
- *Customer Service* replaced Circulation.
- Directors were called what they really are: *President and CEO*.
- *Classes* and *events* replaced storytimes and programs.
- *Library Journal*'s annual award became "*Educator of the year.*"
- Our profession stood for "*The freedom to pursue education.*"
- *Master of Education* (with an emphasis in Public Libraries, Academic Libraries, Government Libraries, Business Libraries, etc.) replaced Master of Library and Information Science.
- The national library symbol were refreshed with a symbol that captured our complete curriculum.
- We all said that magic word, and conveyed to everyone through strong, self-explanatory language that we are what the world values most.

Just think what would happen! People would, intuitively, understand our value.

Figure 12.1   National library symbol—current.

Libraries = Education

Figure 12.2   National library symbol—refreshed.

THE POWER OF US

Together, we have the power to transform our image, ushering in a new era where libraries are viewed as central to our nation's education infrastructure and an economic imperative.

Even in the beginning stages of implementation, you'll see your staff members energized. They'll love their new titles that accurately convey their worth. They'll appreciate the strategic vocabulary that conveys precisely what they do. They'll stand tall as they see themselves in your organization's crystal clear vision—public education for all—delivered through three timeless pillars that ensure a flourishing future for their jobs, their organization, and their profession.

It's time to receive full credit for what we do. It's time to build a powerful brand that unmistakably defines us. With education as our brand, we will command our full value.

Collectively, our strategic language will influence mayors, county executives, governors, and U.S. Presidents to include libraries in their meaning of the word *education* when they declare their highest funding priority in statements such as, "Even as we cut out things that we can afford to do without, we have a responsibility to invest in those areas that will have the biggest impact in our future, and that's especially true when it comes to education."[4]

Let's transform our image and revolutionize our profession by, once and for all, letting the world know who we are, what we do, and why it matters. We are education—what the world values most.

NOTES

1. E-mail to author, September 13, 2011, used with permission.
2. E-mail to author, September 12, 2011, used with permission.
3. "Court Says Libraries are 'Educational Institutions,'" *Library Journal* 136, no. 11 (June 15, 2011), p. 19.
4. Jackie Calmes, "Obama's Budget Focuses on Path to Rein in Deficit," *New York Times*, February 14, 2011, http://www.nytimes.com/2011/02/15/us/politics/15obama.html.

BIBLIOGRAPHY

England, S. Randle. "The Consequences of Promoting an Educational Role for Today's Public Libraries." *Public Libraries* (March/April 2007), pp. 55–63.

Gross, Valerie J. "A⁺ Partners in Education: Positioning Libraries as a Cornerstone in the Education Process." *Children & Libraries* 1, no. 2 (Summer/Fall 2003), pp. 27–31.

Gross, Valerie J. "A⁺ Partners in Education: Linking Libraries to Education for a Flourishing Future." *Public Libraries* 44, no. 4 (July/August 2005), pp. 217–22.

Gross, Valerie J., "Choose Civility: Public Libraries Take Center Stage," *Public Libraries* 50, no. 4 (July/August 2011), pp. 30–37.

Gross, Valerie J. "Transforming Our Image through Words that Work: Perception is Everything." *Public Libraries* 48, no. 5 (September/October 2009), pp. 24–32.

"Library Challenges and Opportunities Tools of Engagement: Attracting and Engaging Library Users." College of DuPage (Glen Ellyn, IL) May 9, 2008, teleconference with speakers Jennifer Edwins, Mary Evangeliste, Valerie Gross, and Jennifer Kelley. Streaming video at www.collegeofdupagepress.com/index.php?id=1671.

Luntz, Frank. *Words that Work: It's Not What You Say, It's What People Hear.* New York: Hyperion, 2007.

Taylor, William C., and Polly G. LaBarre. *Mavericks at Work: Why the Most Original Minds in Business Win.* New York: HarperCollins, 2006.

INDEX

About the Author

VALERIE J. GROSS has served as President & CEO of Howard County (Maryland) Library System (HCLS) since 2001. A passionate promoter of libraries, she takes pride in HCLS's unparalleled curriculum, which continues to earn the system top national rankings. For this achievement, Gross thanks the extraordinary team of educators and support staff that comprise HCLS, as well as the HCLS Board of Trustees, and credits generous funders, most notably Howard County Government. Ms. Gross holds Master's degrees in music and library science, and a Doctorate of Jurisprudence. She received Feature Article Contest awards from *Public Libraries* in 2012 and 2010, and was honored as a *Library Journal* Mover and Shaker in 2004. Valerie, her husband Tri Nguyen, and their son, David, live in Columbia, Maryland.

23340491R00106

Made in the USA
San Bernardino, CA
24 January 2019